~THE~
Mariner's Catalog

Volume 5

Edited by

George Putz

and

Peter H. Spectre

Published by

INTERNATIONAL MARINE PUBLISHING COMPANY

for Marine Annuals, Inc.

PREFACE

An armchair is the only boat to own.
—Fred Brooks

The fifth volume of the *Mariner's Catalog*. Who would have thought it possible? When we started this series five years ago, we certainly were't alone, but neither were we sure that there were enough readers out there with enough interest to sustain the subjective cataloging of the marine world's resources. We're fortunate to have all the company.

But we must retain our perspective here. This catalog is about boats and the sea. We take our work on it seriously, but we are well aware that the subject is not of earth-shattering importance. We are talking about boats, not theology, and so there are times when we are surprised by the intensity of feeling we detect here and there.

While we are delighted to see a revival of interest in building, restoring, and using classic craft, we are sometimes repelled by the dogma that tends to build up around such endeavors. We occasionally see an unusual grimness on the faces and in the words of today's lovers of the sea, a grimness than can be ridiculous at times.

What do we mean and who is doing it? Well here are a few examples that come immediately to mind: The person who says a boat reproduction isn't authentic because power tools were used in her construction. The person who, in the process of dismantling a boat for restoration, discovers an empty screw hole, so does not put a replacement screw in the hole because he wants to be sure the boat is historically accurate. The museum custodian who won't allow the museum's boat plans to be reproduced because boats built from the plans might not meet the museum's standards. The dory aficionado who scoffs at the doryman who uses locks rather than thole pins. The boatbuilder who won't use modern materials on a boat, simply because they are modern, even though they might have been proven superior to their counterparts of the past. The expert who stands around the boat landing and pokes fun at a traditional craft's rigging since it differs in a minor way from that shown in *Steel's Art of Rigging*. No doubt you have a few choice examples of your own.

If we are to develop more than a casual interest in things marine, we must maintain our equilibrium. There are very few right ways or wrong ways to do anything. There are mostly ways that work for us and that in the process make us feel good. After all, for most of us, messing around with boats is an avocation, not a vocation, and we are out to have fun, not torture ourselves with imaginary tests of doctrinal purity. We need more people who say, "Isn't it great to be out on the water in a fine, traditional craft that really goes?" and fewer who say, "I can spot a loose fricket on a topping lift faster than you can." To the latter, all we can reply is, "So's your old man."

Now for a few words about the book itself. Volume 5 is a continuation of its four predecessors, but it has a few changes here and there, the most notable of which is that we no longer use our own bylines or initials, only those of our contributors. So if something you read causes you to become angry, don't blame me; the other editor wrote it.

We would also like to caution you. This is a book that deals with devices, both physical and mental. Devices that aid and protect us can also trap us, much like those screws they use in the stalls of public lavatories, the screws you can't back out once they're in. The symbolic devices—the attitudes and ideas here—can become *magic* and activate the glands after first shutting off the brain. So don't be trapped.

And a final thought. The signs of change are as balanced as anything else, in the longer run at least. For every bird that died in a mine to tell the men to get out, there was another well-fed and loved bird that made someone less alone, to its own advantage. For every social indicator like the Staten Island ferry upping its rates (to tell the citizens to get out?), there is a boat being built with the golden thought that it will serve its owner or to his advantage.

George Putz
Peter H. Spectre

CONTENTS

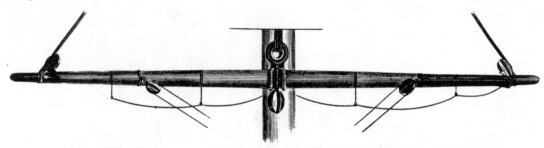

The Cover

The cover design and art was done by marine artist and historian William Gilkerson. It is a watercolor showing the mainsail of a small bark being furled. Gilkerson lives in Mendocino, California, where, he tells us, he divides his time among researching and painting historical vessels, sailing his gaff yawl *Dandy*, fending off any more stray cats, chopping wood, and sweeping bird droppings off the back porch.

The Prices

The prices in this volume, and all others as well, are approximate. They are changed with whim and abandon, so if you order something without checking the latest price with the supplier, be prepared for a gentle reminder for more cash. Don't blame us; blame the Democrats, or the Republicans, or some other convenient group of economic gremlins.

The Books

Many of the titles reviewed in this Catalog are published or distributed by International Marine Publishing Company, 21 Elm Street, Camden, Maine 04843. IM's booklist is revised monthly and contains hundreds of marine books and prints. It's yours free for the asking.

Our Thanks

We thank you all—those who have suggested topics to cover, those who have sent editorial contributions, those who have written us exhortative letters, those who have recommended the *Catalog* to friends, those who have stuck with us. We also appreciate the indexing assistance of Julia Littleton and the editorial advice of Kathleen Brandes and Katherine Campbell.

Our Special Thanks

Our special thanks go to Darrell McClure, who so kindly has allowed us to reprint a few of the cartoons he did for *Yachting* magazine years ago. His humor has a timeless aspect to it, and we are proud to be able to bring his cartoons back to life. We grew up on McClure's characterizations, so we felt our own measure of pride when he wrote us: "Your first four volumes of the *Mariner's Catalog* received with pleasure, but they certainly knocked hell out of my scheduled workday."

Changes

Data we present in past Catalogs has a way of changing—companies go out of business, addresses change, people stop doing what they used to do. If you discover any of these changes, we would be most appreciative if you sent us a card or note advising us. We're in the business of sharing information and need all the help we can get.

Some of the changes we have come across appear where appropriate in this Catalog. Others are:

The traditional watch sweater made by Nelson Knitting Mills and described on page 92 of the 4th Catalog now costs $26. Mr. Nelson cited inflationary wool and labor costs as the cause.

Amateur Boat Building magazine, mentioned on page 23 of the 3rd Catalog, is defunct as far as we know. Neil Thompson tells us that mail to their address comes back "addressee unknown."

Ray Vandermeer, who makes rope fenders, and whose work was described on page 115 of the 4th Catalog, has a new address. It is Ray Vandermeer, 3305 South G Street, Oxnard, California 93030.

INTERESTING
BOATS

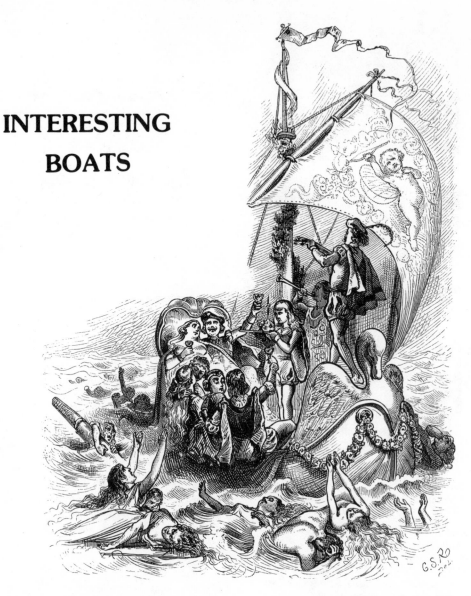

4

In past years we have found craft as interesting as these, but never so many. They are listed here not necessarily because they are "good," but rather because they possess special qualities, often fine workmanship. We look for rarity, character, and the expression of ideas.

Small Craft in Wood

Wherries at $100/foot plus $400 for a sailing configuration; cedar on oak, clinkerbuilt, from:

Duck Trap Woodworking
Cannan Road
Lincolnville, Maine 04849

Left: 12'10" Lincolnville wherry built by Walt Simmons of Ducktrap Woodworking during the winter of 1974-1975. With all her extras, she cost the owner about $1300.

They [wooden boats] are the closest material thing that is built like your own body.
—Royal Lowell

Fine little 13½-foot catboats, the marconi-rigged Wenaumet Kittens, at around $4,000, from:

**R. Bigelow & Company
Monument Beach, Mass.**

Lapstrake boats of many types in the 7- to 32-foot range, with a specialty in Swampscott Dories (12 to 28 feet), from:

**Samuel Connor & Son
Point Hudson Marina
Port Townsend, Wash. 98368**

Lovely blond rowing craft of many types from Kolin; blond from their unusual use of Sitka spruce as plankstock.

**Kolin Boat Works
575 7th Ave.
Santa Cruz, Cal. 95062**

*Top: A Wenaumet Kitten at her mooring
Above: A 16' Swampscott dory under construction at Samuel Connor & Son. The sheer strakes are next.
Below: Kolin Boat Works' Nantucket lifeboat, designed by Pete Culler. She is 17', has Sitka spruce planking, white oak trim and frames, teak floorboards, and copper and bronze fastenings.*

Telephone and mail inquiries are fine. However, since nothing comes off the shelf, serious customers are encouraged to stop by the shop to discuss their requirements. From an extensive library of traditional plans, the customer has much to choose from. We also build custom oars in several styles as well as hatches and other items of custom boat cabinetry. We do not ship or offer brochures. Boat prices are determined individually, depending on the design chosen and discussion between the builder and customer.

—Mrs. Laura G. Kolin

5

Superbly handsome open launches of mahogany on English oak in three sizes. 18′ is £2,200; 23′ is £4,300, and 26′ is £5,700, from:

**Chesford Marine
Bridge Boatyard, Frogmore
Kingsbridge, South Devon
England**

13-foot peapods (rowing model $1,100, $2,100 rigged) are described in a nice note saying ". . . any traditional craft in wood up to 18 feet," from:

**Tenants Harbor Boat Works
c/o Rick Smith
Tenants Harbor, Maine 04860**

Above: Chesford Marine's open launch; LOA 26′, beam 8′3″, draft 2′3″.

Dear Editors:

I am a reader of *National Fisherman* and have purchased numerous volumes from your list of publications. That list is the best I've ever seen and I think other nautical book lovers will benefit if I call your attention to one you don't have. It's *Steamboats on the Western Rivers* by Louis C. Hunter (Octagon Books, 1969) and it cost me $26. I have read several books on this subject and this book is the most definitive one I've found.

Another interesting title is *Life on the River* by Norbury L. Wayman (Bonanza Books) for $6. It is a pictorial history that makes good reading.

Charles B. Fortson
Panama City, Florida

6

Yacht Designs, by William Garden
**International Marine Publishing Company
Camden, Maine
304 pages, illus., 1977, $17.50**

Thirty-seven of the author's designs for cruising boats, both sail and power, with text describing the craft and how they perform.

The interior accommodation plan is practical, and the finish of the cabin will depend upon the owner. Simple bone-white areas with varnished hardwood beams, sole, and trim will suit many. Set off with the right cushions and books, such a scheme is hard to beat, particularly in a hot area requiring a light, airy effect.

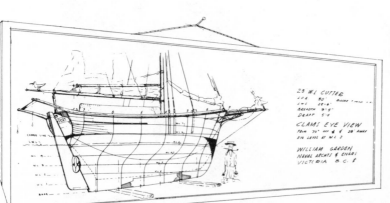

Left, and quote above: From Yacht Designs, *in this case the delectable Spice Island Cutter.*

Small Craft
in Glass-Reinforced Plastic

An 18'8" gaff-headed sloopboat called "Pepper," harkening somewhat to the beloved Muscongus Bay model, for $1,950; and a very slippery skiff called "Glass Slipper" (see Mariner's Catalog No. 4, page 5) at $675, from:

Salt Marine, Inc.
P.O. Box 21584
Ft. Lauderdale, Fla. 33316

Right: Salt Marine's gaff-rigged Pepper, designed by William E. Hitchcock.

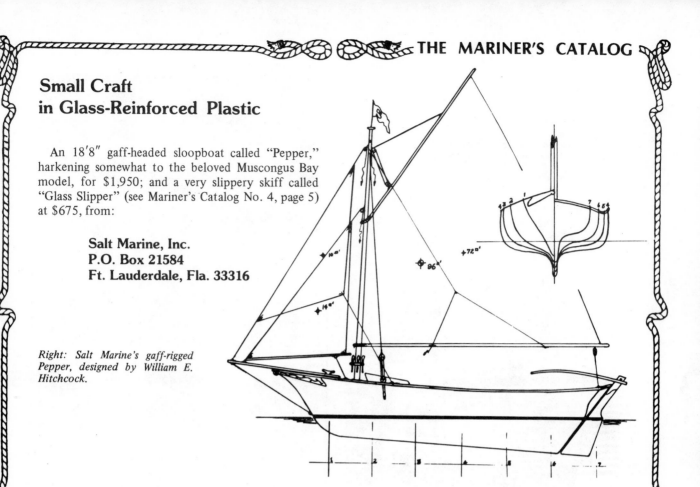

A direct descendant of the reliable Sea Bright model, this 17-foot "Surf Boat" is offered at $1,775 by:

Van Duyne Bros.
113 N. Dudley Ave.
Ventnor, N.J.

Below: Van Duyne's surfboat. 17' LOA, 5'2" beam, 345 lbs. weight, molded fiberglass in 7 layers. Note the oarlocks.

7

Fiberglass Whitehalls are popping out of molds all over the country. An 11'3" rowing and/or sailing model comes from:

**Golden Era Boats
Box 212, Marsh Road
Noank, Conn. 06340**

Drascombe has a new boat to offer, the 21'6" Drifter, a beachable cruising boat with 2 berths, galley, and head. Power options include an inboard Sabb diesel and an outboard in a well.

**Drascombe Boats
878 Sea Street
Camden, Maine 04843**

Lines of the Noank Whitehall were adapted from those of the somewhat larger New York and Boston Whitehalls which were everpresent in eastern harbors at the turn of the century. The boat's unique characteristics are its high wineglass transom and deep keel sections near the stern. This shape not only provides the boat with a traditional graceful appearance but is functional as well. In essence, the boat is a double-ender at the waterline which makes for an easy motion through the water. The rapidly widening stern above the waterline, on the other hand, provides seating capacity.

*Left: The new Drascombe Drifter.
Above: Golden Era's fiberglass Whitehall. Boxed quote is from a Golden Era brochure*

Importing Boats

Dear Editors:
   In the *Mariner's Catalog, Vol. 4,* you asked for information on importing boats. I have written an article on the subject that was published in *Cruising World* magazine (October, 1977) and pretty well sums up the whole experience. I was unusually lucky that everything went so well on my own first try at it, because the potential for trouble is incredible.
   I'm sure you know how it is when you know nothing about something and need to know everything about it. I had to drag information from every source and then screen out the truth. The few people I asked who did import boats refused to show their hand, or, if they did, it would be to my expense, in more ways than just money.
   Here's some advice; if you're going to do it, do it yourself, but get wise to what's going on first and then be prepared to spend your money, because importing is not a poor man's game. The boat you buy had better be a real bargain to justify the expense of the shipping. To show you where the money goes, I'll use the Cornish Crabber* as an example. Whether an Englishman buys a Crabber from the builder or an American buys one from me, it costs £7,897. At the current exchange rate of $1.72, this comes to $13,582.84. To this we add

the expense of customs (2%), customs broker, overseas agent, trucking, customs bond, and ocean freight, a total of about $2,500. This is very cheap, because the Crabber is easy to transport. A wide boat with a deep keel is another story.
   I initially took what for me, anyway, was an expensive risk. I watched the truck, with the boat, leave the builder's yard in England after paying out a lot of money for both boat and shipping. All I had to show for it was a paper saying that in two weeks the boat would reappear in my yard in New York. Would you do it?
   I may sound a little negative, but I'm trying to be realistic. If I can help any of your readers, just let me know. I'll try to keep them from getting a shafting.

David Seidman
Westerly Boats
Box 278
E. Rockaway, N.Y. 11518

*Mr. Seidman is the importer of the Cornish Crabber, a 24-ft. gaff cutter built in England. We are delighted to know that he first learned of the boat through the *Mariner's Catalog* (Vol. 3, p. 15).—Eds.

On Rowing and Oars

Dear Editors:

While happily sculling along with Bill Durham on page 85 of the *Mariner's Catalog,* Vol. 4, I grounded out abruptly. He seems to refer to the oarlocks as the fulcra of a pulling boat, and that set me to scratching the dandruff. In a lever system, the fulcrum isn't supposed to move, but something else does—in this case, the boat. All other things being equal, the most efficient oar would be one whose blade remained stationary in the water without slippage. To this end, the various shovel, spoon, and tulip types have been developed to hold the water better. Since the boat moves and the water doesn't, it seems to me the water's the fulcrum, rather than the oarlocks. (We would welcome debate on this point—Eds.)

Martin Marine Company (Alden Racing Shells), Pepperrell Rd., Kittery Point, Maine 03905, has some very nice imported spruce oars of the spoon and tulip varieties. You can expect to shell out $100 for a pair of 7½-footers.

Recently, the Old Town Canoe people (Old Town, Maine) offered spruce spoons, varnished, leathered, buttoned, and coppered at $5.65 per foot, although you could expect to pay more now—if indeed they're still available. Again, you're probably talking a hundred bucks.

Another route, cheaper and much more satisfying, is to get a pair of first-grade ash oars and go to work with plane and spokeshave—whittle 'em down 'til you don't bust your butt rowing. With care, you can remove enough material to lighten them considerably and give them a little whip.

David L. Register
Damariscotta, Maine

The Sky's the Limit

Given the choice of crawling, sitting, or standing headroom in a small boat, I'm of the persuasion that the latter is the only way to go. I would just rather not spend my time in a boat hunched over like a cripple or crawling on my belly like a snake. But we all cannot afford standing headroom, nor do we all want the maintenance and financial burdens that go with a craft that will provide such a luxury. The choice, then, is an open boat. There's no limit on your headroom, and if it's shelter you want, that can be arranged in all manner of ways, including the time-honored tarp-over-the-boom.

There are two books in print—both British—that sing the praise of open-boat cruising. They both take the sensible, down-to-earth approach and offer some

interesting ideas and guidelines for making your choice worthwhile. Of the two, I prefer Eric Coleman's book because of his easy style of writing, but either one will provide the inspiration to chuck your ideas about shallow-draft head-knockers and get you to sea with a minimum of fuss and expense.

Open Boat Cruising, **by John Glasspool**
Nautical Publishing
Lymington, Hampshire, England
112 pages, illus., index, 1973, £2.75

Dinghies for All Waters, **by Eric Coleman**
Transatlantic Arts, Levittown, N.Y.
160 pages, illus., glossary, index, 1976, $8.75

Below: From Dinghies for All Waters.

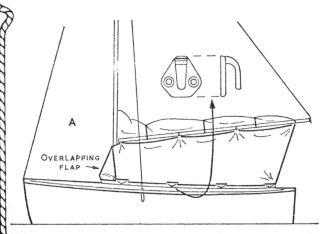

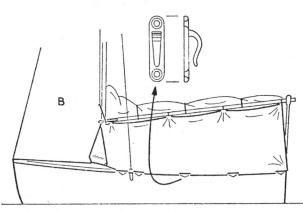

25. Awning arrangements.

9

Medium-Sized in Wood

The Crosby (Chester's) yard on Cape Cod hasn't stopped for a breath in decades. They are noted for craft of all kinds, particularly long-lived catboats and the utility powercraft distinctive to their splendid waters.

**Chester A. Crosby & Sons, Inc.
P.O. Box 490, Bridge Street
Osterville, Mass. 02655**

Right: Two of Chester Crosby's 23' Curlew sloops under sail. Below: A beautiful classic steam launch from Machin, Knight and Sons, Ltd.

Here's a yard that specializes in vintage or veteran craft in England. They recently completed a 22'10" steam launch in cold-molded triple-skinned teak. Her mill is an open inverted compound reversing and condensing steam engine with keel condenser fed by a coal-fired 20" by 30" vertical firetube boiler. Delivery time was one year.

**Machin, Knight and Sons, Ltd.
6 Avery Hill Rd.
London, SE9 2BE
England**

Left: The 3-sail bateau from Virginia Boatshop; LOA 46', LWL 39', beam 13'2", draft 4'8". A modified version of this craft serves in the Long Island dude trade out of Greenport, N.Y.

10

Most of my boats have been very traditional Chesapeake in construction and design. About 50% have been power and 50% sail. My interest is strong for sail. Some rough prices: 16' deadrise sailing skiff, $1,600; 18' skipjack daysailer, $2,300; 24' cruising skipjack, $9,000; 36' centerboard bugeye rig, 25 hp diesel, $40,000; 46' 3-sail bateau (keel), $55-65,000. This includes completed boat, sail away. Our cruising types usually include monkey rails and trailboards.

—C.V. Pedersen
Virginia Boatshop

Solid, traditional Chesapeake craft from:

**Virginia Boatshop
Box 277
Seaford, Virginia 23696**

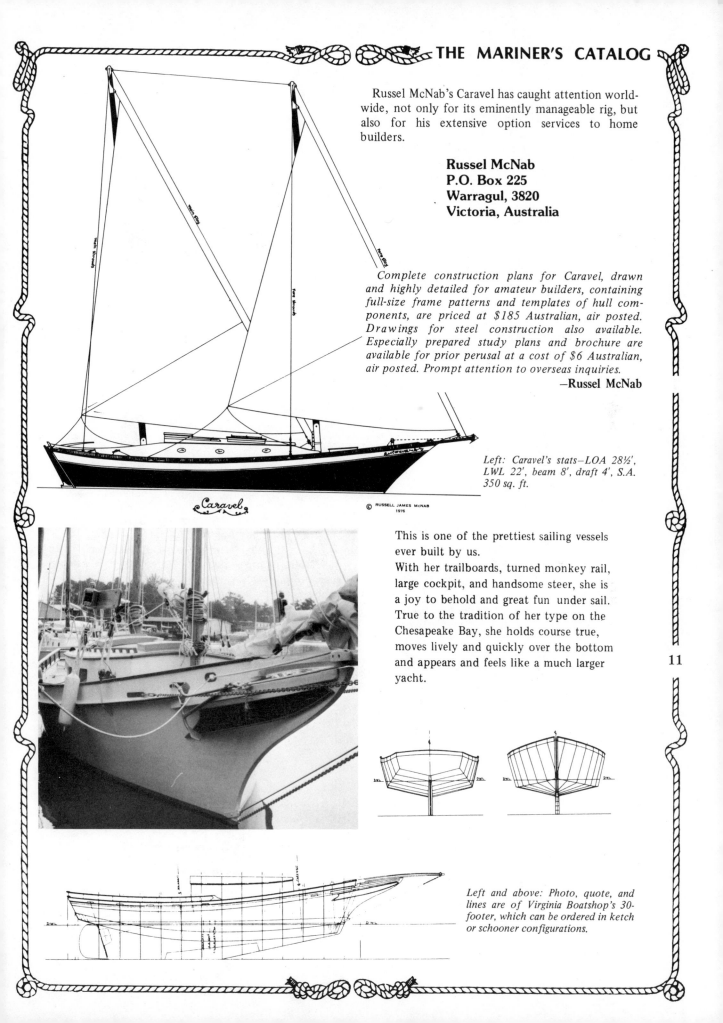

Russel McNab's Caravel has caught attention world-wide, not only for its eminently manageable rig, but also for his extensive option services to home builders.

Russel McNab
P.O. Box 225
Warragul, 3820
Victoria, Australia

Complete construction plans for Caravel, drawn and highly detailed for amateur builders, containing full-size frame patterns and templates of hull components, are priced at $185 Australian, air posted. Drawings for steel construction also available. Especially prepared study plans and brochure are available for prior perusal at a cost of $6 Australian, air posted. Prompt attention to overseas inquiries.

—**Russel McNab**

Left: Caravel's stats—LOA 28½', LWL 22', beam 8', draft 4', S.A. 350 sq. ft.

Caravel

© RUSSELL JAMES McNAB
1976

This is one of the prettiest sailing vessels ever built by us.

With her trailboards, turned monkey rail, large cockpit, and handsome steer, she is a joy to behold and great fun under sail. True to the tradition of her type on the Chesapeake Bay, she holds course true, moves lively and quickly over the bottom and appears and feels like a much larger yacht.

11

Left and above: Photo, quote, and lines are of Virginia Boatshop's 30-footer, which can be ordered in ketch or schooner configurations.

Pleasurable Workboats

When we saw the Potter-25 in an English journal, the old romanticism in us began to scream for food and we sent off in haste for details. The Potter sleeps 2 in the forecastle, has a galley in the pilothouse, and the big waterproof hold will take anything from more bunks (or hammocks), to a laboratory, to a trip of fish. Neat boat, and with an American distributor, too! $23,658 steamaway Annapolis or, possibly, Long Beach.

Larson Yacht Sales
222 Severn Avenue
Annapolis, Md. 21404

Ladd Marine
5933 Naples Plaza
Long Beach, Cal. 90803

Beginning from bare hulls—a 21-footer at $3,250 and a 26-footer at $4,285—Tugs puts together some of the cutest li'l critters that ever twanged a heart-thong.

Tugs
160 Forest Street
Braintree, Mass. 02185

Top right: The Potter-25.
Bottom right: The tugboat configuration from Tugs.
Below: The Little Rhody rigged for fishing.

The Little Rhody 19 is an option-laden stroke of interest costing from $5,900 (outboard version) to $12,500 (75hp Volvo diesel sterndrive). There are mast options, davit and hauler options, even pilot-house-location options. Good idea from:

Hawkline Boat Company
1076 North Main Street
Providence, R.I. 02904

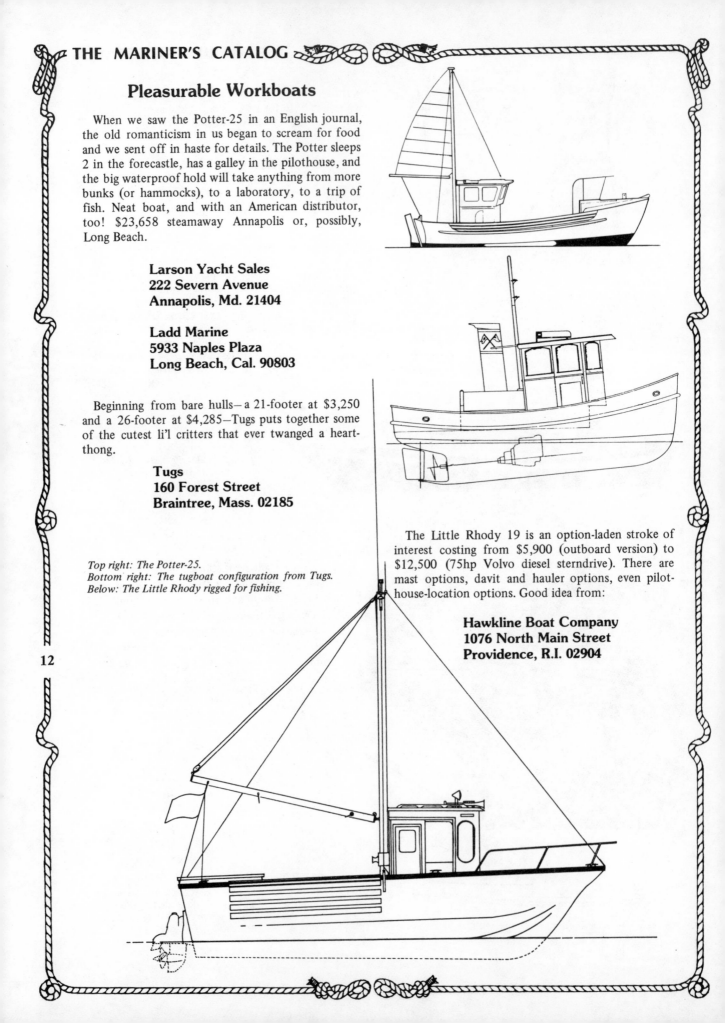

Good Boats, **by Roger C. Taylor**
International Marine Publishing Company
Camden, Maine
224 pages, illus., index, 1977, $17.50

Design commentary and practical advice on 36 traditional cruising boats that the author considers to be good, as opposed to lousy.

The canoe yawl has a fine, hollow entrance, and quite flat buttock lines fore and aft. By her passage, she would disturb the water but little, and she should be a fast little boat. She has a good spread of sail, and with her original Chinese, or battened, lug rig, she could be shortened down quickly in a breeze.

Quote above and sailplan at right: From Good Boats. *This is the 18' canoe yawl* Iris, *designed by J.A. Akester.*

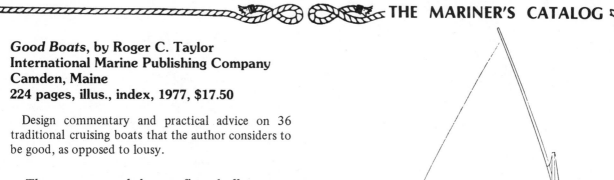

***Four Months in a Sneakbox*,**
by Nathaniel H. Bishop
Gale Research Press, Detroit, Michigan
322 pages, illus., 1879 (reprinted 1976), $18*

Back in print in a facsimile edition is one of the all-time great small-boat voyaging classics. Bishop was one of those late-19th-century romantics who went cruising in very small craft in the most unlikely places. In a voyage prior to the one recounted here, he went solo in a paper canoe from Quebec to the Gulf of Mexico. On this voyage, he went down the Ohio and Mississippi Rivers and along the Gulf Coast in a modified Barnegat Bay sneakbox. His tale is an interesting one and an inspiration to those who prefer cruising in the tiniest boats.

*In defense of the high price of this book: Gale Research Press is basically in the business of reprinting rare books for the library trade. As a result, they, and other reprint publishers like them, deal in very small quantities, which makes the unit cost of their books high.

Right: From Four Months in a Sneakbox. *Anyone who can spend four months in something as small as that deserves to have his book reprinted.*

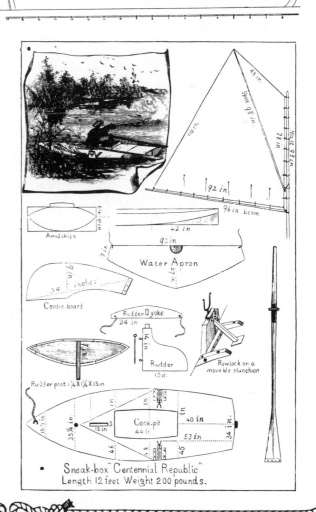

Sneak-box "Centennial Republic"
Length 12 feet Weight 200 pounds.

13

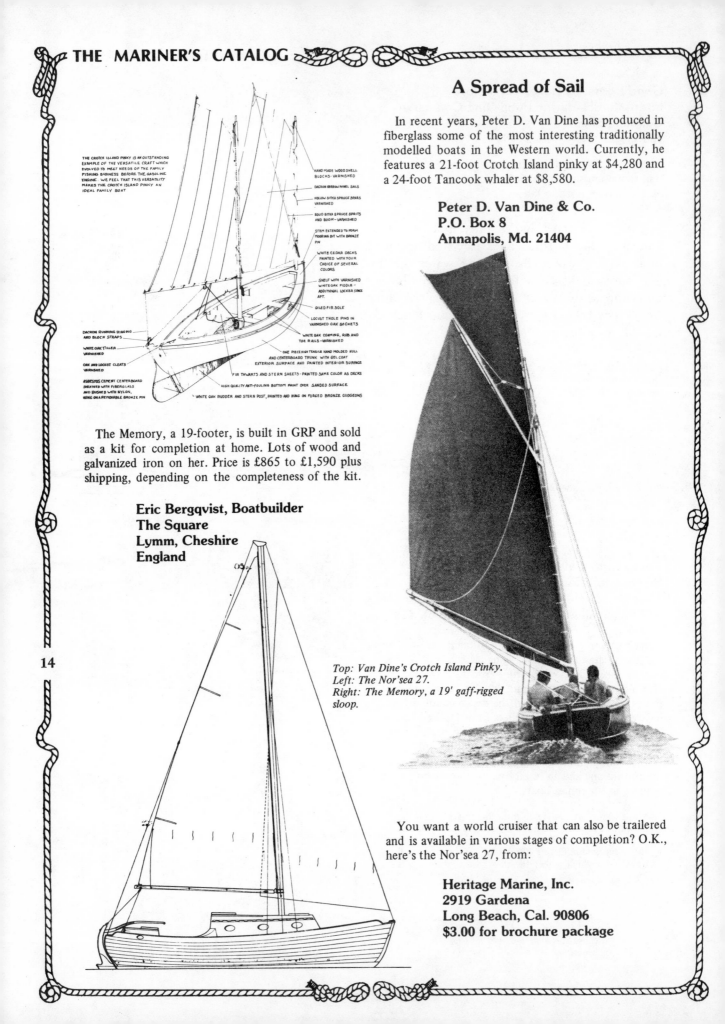

THE CROTCH ISLAND PINKY IS AN OUTSTANDING
EXAMPLE OF THE VERSATILE CRAFT WHICH
EVOLVED TO MEET NEEDS OF THE FAMILY
FISHING BUSINESS BEFORE THE GASOLINE
ENGINE. WE FEEL THAT THIS VERSATILITY
MAKES THE CROTCH ISLAND PINKY AN
IDEAL FAMILY BOAT

HAND MADE WOOD SHELL
BLOCKS - VARNISHED

DACRON TANBARK PANEL SAILS

HOLLOW SITKA SPRUCE SPARS
VARNISHED

SOLID SITKA SPRUCE SPRITS
AND BOOM - VARNISHED

STEM EXTENDED TO FORM
MOORING BIT WITH BRONZE
PIN

WHITE CEDAR DECKS
PAINTED WITH YOUR
CHOICE OF SEVERAL
COLORS

SHELF WITH VARNISHED
WHITE OAK FIDDLE -
ADDITIONAL LOCKER SPACE
AFT.

OILED FIR SOLE

LOCUST THOLE PINS IN
VARNISHED OAK SOCKETS

WHITE OAK COAMING, RUB AND
TOE RAILS - VARNISHED

ONE PIECE HIGH TENSILE HAND MOLDED HULL
AND CENTERBOARD TRUNK WITH GEL COAT
EXTERIOR SURFACE AND PAINTED INTERIOR SURFACE

FIR THWARTS AND STERN SHEETS - PAINTED SAME COLOR AS DECKS

HIGH QUALITY ANTI-FOULING BOTTOM PAINT OVER SANDED SURFACE

WHITE OAK RUDDER AND STERN POST, PAINTED AND RING ON FORGED BRONZE GUDGEONS

DACRON RUNNING RIGGING
AND BLOCK STRAPS

WHITE OAK TILLER
VARNISHED

OAK AND LOCUST CLEATS
VARNISHED

ASBESTOS CEMENT CENTERBOARD
SHEATHED WITH FIBERGLASS
AND BUSHED WITH NYLON,
HUNG ON A REMOVABLE BRONZE PIN

The Memory, a 19-footer, is built in GRP and sold as a kit for completion at home. Lots of wood and galvanized iron on her. Price is £865 to £1,590 plus shipping, depending on the completeness of the kit.

**Eric Bergqvist, Boatbuilder
The Square
Lymm, Cheshire
England**

A Spread of Sail

In recent years, Peter D. Van Dine has produced in fiberglass some of the most interesting traditionally modelled boats in the Western world. Currently, he features a 21-foot Crotch Island pinky at $4,280 and a 24-foot Tancook whaler at $8,580.

**Peter D. Van Dine & Co.
P.O. Box 8
Annapolis, Md. 21404**

Top: Van Dine's Crotch Island Pinky.
Left: The Nor'sea 27.
Right: The Memory, a 19' gaff-rigged sloop.

You want a world cruiser that can also be trailered and is available in various stages of completion? O.K., here's the Nor'sea 27, from:

**Heritage Marine, Inc.
2919 Gardena
Long Beach, Cal. 90806
$3.00 for brochure package**

Nineteenth-century England produced many fine cutter models, some of the best of which were working boats from the West of England, such as those of Itchen Ferry, Falmouth and the Bristol Pilots. These were beamy vessels with firm bilges to enable them to sail well with cargo and to stand up to wind and sea in heavy going. The fishing smacks and other small craft were worked by one man, so the easily handled cutter rig served them well. Speed was an important consideration as weather can rapidly deteriorate in the English Channel and some of these models, particularly the Itchen Ferry, were notable for their performance. Match racing among them was an annual event and even today, on the Channel side of England, you may find these sturdy vessels competing for prizes.

Bristol Channel Cutter

A 28-foot Bristol Channel cutter in GRP, from:

**Sam L. Morse Co.
1626 Placentia Ave.
Costa Mesa, Cal. 92627**

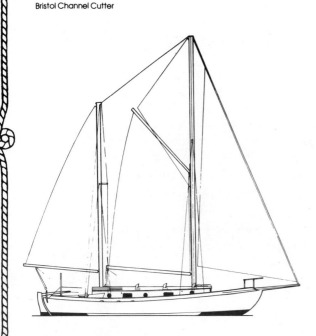

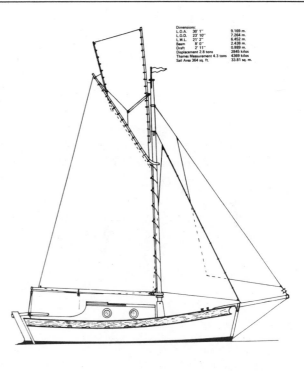

Dimensions:
L.O.A.	30' 1"	9.169 m.
L.O.D.	23' 10"	7.264 m.
L.W.L.	21' 2"	6.452 m.
Beam	8' 0"	2.438 m.
Draft	2' 11"	0.889 m.
Displacement 2.8 tons		2845 kilos
Thames Measurement 4.3 tons		4369 kilos
Sail Area 364 sq. ft.		33.81 sq. m.

Above: The Norske 35 in her ketch rig. She is also available in a cutter rig.
Right: The Tamarisk 24.
The quote at the top of the page is from a Sam L. Morse Company brochure.

The Tamarisk 24 is glass with wooden decks and house, in the £7,000 range, from:

**North Sea Craft
Hall Rd.
Norwich, Norfolk NR4 6DR
England**

Windboats Marine has several craft worthy of a look, especially two ferrocement-hull Colin Archer models, the Norskes 35 and 40.

**Windboats Marine
Wroxham
Norwich, Norfolk NR12 8RX
England**

15

***The Folding Schooner: and Other Adventures
in Boat Design***, by Philip C. Bolger
**International Marine Publishing Company
Camden, Maine
208 pages, illus., 1976, $13.50**

Lines and quote are from The
Folding Schooner *and concern
Little Superior, a 10'3" craft
with a dipping lug rig.*

Sequel to the author's *Small Boats,* with more
designs and comment on innovative small craft for
oar, sail, and engine.

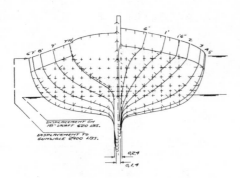

We thought we'd save some trouble by using glued strip planking: a
mistake; we should have stayed with the original sawn frames and steamed
oak planking. Anything on such proportions as these is bound to be hard
to plank, but the strip boat proved to be an absolute bitch to get fair. The
plank sequence had to be changed from the one specified, most of the strips
had to be pre-steamed, the sheer kept trying to get lost; oh my! Larry per-
severed all winter and won through with his equable disposition intact, but
we agreed that it'd have been easier to carve her out of a solid block. The
construction plan is printed as designed; take it as an instructive exercise
in how to drive a builder out of his mind.

16

Dear Editors:

In Volume 1 of the *Mariner's Catalog* you raised a
question of foreign and exotic craft. H.A. Morton's
The Wind Commands (Wesleyan U. Press, Middletown, Conn., $29.95) has good, if brief, information
on most indigenous Pacific craft as well as on the
adaptations forced on European design by the great
sea. Edwin Doran, Jr., has written a convincing
article, "The Sailing Raft as a Great Tradition," that
can be found in *Man Across the Sea* (Riley, et al.,
eds., U. of Texas). Apparently somebody called
your attention to Worcester's works on Chinese
sailing ships but Joseph Needham, *Science and Civil-
isation in China,* vol, 4, parts 1 and 3 (Cambridge
U. Press, N.Y.), is very good on the Chinese development of the compass, its application to navigation, and on the hulls and the rigging. It is worth
noting that the largest sailing vessels afloat in the
early 15th century were Chinese—over 300' LOA
and with perhaps 9 masts.

John R. Pavia, Jr.
Trumansburg, N.Y.

Dear Editors:

The purpose of this letter is to acquaint you with a type of watercraft that may have escaped your attention. I was born and brought up in New York—the Pennsylvania R.R. Station marks my birthplace—and my childhood was punctuated by rides on the horse-drawn open trolley cars. One of these rides took my mother and me down Broadway to the Battery. Here, moored to the seawall, was the Battery Bath. This floating swimming pool was a large, rectangular, two-story wooden structure enclosing waters of New York's upper bay. The structure contained suitable bathhouses and other appurtenances. In the enclosed water I was taught to swim!

Miss Hall, the teacher, had her own technique.

Around my waist went a belt fastened to a long rope whose end Miss Hall held as she walked around the second floor balcony while I paddled happily in the water below. Except for a small built-up platform in one corner, the water was too deep for a nonswimmer. My mother swam, too. Hers was a competent breaststroke only slightly hampered by all the bathing togs she wore.

The "Bath," of course, is long gone. Indeed, it takes a considerable stretch of the imagination to picture a time when the bay water was fit to swim in!

Elsie Parry
Hightstown, N.J.

Elsie Parry's Battery Bath (sketch by Charlotte Putz, from an old magazine photograph).

17

The Observer's Book of Small Craft,
by Gordon Fairley
Frederick Warne, London and New York
192 pages, illus., glossary, index, 1976, $2.95

The *Observer*'s series is a fine example of the shirt-pocket book. For the size and the price, they are packed with information, which, though simple, is accurate. We reviewed the *Observer's Book of Ships* in MC-4; others of interest to mariners are books on *Weather, Sea Fishes, Sea and Seashore,* and now *Small Craft.*

The Observer's Book of Small Craft is, like the others, oriented toward the British Isles, but this shouldn't put you off. Of the modern boats discussed, many of them are of an "international" design, or are imported into the United States and Canada. In addition, the introductory and historical information is pertinent to all boatmen. The emphasis is on sail rather than power, though there is material on the latter.

What audience are these books written for? Beginners, mostly, children most especially (my son has copies squirreled away in different parts of the house), and adults occasionally, especially those who require something light yet factual to thumb through at the bus stop.

Aleutka Stock Plans

John Letcher designed and built a 25-foot cutter, the *Aleutka,* for extended offshore cruising. He had in mind a boat that would meet the following criteria: quick building, low initial cost, low maintenance, and easy handling. She met his demands in every way, logging 17,000 miles to date, so John has drawn up stock plans for the amateur builder. You might want to check them out.

**Letcher Offshore Design
Box 369
Southwest Harbor, Maine 04679**

Right: John Letcher's Aleutka. *For more on this boat, see the* Mariner's Catalog, *Volume 2, page 24.*

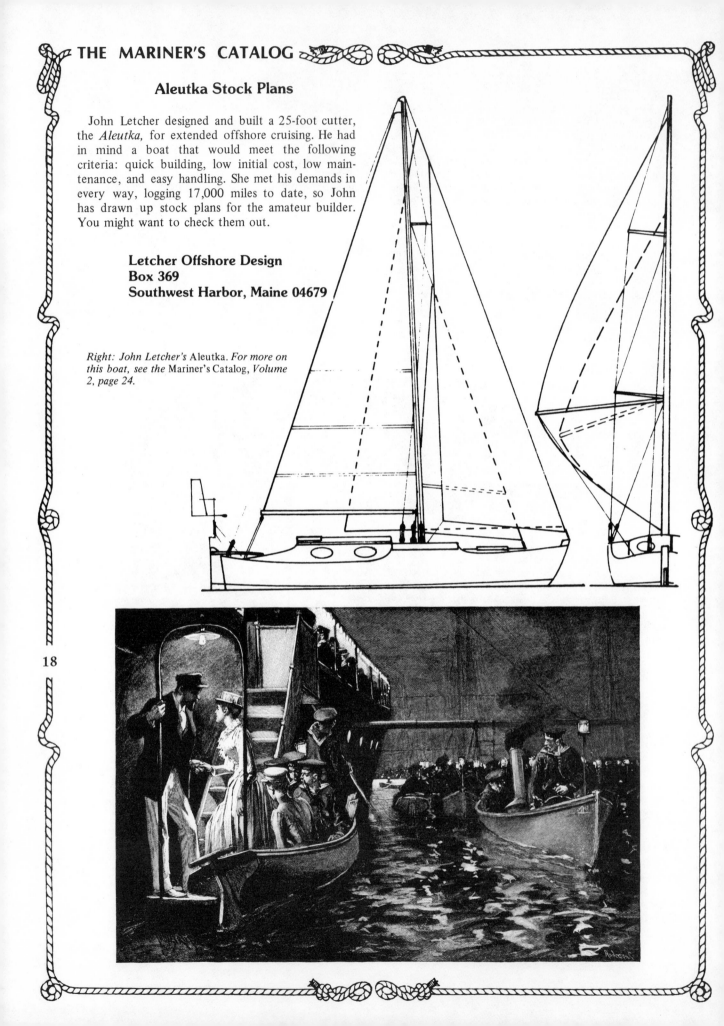

18

Above: The Winninghoff 7M undergoing trials (photo by Samuel Kitrosser).
Below: Data and lines from a Winninghoff Boats brochure.

Working with designers such as Brewer and Bolger, John Winninghoff is coming up with some interesting configurations in aluminum working craft.

Winninghoff Boats, Inc.
Kettle Cove Industrial Park
Gloucester, Mass. 01930

LOA	7M (23 ft.)
Beam	2.4M (7ft. 10½ in.)
Hull Draft @ 3,800 lbs.	.45M (1 ft. 7 in.)
Boat Weight with 70 H.P. Outboard	approx. 1150 lbs.
Boat Weight with 53 H.P. Diesel	approx. 1750 lbs.
Construction	1/8th Aluminum (welded)

Phil Bolger, the designer of my aluminum semi-displacement deep-vee lobsterboat, has been called an iconoclast, an innovator, and numerous other adjectives; given a chance, he will depart widely from the conventional wisdom and currently fashionable design approach. I would describe him as a functional designer, i.e., he comes up with the best possible functional approach to a design problem.

Since the boat is rather light for her size, she rides, even relatively heavily loaded, with the chine out of the water, thus providing the benefits of a long, narrow boat, while providing the deck and cockpit space of a boat having the usually modern length-to-beam ratio of about 3:1. When the lobsterman hauls his traps, the chine goes into the water, thus providing low freeboard for hauling, but relatively high freeboard while underway. The boat is constructed of 1/8″ plate, and weighs about the same as if she were made of 1/2″ wood, but is a great deal stronger. Moving up to 3/16″ plate, which we recommend for really heavy-duty use, adds an easily digestible weight penalty—a matter of 400 or 500 pounds—and provides an approximate structural equivalent to 1¼″ to 1½″ oak at about half the weight.

—John D. Winninghoff

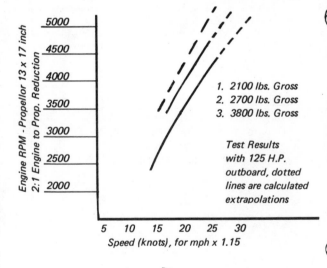

1. 2100 lbs. Gross
2. 2700 lbs. Gross
3. 3800 lbs. Gross

Test Results with 125 H.P. outboard, dotted lines are calculated extrapolations

19

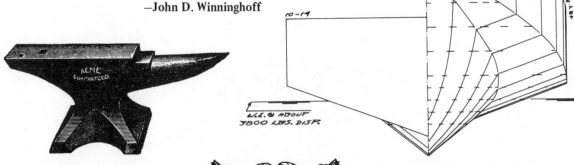

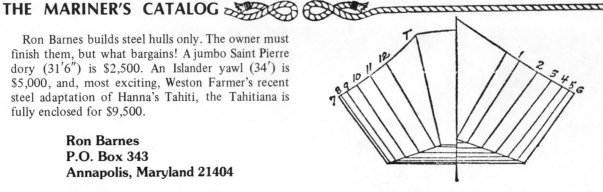

Ron Barnes builds steel hulls only. The owner must finish them, but what bargains! A jumbo Saint Pierre dory (31′6″) is $2,500. An Islander yawl (34′) is $5,000, and, most exciting, Weston Farmer's recent steel adaptation of Hanna's Tahiti, the Tahitiana is fully enclosed for $9,500.

Ron Barnes
P.O. Box 343
Annapolis, Maryland 21404

I used to build wooden boats, but today wood is economically feasible only if (1) you have your own source of timber and the means to saw it into lumber, and (2) you are satisfied with iron fastenings.

Wood from the lumberyard is generally of poor quality and grossly overpriced. Steel, on the other hand, is of uniformly high quality and cheaply fastened by arc welding. For example, steel and welding rods for a steel hull should cost less than non-ferrous fastenings for a wooden hull of equivalent size. The wood (if you have to buy it) might cost more than the fastenings. Finally, wooden boats require more labor to fabricate than any other material except ferrocement (which has other disadvantages).

How much should a steel hull cost? That depends on four factors:

1-*Displacement.* Heavy boats need more steel than light-displacement designs. For a given length, heavy-displacement boats are more seaworthy, roomier, have more headroom, and can carry more weight without overloading. But they also cost more because they need more materials.

2-*Hull shape.* A multi-chined or round-bilge hull like the Tahiti ketch requires much more cutting, fitting, and welding than a hard-chine, vee-bottom design like Harry Pidgeon's famous *Islander.* Even less labor is needed for a flat-bottomed dory design.

3-*Degree of finish.* Integral welded fuel and water tanks, steel decks and house, and other extras involve extra materials and labor, which have a great effect on the price.

4-*Labor charges* can run anywhere from $25 to as low as $8 per man-hour. I have worked in large shipyards (which tend to charge the highest labor rates) where most employees did only two or three hours' productive work in an eight-hour shift. Smaller operations with lower overhead tend to charge lower hourly rates for labor, but be sure the builder is equipped and experienced in the type of craft you want built. Examine other boats he has built. An experienced shipyard welder may make a mess of a steel yacht because the skills, techniques, and experience of big ship construction are not readily transferred to small boat fabrication. On a good design, the builder should be willing to quote on a fixed-price basis, so any lack of productivity will be at his expense, rather than yours.

—Ron Barnes

Dunlop inflatables have no representative in the U.S., so we wrote to England. Their C100 would seem most useful and competitive at £285 plus shipping.

Dunlop Ltd., GRG Division
Atherton Road, Hindley Green
Nr. Wigan WN2 4SH
England

Left and below: The Dunlop C100, a sensible-looking inflatable.

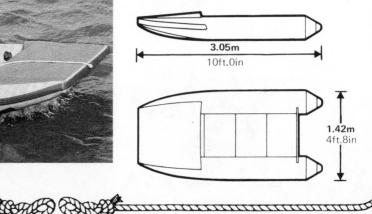

3.05m
10ft.0in

1.42m
4ft.8in

It was only a matter of time before someone came along with ferrocement building kits. Here they are, by Ferro-Marine Services; many models, traditional to ultramodern, small to very large.

Ferro Marine Services, Ltd.
7 Ship Road
Burnham-on-Crouch
Essex CM0 8JX
England

Left: The Harris Deck-Craft, everything you ever wanted in a boat and more.

Smirk. Nudge. Wink.

Harris
2801 W. State St.
Fort Wayne, Indiana 46808

MORE LORE ON SPRAY

by Weston Farmer, NA

Avid students of the occult art of yacht design sooner or later become enamored of the exploits of Captain Joshua Slocum's old *Spray*. She was the first small vessel to be sailed singlehanded around the world.

Her lines were published in *Sailing Alone Around the World* (reprinted by Sheridan House, New York, $7.50), Slocum's classic, simple, and engrossing tale of his adventures in replacing the old boat's timbers completely in a pasture near Fairhaven, Massachusetts, after which, in a sort of "Well, here we go!" mood, he shoved off unsung for four years afloat, ending up off the Battery in New York City.

There, Captain Slocum made himself known to Thomas Fleming Day, founding editor of *The Rudder* magazine. The newspapers of that day, no different in cynicism than now, scoffed at Slocum's story, claiming it to be a fake. Day knew differently, realizing that Slocum's story had worth and merit that *The Rudder* could not pay for. Day sent Captain Slocum to the publishers of *Century* magazine. Slocum's simple, unaffected yarn became a national best seller and went into book form and many printings. It is still the classic of all sea adventure tales.

Now, any boat that "has done it" becomes a model for future generations of sailors, and *Spray* developed her own cult of admirers, imitators, analysts, proponents, and adversaries. For fifteen years the cult of *Spray* had the hot-stove league buzzing, and she has been dissected by a lot of good and earnest men.

Most of the chatter centered around the discovery by Cipriano Andrade in the late 'teens of this century

that *Spray*'s docility and self-steering was caused by the "fact" that all of her centers fell amidships: the CLR, the CG, the CB (naturally), and that her center of effort of the sail plan was fortuitously so placed that she could carry 1,495 square feet of sail, all of it handled by a single hand!

None of the statistics I have seen printed ever showed either offsets or proof of her architectural engineering. Last spring, in re-working Hanna's famed *Tahiti* into a steel version called *Tahitiana,** I had need to pin these factors down. I made some discoveries that I believe students of *Spray* will find interesting.

To get an accurate fix on *Spray*'s weight, her metacentric height so as to establish her stability, her center of lateral resistance so as to establish the magic lead of her sailing center of effort, it became necessary to reconstruct her lines on an accurate engineering basis. I have a well-worked-out method for doing this.

Photostats of lines can be made. They are never hairline accurate, because few large cameras have lenses that are accurate orthographically. Lines at the edges of the enlarged plate always bend a bit and are out of whack. The trick is to make stats nearly large enough, and then, with a steel straightedge, set proportional dividers to final scale, and working to

(Continued on next page)

21

*Weston's too modest. His steel version of the Tahiti ketch is an instant success. For more details, write Weston Farmer, 18970 Azure Rd., Wayzata, Minn. 55391—Eds.

(Continued from preceding page)

known beam and length, lay in dimensioned lines. It is from Mower's set of lines in Slocum's book that I worked up a profile that was accurate, and a set of lines in plan half-breadth from which I could determine sectional areas.

Using this method, I discovered that in Mower's published body plan, the midsection of *Spray*, station 6, was missing!

What value, then, was all the yammerschoonering worth in previous analyses? I leave it to you. Ciprinano Andrade and John G. Hanna said *Spray* had all her centers on station 6. How could they calculate it from Mower's body plan if it wasn't there?

I found her fabled CLR to be 2½" abaft the mid-

section. For the hell of it, I went on and worked up her offsets and vital statistics. For posterity's sake I venerated the Old Classic's elements in an inked plate, and present it here to add to the lore of the *Spray*.

I believe the offsets to be accurate. The scale of the profile and the lines half-breadth will bear up under scrutiny. The body plan is slightly off scale—about the width of 1½" planking—but this was due to a slight slip in my dividers when inking *after* her areas were taken, and it is still visually adequate. The offsets are from the profile and plan view. "Believed accurate, but not guaranteed," as all good shipyard drawings state.

So here, then, is some data for your Gee Whiz Department, to be filed under Lore: *Spray*.

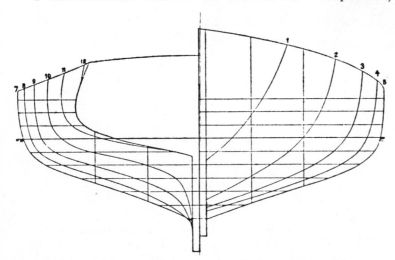

Left: The body plan of the Spray, *with the missing midsection (station 6), as originally published in* Sailing Alone Around the World.
Below: Weston Farmer's redrawn lines of the Spray.

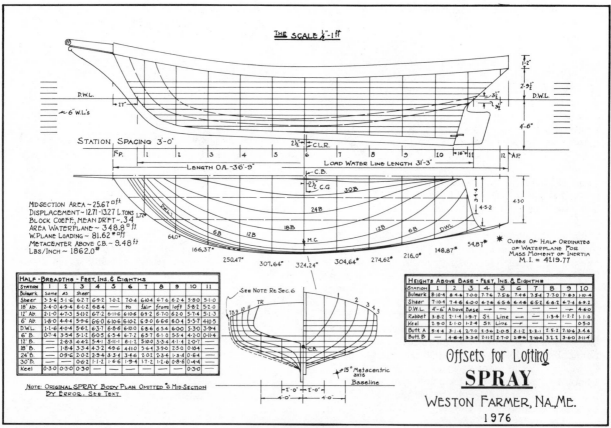

THE SCALE ⅛"-1 ft

MIDSECTION AREA ~ 25.67 □ft
DISPLACEMENT ~ 12.71 -13.27 L. tons
BLOCK COEFF. MEAN DRFT ~ .34
AREA WATERPLANE ~ 348.8 ft
W. PLANE LOADING ~ 81.62 #ft
METACENTER ABOVE C.B. ~ 9.48 ft
LBS/INCH ~ 1862.0 #

Cubes of Half Ordinates of Waterplane For Mass Moment of Inertia M.I. = 4219.77

Note: Original Spray Body Plan Omitted 6 Mid-Section By Error. See Text.

HALF-BREADTHS - FEET, INS. & EIGHTHS											
Station	1	2	3	4	5	6	7	8	9	10	11
Bulwark	Same	as	sheer								
Sheer	3·3·6	5·1·6	6·2·7	6·9·2	7·0·2	7·0·4	6·10·4	6·7·6	6·2·4	5·8·0	5·1·0
18" Ab.	2·4·0	4·9·4	6·1·2	6·8·4	—	to	fair	from	loft	5·8·2	5·2·0
12" Ab.	2·1·0	4·7·3	5·11·2	6·7·2	6·11·6	6·10·6	6·9·2	6·7·0	6·2·0	5·7·4	5·1·3
6" Ab.	1·8·0	4·4·4	5·9·6	6·6·0	6·10·6	6·10·2	6·9·0	6·6·6	6·0·4	5·5·7	4·10·5
D.W.L.	1·1·6	4·0·4	5·6·2	6·3·7	6·8·6	6·10·0	6·8·6	6·5·4	6·0·0	5·3·0	3·9·4
6" B.	0·7·4	3·5·4	5·1·2	6·0·5	6·5·4	6·7·2	6·5·7	6·1·0	5·5·4	4·2·0	0·11·4
12" B.	—	2·8·3	4·4·2	5·4·1	5·11·1	6·1·2	5·10·0	5·3·4	4·1·4	2·0·7	
18" B.	—	1·8·4	3·3·4	4·3·2	4·9·6	4·11·0	5·6·4	3·9·0	2·5·0	0·10·4	
24" B.	—	0·9·6	2·0·2	2·9·4	3·3·4	3·4·6	2·0·2	1·3·4	1·8·4	0·6·4	
30" B.	—	—	0·6·2	1·1·2	1·6·6	1·9·4	1·7·2	1·2·6	0·8·6	0·4·4	
Keel	0·3·0	0·3·0	0·3·0	—	—	—	—	—	0·3·0		

See Note Re Sec. 6
15° Metacentric axis
Baseline

HEIGHTS ABOVE BASE - FEET, INS. & EIGHTHS										
Station	1	2	3	4	5	6	7	8	9	10
Bulwark	8·10·4	8·4·6	7·0·0	7·7·6	7·5·6	7·4·6	7·5·4	7·7·0	7·8·3	1·10·4
Sheer	7·10·4	7·4·6	6·0·0	6·7·6	6·5·6	6·4·6	6·5·2	6·6·2	6·7·4	6·9·2
D.W.L.	4'-6" Above Base		—	—	—	—	—	—	4·6·0	
Rabbet	3·8·2	2·1·4	1·9·7	St.	Line	—	—	1·3·4	1·2·7	1·1·0
Keel	2·9·0	2·1·4	1·2·4	St.	Line	—	—	—	0·5·0	
Butt. A	5·4·4	3·1·4	2·7·0	2·3·6	2·0·5	2·1·2	2·2·1	7·5·2	7·10·6	3·4·6
Butt. B	—	4·6·4	3·3·6	2·11·2	2·7·0	2·8·4	2·10·4	3·2·2	3·6·0	3·11·4

Offsets for Lofting
SPRAY
WESTON FARMER, N.A., M.E.
1976

CANOES AND KAYAKS

Time takes its toll, but it renews as well. As Alan Watts said, the ends of times provide the groundwork for beginnings, and such would seem the case for canoeing, and kayaking as well. Canoes and kayaks, and the sport of using them, are in renaissance everywhere. This may be a mixed blessing—increased use will place stresses on some environments and create demands for access and services—but it is a blessing of sorts for reasons of personal and national health and quiet, and the economy that it creates attracts talented people who in other times did other things.

Strippers

Two more of the sort have emerged at RKL and Sundance. Robert K. Lincoln builds stripped (white cedar) canoes covered with clear glass-epoxy, 16', 17', and 18' river and lake models, all under $750, and 16' and 18' "Ugo" model canoes at around $750. Beautiful craft.

RKL Canoes
Pretty Marsh
Mt. Desert, Maine 04660

An RKL canoe being stripped up (left) and at rest (above).

Sketch of canoe and specifications from a Sundance brochure.

A similar technique is used at Sundance, only the wood is "B.C. cedar," which we assume to mean western red cedar, Alaskan yellow, or a near relative, and the final coat is not marine varnish, as at RKL. 14', 15', and 16' models are offered. Customers may order their own keel size, and may determine thwart, seat, and even bulkhead (storage) preferences. Because of exchange rate fluctuations, no prices were quoted to us.

**Sundance
851 Bay St.
Gravenhurst, Ontario
Canada**

SPECIFICATIONS

Length	Beam	Depth	Capacity	Weight
14'	34"	12.5"	600 lbs.	46 lbs.
15'	35"	12.5"	700 lbs.	50 lbs.
16'	36"	12.75"	800 lbs.	54 lbs.

OPTIONS	Add
Yoke	0 lbs.
Additional Thwart	1 lbs.
Stowage Bulkhead	4 lbs.
Brass Keel Moulding	2 lbs.
White Water (Additional Fiberglass)	3 lbs.

Above: A freshly built Sundance canoe awaits her owner.

Exit Hazen

Dear Editors:

I sold Wilderness Boats (see MC-2, page 32) two years ago, and the rights to my book (*The Stripper's Guide to Canoe Building*, see review MC-3, page 36) were sold this summer. The publisher of the new, enlarged, and more glorious third edition is:

The Book Bin
547 Howard St.
San Francisco, Calif. 94105

The book's now priced at $7.95, including the plans, and has extra chapters on making canoe sails and making your own canoe paddle. There's a beautiful color photo on the cover, the type and layout have been redone . . . it's more readable and understandable.

David Hazen
Eugene, Oregon

Construction Techniques for Wood Strip Canoes, by Charles W. Moore
U.S. Canoe Association
P.O. Box 9, Winamac, Indiana 46996
18 pages, paperbound, 1976, illus., $5.00

Not as detailed as the *Stripper's Guide to Canoe Building* by David Hazen (see review, MC-3, p. 36), yet covers the territory. The instructions are for building a cedar strip canoe, covered on the inside and outside with fiberglass. The USCA also sells full-scale plans for canoes built with this method—an 18'16" cruiser, a 17' flatwater C-1, a 21' flatwater C-2, and a 24' Club Four C-4—all available at $2 apiece for non-members.

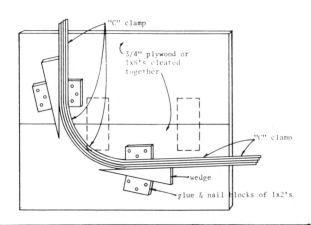

To build stem pieces using laminations, obtain a piece of hardwood, preferably ash, that is 1" thick x 36" to 40" long with a flat grain. Rip off a series of strips that are approximately 3/32" thick. These strips will be edge grain and will bend quite easily. The tighter the radius to be used on your stems, the thinner the strips must be. The 18'-6" U.S.C.A. "Cruiser" model plans will require stem laminations no larger than 3/32".

Boxed quote and diagram above: From Construction Techniques for Wood Strip Canoes.

Below: From a Riverside Canoe Company brochure.

Fiberglass Kits

It is, of course, the emergence of one's self that's at issue and often that means building a canoe one-self. Scratch building is the best way to do this, but a natural reticence makes kits mighty attractive the first time around, and there is a zillion of them available. Well, almost. Not pretty, probably not good at all as a canoe, but the cheapest kits we have found are at Riverside, the so-called Adventure line, kits 14' to 18', $70 to $90 plus shipping.

The Riverside Canoe Co.
P.O. Box 5595
Riverside, Cal. 92507

25

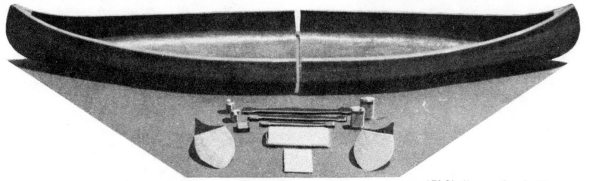

17' Challenger Canoe Kit

*Above: The 13' duckboat from American Fiber-Lite.
Below: Seda's Explorer—length 15', width 33", weight 59 lbs.*

Two Notables

A perusal of our annual mountain of canoe-company literature produced two interesting models, a 13' duckboat from American Fiber-Lite, and the 15' Explorer from SEDA.

**American Fiber-Lite
P.O. Box 67
Marion, Illinois 62959**

**SEDA Products
P.O. Box 41
San Ysidro, Cal. 92173**

EXPLORER — Touring Canoe

This is a true wilderness expedition boat. It is partially decked and has one long oval cockpit which can be covered with the optional spray cover. The spray cover is tightened with stainless steel cable   and special device   to form an integral part of the boat. Two large cones are sewn in to allow entry of paddlers. Should the boat capsize in heavy whitewater the paddlers may leave the boat and the cones will press together sealing the boat. Because of this the boat stays practically dry inside and floats high to avoid damage. The EXPLORER has plastic molded seats allowing paddling either in a sitting or kneeling position. Also the built-in flotation in both ends keeps the boat afloat if used without a spray cover. Foam knee pads, webbed knee braces, hooks to secure your gear and grab loops are features included. The EXPLORER is very maneuverable and stable and will provide the owner with a multi-use boat for all types of waterways from little mountain streams to the ocean.

A Guide to Paddle Adventure,
**by Rick Kemmer
Vanguard Press, New York
295 pages, illus., no index (!),
paperbound, $6.95**

26

The title makes it sound like an insipid book patronizingly written for black bass tournament amateurs, but last year I gained a healthy portion of advice from it when I went out and bought a canoe. The subtitle tells the scope of the book: "How to buy canoes, kayaks, and inflatables. Where to travel and what to pack along." For someone like me, who wanted to get involved in canoeing but whose only experience in it was renting them on sunny afternoons on the Potomac River, the information provided was sound, clearly stated, rational (i.e., no ideology), and detailed. As a result, I bought a 17-foot Grumman aluminum canoe and haven't had a single twinge of guilt or regret since.

Boxed quote at right from A Guide to Paddle Adventure.

Fiberglas Engineering Corporation of Wyoming, Minnesota, manufacturer of Oswego canoes, produces two fine fiberglass models 16 feet long: the double-ended Whitewater and the square-stern Osage. The Whitewater features expanded foam flotation in its bow and stern, two thwarts, and two seats. The Osage has one thwart and two seats; its sawed-off stern is shaped to a narrow "V" configuration. Capacity for the Whitewater is 800 pounds, while the Osage is rated at 900 pounds. The Osage accepts small outboards up to 3.5 horsepower. Both canoes are available in red, blue, green, gold, coral, and dead grass, the latter being used as camouflage when hunting. These canoes are average in size and weight, and they feature stylishly rounded ends with moderate upsweep. The Oswego warranty is for two years to the original owner, but cost of transportation to the factory must be borne by the owner.

Algonquin, a 16-foot touring canoe that also handles whitewater, is typical of the excellent specialty designs emanating from Vermont Tubbs. It features a low bow and stern for minimum wind sensitivity and better visibility when portaging. It has two woven seats and ash thwarts and rails, giving a handsome, traditional appearance. Large whitewater decks of ash keep out the spray. Its V-shaped hull is designed to hold course well yet provide good maneuverability. Overall, the canoe is constructed of an all-cloth layup similar to that of an Olympic-style kayak. There is no matt or roving to add weight. Although normally rigid, the hull flexes on impact without shattering. Urethane-filled tanks provide flotation. Despite its high price, the fast, comparatively narrow design of this canoe makes it worth considering. Here is a fine craft for people interested in entering marathons and in racing. But its design does not preclude touring and camping.

Boatbuilder's Manual, by Charles Walbridge
Wildwater Designs, Penllyn, Pa. 19422
70 pages, illus., paperbound, 1973 (2nd ed.),
$4.50

Subtitled "How to build fiberglass canoes and kayaks for whitewater." From a bookman's point of view, this is a pretty crude example of the trade; but you don't buy this book because you like to read or you like to fondle calfskin-bound volumes.

You buy this book because you want to build canoes and kayaks out of fiberglass and other synthetics, such as Kevlar, nylon, polypropylene, etc. You also buy this book because the information it contains is worth a building lot in midtown Manhattan, especially to the home builder who wants to experiment with designs. To reduce it to a simple statement: if you want page after page densely packed with technical and practical advice for building small, strong, lightweight craft, this is your manual.

CLOTH:	WEIGHT oz/ sq yd	TEAR STRENGTH		RIGIDITY/ FLEXIBILITY		FLEXURAL MODULUS		ABRASION RESISTANCE		RESIN ABSORPTION	
E-GLASS MATT	18	LOW	(1)	V. RIGID	(2)	LOW	(1)	MODERATE	(2)	VERY HIGH	(1)
E-GLASS ROVING	32	MODERATE	(2)	V. RIGID	(2)	LOW	(2)	MODERATE	(2)	HIGH	(2)
E-GLASS CLOTH	7.5,20 10	MODERATE	(3)	RIGID	(3)	MODERATE	(3)	MODERATE	(2)	MODERATE	(3)
NYLON CLOTH	4.2	VERY HIGH	(5)	VERY FLEXIBLE	(5)	HIGH	(4)	VERY HIGH	(4)	LOW	(5)
POLYPRO-PYLENE	4.6	VERY HIGH	(5)	VERY FLEXIBLE	(5)	HIGH	(4)	VERY HIGH	(4)	LOW TO MODERATE	(4)
DYNEL CLOTH	4.0	LOW	(1)	RIGID	(2)	LOW	(2)	UNUSUALLY HIGH	(5)	VERY HIGH	(1)
DIOLEN MATERIAL	-	MODERATE	(3+)	MODERATELY FLEXIBLE	(3)	MODERATE	(3+)	MODERATE	(3)	- - - -	
S-GLASS CLOTH	6,12	MODERATE TO HIGH	(4+)	MODERATELY FLEXIBLE	(4)	VERY HIGH	(5)	HIGH	(4)	HIGH	(2)
PRD 49 KEVLAR	6.0	HIGH	(5)	RIGID	(2)	VERY HIGH	(5)	HIGH	(4)	MODERATE	(3)

"E-Glass" is the industry designation for regular fiberglass.
"The Synthetics" (Nylon and Polypropylene) should not be heat cured. Pre-shrunk (heat treated) cloths are available at extra cost. As they tend to delaminate, epoxy is more effective as a resin system than polyester.

To maintain rigidity with layups using the more flexible cloths: use a more rigid resin system. Polyester is easy to regulate by varying the ratio of rigid: flexible resin. Epoxies are more difficult, and may require the use of a different hardener.

Most synthetic cloths were developed for the tire industry. If you hear of some great new material for making automobile tires, you might want to try it for boatbuilding!

On the River, by Walter Magnes Teller
Rutgers University Press
New Brunswick, N.J.
331 pages, illus., index, biblio., 1976,
paperbound, $5.95

This is an anthology of accounts of canoe and small boat voyages, most on fresh water but a few on salt. The selection is intelligent and varied, ranging from well-known authors, such as Henry David Thoreau and Nathaniel Holmes Bishop, to the practically unknown, such as Ralph K. Wing and Isobel Knowles. A nice feature of the book is the maps, which help more than you would imagine.

Middle-of-page chart from Boatbuilder's Manual.
Sketch above from On the River.

It's True
Fiberglass Craftsmanship Lives

We were nearing the end of a deep-winter's day of searching the countryside for material for the *Mariner's Catalog*. We were tired, we were reeling from the accumulated mounds of data we had collected, we were within sight of Weston, Massachusetts, the home of Bart Hauthaway, a legendary canoe-builder and vanishing-breed outdoorsman. We almost packed it in and holed up in a motel until we could clear our brains for another assault on our subject. To our credit, we didn't.

We turned off Route 128 to find Bart and talk about boats. Find him we did—up to his neck in resin and glass cloth, putting the finishing touches on a mold for a new seagoing kayak, surrounded by paddles, fishing rods, stuffed ducks, shotguns, hand-tied flies, books, magazines, photographs, correspondence, and canoes and kayaks of every description, all to his own design. His backyard was a sea of boats, some completely buried in snow, some half showing through, others perched like gulls on top of drifts. Off to the side was the most gorgeous fisherman's featherweight canoe we had ever seen: a Rob Roy model measuring 10½′ x 29″ x 12″, weighing a mere 30 pounds, tearing our hearts out. Who ever would have thought it possible?—a fiberglass canoe built by a craftsman, a boat to make your hands shake and *not* made of wood. $350, from:

Bart Hauthaway
640 Boston Post Road
Weston, Mass. 02193

Bart also custom-builds fishing canoes, hunting canoes, duckboats, competition kayaks, cruising kayaks, single and double paddles. Send him a stamped, self-addressed envelope for his latest catalog and price list.

28

Above: The happy owner of a new Hauthaway Rob Roy tries her out on the mighty Megunticook River (photo by Brooks Townes).
Right: From the Wildwater Designs Kits catalog.

Skirts

We notice that more and more kayak outfits are offering spray skirts and kits for them. A kit in *Neoprene* is offered by:

Wildwater Designs Kits
Penllyn Pike & Morris Rd.
Penllyn, Penn. 19422

Oars and Paddles

Maine seems to be teeming with oar and paddle people. Two newly discovered ones are Joe Hasenfus, who, at $25 per, makes custom-laminated spruce paddles—has done it for 37 years—and Shaw & Tenney, a company that has made first-class wholesale oars and paddles since 1856.

**Joe Hasenfus
Kents Hill, Maine 04349**

**Shaw & Tenney, Inc.
20 Water Street
Orono, Maine 04473**

OAR LENGTH FORMULA:

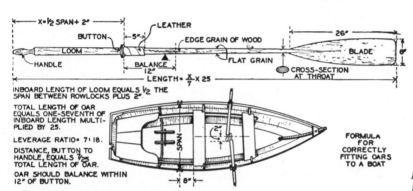

INBOARD LENGTH OF LOOM EQUALS ½ THE SPAN BETWEEN ROWLOCKS PLUS 2".

TOTAL LENGTH OF OAR EQUALS ONE-SEVENTH OF INBOARD LENGTH MULTIPLIED BY 25.

LEVERAGE RATIO= 7:18.

DISTANCE, BUTTON TO HANDLE, EQUALS ½₅ TOTAL LENGTH OF OAR.

OAR SHOULD BALANCE WITHIN 12" OF BUTTON.

FORMULA FOR CORRECTLY FITTING OARS TO A BOAT

Paddles, oars, and oar length diagram from Shaw & Tenney brochure

KAYAK NOTES

There is a wellspring of kayak information for the serious inquirer at the National Museum of Man in Ottawa, including a 17-page kayak bibliography (Xeroxed), an illustrated *Glossary of Kayak Terminology* (published pamphlet), an extensive photo collection of Indian and Eskimo craft, and more than forty kayaks on exhibit. Millennia of development leaves much for the student, little for the inventor. Those interested should write:

**David W. Zimmerly
Canadian Ethnology Service
National Museum of Man
Ottawa K1A OM8
Canada**

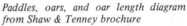

Left: From An Illustrated Glossary of Kayak Terminology *by David W. Zimmerly.*

Sea Canoeing
by Derek C. Hutchinson
Adam & Charles Black, London, 1976
from Transatlantic Arts
Levittown, N.Y. 11756
$15.00

Don't ask questions, just buy it. Based solidly on native practice, these are the techniques of ocean kayaking in every aspect; thoroughly illustrated, by one of the best authorities in Britain and Europe.

Seal Launching and Landing

Many of the areas which provide beautiful scenery and freedom for the sea canoeist also provide rocks, cliffs and many difficulties for landings and launchings. Fortunately or unfortunately, seas have a habit of calming down while one is asleep in a tent. Upon walking down to a large flat slab which was regularly awash the day before, you may discover it many feet above a placid sea. The seal launching method in Figure 29 shows a way of getting your canoe safely into the water.

A couple of readers have mentioned that the use of butyrate airplane dope, recommended in MC-4, has excessive shrinking characteristics and that its use presupposes a uniformly loose skin before application. Otherwise, the shrinkage severely compresses the framework and creates a scalloping effect, unsightly on some framing schemes and a slight addition to wetted surface on all of them. Butyrate's advantages remain, however (but see differing opinion in accompanying letter).

If one does wish to use oil-based fillers, two or three coats can be saved by using Interlux 244 Boatyard Sanding Surfacer White Paint. We used it for the first time last year, and the stuff is dynamite for killing the weave on 10-ounce duck. If you ever wondered how yards could, relatively speaking, get so much done so fast in the springtime, this is one of the reasons, and if you don't see it on the "consumer's" shelves meant for us, create an embarrassing, obnoxious fuss about it.

Figure 29. A seal launching.

Boxed quote and diagram above from Sea Canoeing.

Dear Editors:

I used butyrate dope (see MC-4, p. 53) from my local airport on my old-fashioned wood and canvas kayak ten years ago. It *does* crack, imperceptibly, causing leaks and coatings on top to crack. I sealed leaks by flooding the inside with old-fashioned smelly canvas waterproofing liquid.

I'm still looking for a canvas dressing to replace the butyrate, which I will sand off.

Jerome L. Kligerman
Philadelphia, Pa.

30

Scull, Shell, & Sweep

In the MC-4 we listed the Pocock shells in Seattle, which piqued enough interest to have us look more deeply into sport rowing, that most enervating of competitive sports and pleasant of individual ones.

Harry Parker, crew coach at Harvard, kindly directed us to the National Association of Amateur Oarsmen, the hub of the sport in this country. They've the *Oarsman,* a journal, books, plans, paraphernalia, and, most helpful, a list of scull and shell sources worldwide, a few of which are listed on the opposite page.

**National Association of Amateur Oarsmen
#4 Boat House Row
Philadelphia, Penn. 19130**

Thirty-four pounds of "single" plus oars for $1,300 makes beef look quite reasonable. This one is made in Japan and sold in this country by:

**Lyman S.A. Perry
311 Newtown St. Road
Newtown Square, Penn. 19073**

Oars and sweeps, as well as shells (up to eights) are offered by:

**Worcester Oar & Paddle Co.
660 Franklin St.
Worcester, Mass. 01604**

	SINGLE	PAIR	DOUBLE	FOUR	QUAD	EIGHT
Joseph Garafolo, 660 Franklin Street, Worcester, MA 01604	X	X		X		X
George Pocock Racing Shells, Inc., 509 NE Northlake Way, Seattle, WA 98105	X	X	X	X	X	X
Helmut Schoenbrod Racing Shells, 596 Elm Street, Rt. 1, Biddeford, ME 04005				X		X
Ted Van Dusen, 22 Heritage Lane, Duxbury, MA 02332	X					
Alden Ocean Shell, Martin Marine Co., Box 2510 Peperell Rd, Kittery Pt., ME 03905	X		X			
Alfred Stampfli Bootswerft, Seestrasse 489 8038 Zurich, Switzerland	X	X	X	X	X	X
Donoratico, c/o Harry A. Goetschi, a/s FQSA 1415 Est, rue Jarry, Montreal, Que. H2E 2Z7	X	X	X	X	X	X
Kaschper Racing Shells, Ltd, P.O. Box 40, Lucan, Ont., Canada	X	X	X	X	X	X
Edwin H. Phelps, 34 Robin Hood Lane, Putney, London, England	X					X
Sargent & Burton Pty, Ltd., 20-22 Bennett St., Mortlake NSW 2137 Australia				X		X
Scandia Marine & A/B Scandia Boats, Uddevalla, Sweden						
George Sims, Eel Pie Island, Twickenham, Middlesex, England	X	X	X	X	X	X
Fuji Sculls, L.S.A. Perry, Agent, 311 N Newtown Street Road, Newton Square, PA 19073	X					
Croker Oars, 108 Bowden St Meadowbank, 2114 Sydney, Australia						
Charles Butt, 977 Spencer Road, McLean, VA 22101	X					
Coffey Corporation, 32 Linnarean St., Cambridge, Mass. 02138	X	X	X	X	X	X

31

Canoes of Oceania, by Haddon and Hornell
Bishop Museum Press, Honolulu, Hawaii
908 pages, illus., index, 1975 (reprint),
paperbound, $25

The book might be paperbound, but the monumentality of this study, the depth of the detail, the plans and drawings, the notes, and the scholarliness of the text makes this a definitive work that is well worth the price. This large-format reprint (7″ x 11″) combines in one volume *The Canoes of Polynesia, Fiji, and Micronesia* (1936); *The Canoes of Melanesia, Queensland, and New Guinea* (1937); and *Definition of Terms, General Survey, and Conclusions* (1938). Students of small-boat evolution and design shouldn't pass up this one.

Below: From Canoes of Oceania.

Anson's drawing also shows what appear to be pulley blocks in use, though perhaps they are thimbles, but there is no reference to them in the text and so far as known such a device was never employed by any Micronesians till after long contact with Europeans. Anson continues:

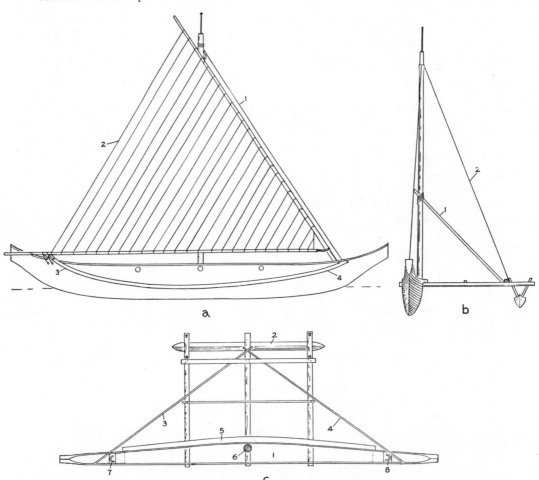

FIGURE 300.—"Flying proa" of the Marianas Islands. *a*, view from leeward with sail set: 1, one of two stays supporting mast, the other hidden behind sail; 2, matting sail; 3, 4, running stays. *b*, head view, outrigger to windward: 1, mast shore; 2, shroud. *c*, plan: 1, proa; 2, "boat" at end of outrigger frame; 3, 4, braces from the ends to steady frame; 5, thin plank placed to windward to prevent shipping of water, to serve as seat for native who bales, and sometimes as rest for goods transported; 6, part of middle outrigger boom on which mast is fixed; 7, 8, horseshoe sockets, in one of which yard is lodged according to tack (after Anson, 1748).

32

TOOLS

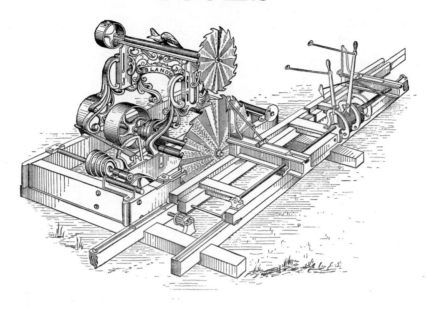

Sadder But Wiser Are We

The following is a true and extremely sad story. It's also a hideous joke for people who miss nice hand tools.

Time: Last week.

Place: Sears Store, hardware department (Topeka, Kansas).

Me: "Do you have a saw set?"

Them: "Oh no . . . all of them are sold separately."

—Mark Roeyer

Caulking Mallet

. . . Don't know how, who, or what, but there is a hardware store in Belfast, Maine, and they have a catalog, and it lists a caulking mallet; to our knowledge, the only one in the country.

**Hall Hardware Co.
Belfast, Maine 04915
Catalog on request**

Old and Good

Woodworker is 75 years old, the oldest woodcraft journal yet in print. It is monthly, English, and now published by our old friend:

**Model and Allied Publications
P.O. Box 35, Bridge Street
Hemel Hempstead
Herts 1HP 1EE
England
$15/yr.**

33

Below: Caulking mallet from Hall Hardware catalog, which also shows a number of other essential tools for the practical boatman.

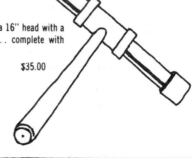

Caulking mallet with locust handle . . . a 16" head with a 16" handle mallet is well balanced . . . complete with polished steel rings.

Caulking mallet $35.00

One Man's Workshop

by C.A. Campbell

I am a consulting engineer normally travelling a great deal, but for over 30 years my avocation has been "do-it-yourself" in woodworking for my home and my boats. Building small sail and row boats (up to 19') of good hull form by relatively cheap and simple modern techniques has been of interest for several years, and I always have some project underway. After musing over what equipment or techniques have been most useful to me, I offer the following:

Work Bench Setups

My indoor area has always been limited to a portion of my garage and basement, so setups which can be readily erected, dismantled, and stored are of prime consideration. Also the size, type of surface, and working height should change for different people and type of job to avoid fatigue and provide convenience. I have one long bench about 28 inches high along a wall, which is really only the center for storage above and below, and a surface for collecting, sorting, etc. I almost never actually work at it.

My working benches are set up on sawhorses, as this provides access from all sides and above. These sawhorses use sheetmetal brackets which take 1" x 4" nominal stock lumber tightened with ¼" carriage bolts and wing nuts. I have several sets of brackets and with these get several degrees of versatility.

Height above floor: I have sets of legs which allow working from 18" to about 36". Each set was made when I had a project which needed it. When not in use, the 4 legs for each horse are stacked, held together with a rubber band cut from an old tire inner tube.

Width: Horizontal cross members vary from about 30" to 60". One set has V notches quite useful to hold long stock for spars, oars, etc.

Work surface: Most surfaces are of plywood, ½" to 1" thick, from 1' to 4' wide, and 3' to 8' long. These were all leftover pieces from other projects. Cleats are screwed on the underside to bear against the sawhorse cross members. If rigidity is needed, 1" x 2" or 1" x 3" cross braces are temporarily nailed (use double headed nails) between sawhorse legs and/or cleats. When not in use they stack against a wall.

Other surfaces are 2" x 4", 2" x 6", or 2" x 10" planks of 6' to 16' in length. These stack on horizontal wall brackets when not in use.

The plywood tops are covered with various cleats, holes to take stops, dogs, holddowns, various styles of bench hooks, etc. A couple are specialized, with forms for gluing picture frames, laminating breast hooks, knees, built-up paddles, oars, etc. Final gluing pressure is usually supplied by wedges. Using one screw vise face, you can get the multipoint surface-hold system touted by those $500 workbenches.

The planks as tops serve many purposes:

— to support plywood sheets for layout & trimming with a sabre saw.

(Continued on next page)

Tool Supply Houses

With a few exceptions, of course, these previously unlisted general handtool supply houses have much of the same array as those listed in previous volumes of the *Catalog*. We list them on the good theory that people should shop for their shop, and keep it hot for all of them.

Leichtung, a generally well-known house for their fine Danish workbenches, Bracht chisels, and generally excellent range of woodworking tools, also lists a joist brace.

**Leichtung, Inc.
701 Beta Drive #17
Cleveland, Ohio 44143**

JB2 - JOIST BRACE
Ordinary braces are available most anywhere. Joist braces should be. As the name signifies, it was first a house carpenters' tool meant for work in very tight corners or between joists, because it doesn't require the 360° sweep of an ordinary brace. Mahogany tinted beech handles, ball bearing head, nickel plated with a superior ratchet and universal chuck. 10" from handle end to shaft. **$17.95**

Above, left, below: From the Leichtung catalog, which has some fantastic color photography.

BR844 - 8 PIECE FIRMER CHISEL SET -
These are really tough! Tungsten-Vanadium alloy steel (Rockwell C61-63) with the comfortable Bracht ribbed-ash handle and nickel-plated, double hoops. From 10-12½" in length (depending on blade size). Set contains: ¼", ⅜", ½", ⅝", ¾", 1", 1¼", and 1½" sizes.
$44.95

BR844-1½"

34

(Continued from preceding page)

— two 2″ x 4″s with clamps make a fine vise for tapered or odd-shaped pieces.

— a long 2″ x 10″ is perfect for getting out a spiled strake or working on any long board. I use a Zyliss edge-clamped vise; it's expensive but versatile; there are cheaper versions.

— to make ladder frame setups for mounting molds and backbone for small boats.

I usually nail for temporary setups, use screws for more precision or strength, and thrubolt for long-term or repetitive use.

Some useful tools

My principal power tool is a *Shopsmith Mark 5* to which attachments, jigs, and cutting tools have been added as I needed them for a job. It is a versatile precision machine, and setup time is no trouble to me—it might be a problem for production work.

Hand power drills: Sears heaviest duty bought on sale in 1/4″ and 3/8″ sizes. Each over 10 years old, each rebuilt once, and each serviced by me once a year. Each has a versatile mounting bracket for bench use. There are many attachments, acquired as a good use arose.

Sabre saws: Again Sears best bought on sale 7 years ago, never overhauled except by me. The secret is not to overload it by using the correct blades, and just expect some breakage. I do not have a bandsaw, so this sabre saw gets some heavy-duty use, e.g., curves on 2″ oak, 5/4 maple, locust for cleat blanks, and blanks for knees from apple and beech.

Rasps: both hand and power. It is my experience that rasps are the most useful tool for quickly and precisely removing large amounts of wood after you have used a saw. I have hand rasps of different cuts, both flat and rounded. Also included are the various shapes of Stanley Surformers for hand use (including the Stickleback, a sort of rough, non-clogging, rattail-type file). Equally useful are power rasps as drums in several lengths and diameters, and flat discs. I use these in the hand power drills, drill press, and the discs in place of a table-saw blade to surface rough-cut stock. Rasp blades are also available for a sabre saw, and have proved useful to finish the bevel on long plywood plank sheets instead of a plane.

Japanese saws: These cut on the pull stroke, have very little tooth set, and very thin blades. Used with guides, I find them much better than back saws or tenon saws for close work in either plywood or regular stock. They stay sharp for a long time, but a

(Continued on next page)

The Princeton Company is another one of the new, rather a bit too precious "tools-for-the-connoisseur"-type places, but their growing inventory would seem worth our continuing attention. We are impressed with their double-pump oiler, for example, and their leather tool apron.

The Princeton Company
P.O. Box 276
Princeton, Mass. 01541

35

FORTY-FIVE DEGREE
Outside The Table

VERTICAL
Outside The Table

HORIZONTAL
Outside The Table

HORIZONTAL
Inside The Table

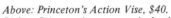

Above: Princeton's Action Vise, $40.
Right: Princeton's carpenter's leather apron, $23.

(Continued from preceding page)

special fine file is required to resharpen. I have used these to cut continuously varying bevels on molds, chines, and transoms, except for a final touch with a rasp or plane, to notch for keel, ribbands, etc., to cut scarf joints in place in strip planking, and finally to fit "dutchmen." My advice is—don't bear down, let the saw do the work.

Other saws: For small-boat work I prefer short blades, and I own two that seem to get a lot of work. First is a cut-anything type about 16″ long with a handle that angles into many positions—very handy. Second is a Swedish set of six blades (keyhole, rip, crosscut, backsaw, floor cutter) with one handle also about 16″ long. My advice is, keep them sharp; I touch up with a file as soon as they show any sign of dullness. A third saw, not often used, but excellent when I wanted to remove old pieces during renovation without taking everything apart, is a thin, coiled blade (also Swedish) which I bought at a camping outfitters some years ago.

Knives: Good drawknives, spokeshaves, inshaves, etc., are now available, though expensive. But I use other knives extensively. First is a hefty two-blade pocket knife (4-inch) that I have owned for 40 years; the large blade is kept sharpened to a V edge for heavy cutting; the smaller blade is kept razor sharp. My natural inclination is to use this first for any small, fine trimming rather than locate the special tool. Second is the multigadget Swiss army knife; I have used every gadget on it in small-boat work, including the toothpick and tweezers. Third is one that I had a machinist make for me some years ago

from a 1″-wide heavy file; the blade is about 4½″ long, heavy at the back, sharp-pointed on the straight-edge, which is ground veed like an axe. It was made to be pounded on the back; I use it to chip glue, putty, cut cable or rope, make small notches, etc. My machinist only tempered the edge to be ground. Fourth is my "crooked knife"; this is an old woodsman's type, about 6-inch blade with a hook in the end, one edge ground; it is designed to cut by pulling toward you, and the hook acts like a gouge. Mine was made from a heavy hacksaw blade, and I left the teeth on the back edge. I use it mostly as a small drawknife in boat work. Fifth is really not a knife but a scraper; I use one with 4-edge replaceable blades of which two edges are serrated; for me, scraping to produce a fine joint or smooth finish is better than fine planing or sandpaper.

Hatchets: I have never had to try to learn to use an adze, broadaxe, etc., for shaping large timbers. However, I do often use several smaller hatchet types to rough out work, because it is less effort than a handsaw or getting to a bandsaw. First, and most usual, looks like a butcher's meat cleaver, or an extra-heavy Chinese chef's knife. Second is an ancient light lather's hatchet. Third is a Japanese carpenter's hatchet weighing a bit over one pound, but with a 4½″ cutting edge. Fourth is a machete. These are all kept sharp with a fine file, not honed with a stone. My only advice besides practice is don't bear down; take it easy and let the tool do the work.

Sharpening: I own and use guides for filing hand and circular saws, and also an assortment of grinding

(Continued on next page)

Consumer's Bargain's catalog beats some suppliers' prices and loses to others. They are going for the "hard-to-find" and "ingenious device" market, so it is worthwhile to hold this one up to the others. I've got one of their shop knives, and it is the best of several in the shop. It's the only one that has held its edge all the way around while trimming 10-ounce deck canvas, for example. Also, they have a good buy on a breast drill.

Consumer's Bargain Corp.
109 Wheeler Ave.
Pleasantville, N.Y. 10570

SHOP KNIFE
Of Finest Tool Steel

You'll want this top quality knife handy at all times in the shop or in the home. It's made of hard tool steel and has a comfortable handle that will do the toughest jobs easily. The blade is guaranteed to keep it's sharpness and durability. It will handle all your wood carving jobs. It works on plaster, linoleum and plastics. Good for the sculptor or woodworker.

M-1 Shop Knife ....$2.49 ppd

Just as Consumer's Bargain *sort of* goes after Brookstone, so Woodworkers Supply of New Mexico *sort of* goes after Woodcraft. Nice catalog, competitive prices, and a unique trick or two as well.

Woodworkers Supply, Inc.
P.O. Box 14117
11200 Menaul NE
Albuquerque, N.M. 87112

Grinding and Lapping Compound
Since 1903 Clover compound has been used to solve tens of thousands of different grinding and lapping problems. Some of these applications include honing tools with compound on a flat piece of glass, "running-in" gears and lapping iron plane bottoms. Offered in silicon carbide grain in a highly-developed blend of honing oil and grease. Two assortments are available: 3 one-pound cans each of 120, 280 and 500 grit or 12 ¼-pound cans of 80 through 1000 grit.
140-001 3 one-pound can assortment   **$16.25**
140-002 12 ¼-pound can assortment   **$29.00**

Above: From Woodworkers Supply catalog.
Left: From Consumer's Bargain catalog.

(Continued from preceding page)

wheels and honing stones. My most useful wheel is rubber bonded with abrasive which I obtained through Shopsmith. With a good adjustable tool rest and a bit of practice, you can hone chisels, gouges, plane blades, knives, etc., almost to perfection. A few swipes on a hard Arkansas stone, plus stropping, will give a razor edge.

Sandpaper: I have watched this disappear in shops and boatyards by the ream because it is often used by the uninformed where they should use other tools. But more important is that when it should be used, there is a much better modern product. This is carbide grit bonded to metal. I have it in coarse to fine grits for circular, orbital, and hand block sanders. It just never seems to wear out. Another product with which I have only a little experience is an open-weave nylon impregnated with grit; it did not clog up when I tried it.

Rotary Sanders with universal-joint padded heads do a good enough job in sanding curved boat surfaces for rough work, but for fine finishing, I prefer a flexible batten with paper tacked to it.

Clamps and wedges: I will agree with everyone who has written that you never can have too many. The tool catalogs are full of all kinds, all sizes, and all expensive. I probably made my first homebuilt clamps as a Boy Scout, and I have no count of either the types or sizes that I have made since. But, for the uninitiated, start by reading something like Sam Rabl's book (*Boatbuilding in Your Own Backyard,* Cornell Maritime Press) and catalogs for ideas. Here are a few tips that have worked for me:

Use ¼" threaded rod and wing nuts available in hardware stores to pull your wood clamps together—much cheaper than carriage bolts.

Cut pieces of aluminum tubing to slip over the ¼" rods when you need spaces. It's a lot easier than fitting blocks or dowels.

Use a small hydraulic screw jack, available in auto stores, with proper blocking to put pressure on heavy members.

Use a come-a-long multipart tackle or Spanish windlass to haul on a lever arm.

Use blocks and wedges (always in pairs with shallow angles). My wedges range in size from about ½" to 2" to 2" x 20". Use the scrap material that you have on hand; hardwoods are better than soft, but both will work.

Use rope, straps, webbing, rubber tire tubes, etc., to go around large girths or awkward shapes.

Vise-grip pliers (in their many forms) are powerful clamps.

American Perfect Pattern Screwdrivers

Forged from one solid bar of tempered, high carbon steel, these classic screwdrivers are built for rugged use. Lacquered hardwood handle inserts form an extremely comfortable grip.

113-027	4" Blade	$2.55	113-029	8" Blade	$ 4.10
113-028	6" Blade	$3.15	113-030	10" Blade	$ 4.20
113-401		Set of 4 above			$13.60

It is not clear just what bad habits are developed by firms that cater to ordinary amateur craftsmen, but surely there are some. Woodworker's Tool Works caters to professional shops in the woodworking industry, everything from sandpaper to big, expensive machines.

Woodworker's Tool Works
222 S. Jefferson St.
Chicago, Ill. 60606

37

Above: American Perfect screwdrivers from Woodworkers Supply catalog.
Right: Adjustable countersinks from Woodworker's Tool Works catalog.

NO. 122 ADJUSTABLE COUNTERSINKS

(for flat bottom holes)

NO. 122-V ADJUSTABLE COUNTERSINKS

(for seating flat head screws)

Above tools made of finest grade carbon steel, carefully heat treated to give maximum tool life. Twist length is 2½". Shank ½" x 2". Overall length is 4½". Center drill is held securely by set screw in addition to the split shank. Center drills are not included in prices shown below.

Several machine tool, truck and diesel, and body shops we know use Wholesale Tool. Their 148-page catalog is jammed with the ingredients of cataclysmic mechanic's clutter.

Wholesale Tool Co., Inc.
12155 Stephens Drive
Box 56
Warren, Michigan 48090

Right: From the Wholesale Tool catalog.

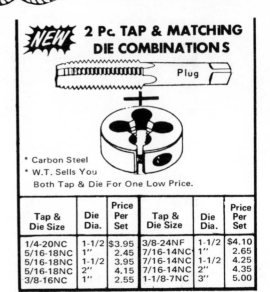
Tools for Your Safe Deposit Box

There is a new development in England that will interest only the stark raving gonzo tool discernist— two planes, the first of what will be a collection, made by a British optical firm. Their finish is microscopic and price astronomical. The last we heard, the mitre plane was around £185, plus shipping, and the shoulder plane £260, including shipping, from:

Henley Optical Co.
4 Hart Street
Henley-on-Thames
Oxon RG9 2AU
England

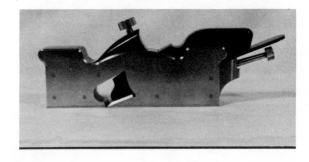

Above: Henley Optical's shoulder plane.
Below: Henley Optical's mitre plane

38

Buck

It would not be right to continue tool coverage without saying for the record . . . Buck Bros.

Buck Bros., Inc.
Riverlin Works
Millbury, Mass.

No. 15¼ Handled Paring Chisels—Beveled Edges, Bent Shank

The 1 inch is 8½ inches long from bolster, supplied with fancy handles.

Available in the following sizes:

¼	⅜	½	⅝	¾	1	1¼	1½	2	inch

Left: From the Buck Brothers catalog

**Model 2006
CORDLESS 3/8" DRILL
& SCREWDRIVER
The Quick Charge**

- Operates forward and reverse
- Full recharge cycle, 1 hour
- Ready-light indicates full charge
- Can be recharged hundreds of times
- Recharger included
- Has on/off trigger lock
- Chuck key stores in handle

WORLD'S
LARGEST

MAKITA SUPER PLANER, 6-1/8" (155 mm) wide
amply powered by 1-1/2HP motor (rated 12 AMPS at 100V) 1140 Watt
15000 RPM, length overall 17-3/4"(450 mm), weight – 18 lbs.(8 kg)
will take as much as 2 mm (5/64") off in one pass. All bearing
construction throughout. With optional stand makes the ideal
small jointer. Standard equipment includes: Wooden carrying case,
blade guage, holder assembly for sharpening knives, socket wrench,
& screw driver From Japan
Order Nr. 18F1805 for 115V

Why don't shop manuals and tool catalogs list
stools, bottle openers, dart boards, radios, stoves,
kitsch, porn, and sources of interesting spiders for
shop windows? Every good shop has them. Sanity
demands it.

—Eds.

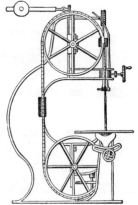

Skil

Skil has their cordless drill recharging time down to
one hour now. These geared-down 3/8" tools can be
extremely handy out on the mooring, on the ways, at
the masthead, and on mountain summits. From your
local dealer, or:

> **Skil Corp.
> 5033 Elston Ave.
> Chicago, Ill. 60630**

World's Largest

I have been delighted with my Rockwell Versa-
plane, but, just out of curiosity, I decided to look for
the largest hand-operated power plane in existence,
and I think I found it at Bimex, another supplier to
industry. Eight-side the schooner's mainmast in one
afternoon!

> **Bimex, Inc.
> 487 Armour Circle, N.E.
> Atlanta, Georgia 30324**

Left: From the Bimex catalog.
Left, above: From a Skil Corp. brochure.

A Screw-Slot Cleaner

Mr George Clapp, one of our avid readers, sent us
an interesting tool he has developed for cleaning
putty, paint, or glue out of screw slots during boat
repair/restoration jobs. Here's what he has to say
about it:

> On the theory and experience that a screw driver
> does a very poor job, usually, of cleaning the slot of an
> old screw prior to its removal, this little device helped
> me clean both slotted and Phillips head screws.
> Especially does it seem to work well after the plug has
> been gotten out and "ye ice pick" does a halfway job.
> You will notice that it will cut on the push or pull
> stroke. When I'm working on an antique car with a
> badly rusted (steel) screw, it is often possible to re-slot
> the screw sufficiently (with patience) to get enough
> bite of the screwdirver bit so it will back out.
> The "bit" is a water-hardening drill rod soft-soldered
> into the hex brass. Of course it can be touched up
> with a fine stone to keep it sharp.

We tried the tool out on some pretty tough screw
slots and found it very effective; we also found it to
be a well-made tool with just the right amount of
"heft" to it.

George will make one up for you for $5, postpaid.
Be sure to give him a couple of weeks, though, since
each tool is custom-made.

> **George Clapp Company
> 3993 Chase Rd., RD#1
> Burdett, N.Y. 14818**

39

Knice Knife Knotes

Dear Editors:

Volume 2 of the *Mariner's Catalog* contained a letter by Robert A. Compton recommending Ibberson knives. The latter are excellent. And yet, the most useful and versatile English product of this type—to my knowledge and on the basis of other sailors' comments—is one manufactured by Rodgers Wostenholm Group (Guernsey Road, Sheffield, England). Last year when my wife and son visited a friend in California for a brief sailing visit, I sent a Rodgers Yachting Knife with a self-made sennit lanyard and carbine hook as a memento, and here are his comments after a difficult period with a Contessa boat: "The lovely combination emergency tool you gave me with all the beautiful fancy ropework certainly had a lot of use in the Contessa sail. It was in continuous use the four days we were working on the boat. While we had a big tool box, [the Rodgers knife] saved so much time as it was always handy. The other fellows bought similar ones but they just didn't have the last 10% of workmanship that yours had." On another occasion, the same user wrote, "We have seen endless variations of the idea, but this is distinctly better than the rest." If any confirmation is required, the Sailing Club of Bonn uses no other yachting knife for basic ropework, splicing, and marlinspike seamanship training.

Karl Freudenstein
Bonn, West Germany

We contacted Rodgers Wostenholm and their stainless steel yachting knife with marlinspike, shackle, blade, can opener, and shackle slot is £2.69, FOB Sheffield.—Eds.

To give domestic cutlery some parity, those we know who use Russel Harrington around the fish plants (and there are several) like them a lot. They don't have one fileter, but many; not one "clam," "oyster," or whatever knife, but many, filling the traditional style preferences of different parts of the country.

Russel Harrington Cutlery, Inc.
Southbridge, Mass. 01550

Below: From the Russel Harrington catalog; from top to bottom—½" narrow fillet knife in super stainless steel; one-piece forged crab knife in stainless steel; beech-handled clam knife in super stainless steel.

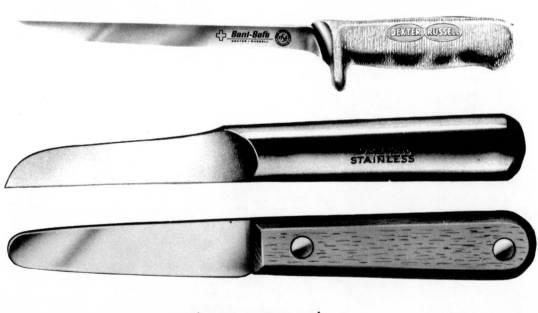

Knife Digest, edited by William L. Cassidy
Paladin Press, Boulder, Colorado
160 pages, illus., 1976, paperbound, $7.95

An annual publication (the latest edition is the
second annual edition), this is to knives what the
Mariner's Catalog is to the sea. The content ranges
from practical advice to historical articles, with heavy
emphasis on custom knives and knifemaking. Production knives are not ignored, however: witness excellent articles on the cutlery business in Solingen,
Germany ("The City of Blades"), and a tour of the
Smith & Wesson knife works. We found this publication to be of immense interest, even though we have
only a casual interest in knives—credit our fascination
with this book to a fine layout, good photography
(color as well as black and white), provocative
writing, and honest reporting.

Another book on knives to come our way is:

An Encyclopedia of Knives,
by Norman M. Strung
J.B. Lippincott, Philadelphia, Pa.
219 pages, illus., index, 1976, $12.50

We would rather not call it an encyclopedia, though.
The subtitle describes it better: "An illustrated consumer's guide to buying, using, sharpening, and caring
for all over-the-counter knives." A good book to help
you sort out the good cutlery from the bad.

Is there anything "custom" left in custom
knives? The field got its start catering to the wishes
of an inventive public, it got its big push selling quality instead of quantity, and now it seems that anything goes. A whole new market has been built
around the assembly of outlandish "art knives,"
which sell for equally outlandish prices to a gulible
public.

We had a long talk about the phenomena with
several knowledgeable collectors: all of whom an-
nounced they were rapidly getting fed up. We heard
them air their gripes during the long weekend of the
1975 Guild Show, and by the end of that weekend,
we were forced to admit that we were beginning to
see things their way.

There's a new rudeness going around: the
rudeness that comes from thinking that all a knife-
maker has to do is to whip up something "arty,"
stick a fat price sticker on it, and sell it to the first
sucker that comes along. There's also a new ego-
tism abounding that prompts certain makers to treat
their customers like so much garbage.

We don't like it, and we won't support it.

41

Etching by Shaw-Liebowitz: three-tone selective electroplating, enamel
work, and total coverage are options.

Boxed quote and photo from Knife Digest.

To Fight Collectors You Must Join Them

To nail down the obvious, persons who build traditional small craft are traditional craftsmen using traditional tools in traditional ways. Certainly, many of the traditional tools are available in modern configurations, but most of these just do not have the feel and balance of the old ones—custom forging and fifty years of palm grease cannot be duplicated artificially. And so the boatbuilder is in direct competition with tool collectors, museums, and decorators and would do well to join them rather than fight them. The tool user is as good a curator as can be found. All properties in life are only on loan anyway, even for museums.

The Early American Industries Association is the largest tool collector's organization in the country. They've a journal called *The Chronicle* and a newsletter, *Shavings*. Subscription alone is $8.00. Membership is $14.00 for individuals. There are, of course, regional, state, and local groups that one can join.

Subscription application:

John S. Watson, Treas.
E.A.I.A.
Office of State History, Building 8
Rotterdam Industrial Park
Schenectady, N.Y. 12306

Membership application:

Earl Soles
Blaikley Durfee House
Williamsburg, Virginia 23185

Regional Groups

Midwest Tool Collectors Association
c/o Mr. Marion Henley
808 Fairway Dr.
Columbia, Missouri 65201

E.A.I.A.-West
c/o Mr. Richard G. Frizzell
2018 Farrell Ave.
Redondo Beach, Cal. 92078

South West Tool Collectors Association
c/o Mr. Sam Scott
3001 Walnut Hill, Apt. 2011
Irvine, Texas 75062

Woodshop Tool Maintenance
by Cunningham and Holtrop
Charles A. Bennett Co.
Peoria, Illinois
307 pages, illus., index, 1974 (rev. ed.), $13.25

A shop text for the serious craftsman. The authors cover both hand tools and power tools and go into considerable detail about sharpening, lubrication, adjustment, and general maintenance. As an example of the depth of coverage, there are seven pages, with step-by-step illustrations, on coiling and uncoiling bandsaw blades—a subject we've never seen discussed anywhere else. You won't be disappointed by this book.

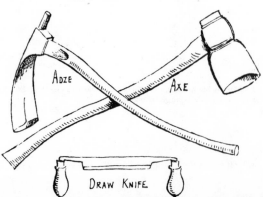

THE SPARMAKER'S TOOLS.

Adze

Axe

Draw Knife

Dear Editors:

I have built and operated a 10-inch tilt arbor table saw I got as a kit from Gilliom Tools in St. Charles, Mo. (1109 N. 2nd St.). I can tell you that their kit worked and worked well, for what it was. It certainly was plenty for me. Have used it for everything, including 8/4 teak. Got some carbide blades from Sears for it, plus a rebuilt 1 h.p. motor (from Sears again), and I had a nice saw for a total layout of $40 or so for Gilliom's kit, $20 for 1 piece of 3/4-inch fir ply, and $35 for the motor.

I haven't seen mention of an item I think deserves to be in the *Catalog*—or at least a comment somewhere. That is a weird saber saw made by the Bosch Corporation. This machine (their #1578) has an electronic speed control plus—and this is most important—a variable orbiting-action blade. Meaning that if you desire, the blade goes back and forth at the same time it's going up and down. By golly, the crazy thing eats 8/4 oak for breakfast, 1/4″ mild steel for lunch and up to 1/8″ stainless for dinner. With one of the huge selection of blades available for it, I fed it a Coke bottle. Cut the neck off—zip. You can get three kinds of rasps for it, too. The machine lists at somewhere around $140, but it's only about 7.6 zillion times more saw than you can get from Sears or Wards for $80 or so. There is nothing else to compare, nothing.

Mark Roeyer
Lawrence, Kansas

Dictionary of Tools
by R.A. Salaman
Charles Scribner's Sons, N.Y., 1975, $47.50

During 1976, most every tool, craft, woodworking, and traditional boating publication in the Western World reviewed this book. They did not do it because it retails for $47.50 and were afraid they'd lose it if they didn't review it; they reviewed it because it is so very full and very beautiful. All the editors and reviewers who received it bubbled and shrieked, and only a few cranks here and there sent in letters of complaint about the reviews to point out some tool that was excluded or missed or some error or other that marred the nice rug. Perhaps the book could be twice as long, twice as complete. It would, then, be excessive. As it is, it's seminal. Encourage your local librarian.

Axe, Blocking (Squaring Axe) *Fig. 55*
An asymmetrical, parallel-sided blade, sometimes as long as 22 in when new. The poll is light and flat, the lugs pointed below and flat on top, and the eye is sometimes set at an angle so that the blade leans towards the handle. Ground either as a Side Axe or with a double bevel.

Used for squaring heavy timbers, for example in shipbuilding and dock works. The extra length of blade is needed for reaching the bottom of wide pieces. The word blocking probably refers to the 'block' – a word used for the 'heeling' of the main mast, and also to other solid pieces of wood on a ship and elsewhere.

and smash through a bulkhead. We have one in the Museum which comes from H.M.S. *Captain*. The ship capsized in the Bay of Biscay in 1870 and was an iron clad . . . It was a weapon of destruction, but, of course, still basically an axe with a spike at the back. It was also useful in emergencies for cutting away ropes or spars which threatened to endanger the ship.'

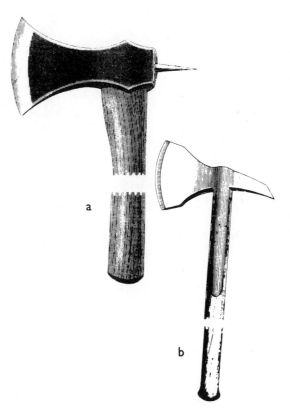

Fig. 56

(*a*) From Sheffield List 1888
(*b*) From William Gilpin 1868

Fig. 55

Axe, Boarding (Boarding Hatchet) *Fig. 56*
Illustrated in the Sheffield List of 1888 as a light Axe (1¾ lb), with a flared blade and a square poll on which is mounted a sharp spike. Mr. G. P. B. Naish (National Maritime Museum, 1970) has informed us: 'The axe was carried by boarders and used to damage the enemy's ship, cut up his rigging, hack through a spar

Quote and illustrations from Dictionary of Tools.

43

BOATBUILDING

Above: Sketch by Buck Smith.
Below, left: Cartoon by Darrell McClure.

One-Stop Builder's Supplier

We heard rumors that the Clytie Corporation was setting itself up as a one-stop shopping center for boatbuilders. It's true, it's true.

44

Clytie Corporation
60 River Street
Beverly, Mass. 01915

There is nothing an amateur cannot do if he lives long enough

Dear Editors:

We are basically boatbuilders, doing new construction and major reconstruction work, principally on yachts. As a part of that business we maintain a stockroom whose inventory is designed to fit our needs as boatbuilders; selling materials to others came naturally after the first few inquiries.

Our typical materials customer is building a small boat, owns a bandsaw but not a planer, and needs wood finished to thickness, fastenings, resin, paint, and hardware. We have gone so far as to scale all the wood off the drawings, although most come to us with a list. For the professional we probably have less to offer, although we do stay on top of fastenings, with five different suppliers, and on the New England woods, particularly bending white oak, we are a good source.

I answer all inquiries; everyone who mentions what he has in mind gets a personal note and suggestions, if warranted. A stamped, addressed business envelope would be helpful. Sooner or later we will go to a booklet form for the list (we now offset them 100 at a time), but we are continuing to revise it, and a booklet is somehow very final.

James L. Woodward
President
Clytie Corporation

Fastenings

Responding to our inquiry, Marine Screw-Bolt indicated that they distribute the following items:

Stainless Steel	*Silicon Bronze*	*Brass*
Wood screws	Wood screws	Wood screws
Sheet-metal screws	Carriage bolts	Machine screws
Machine screws	Bolts	Nuts
Bolts	Nuts	Washers
Nuts	Washers	Cotter pins
Washers		
Cotter Pins		
Threaded Rod		
Crimp-on electrical connectors		
Stainless steel hose clamps		
Twist drills—cobalt (for SS)		
Nylon cable clamps and ties		
Paint brushes		

**Marine Screw-Bolt
Box 421
Valley Stream, N.Y. 11580**

Youth Shall (possibly) Be Served

We all can be enthusiastic about the many new craftsmen around the country who are taking a crack at boatbuilding. Considering the number of make-work jobs, lousy jobs, and non-jobs in which many find themselves, there is no blaming the pride some feel when asked what they do and are able to answer, "I'm a boatbuilder."

However, with the apprentice system generally gone in the teeth, the new builders must pay their dues to themselves, and one or two boats does not a journeyman make. A boat may be worth five or six dollars an hour of its building, so long as it is abuilding during those hours.

Inevitably, though, a craft building under new hands does not come together with the easy, steady pace that the journeyman can give to it. There are hours, sometimes days, of just staring at it, trying to figure something (it) out, cigarettes or other attendant vices under intimidation, and those trips to town for the do-dads that should have been at hand. This is *education,* not boatbuilding, and its costs should not rest upon the customer.

Too, we have noticed that *speed* and *quality* of workmanship are more often independent variables than not. Slow work is not necessarily the better work, and the old saw of "starting out slow" may be nothing more than the fixing of a poor habit from the beginning. It is probably easier for a fast workman to improve his craftsmanship than it is for the crafty workman to become a fast one. (Don't get us wrong, though; we completely disapprove of a customer getting his boat on time. That would be untraditional.)

In any case, it would seem better for all concerned to settle on a reasonable price plus materials costs when engaging the self-apprenticed.

—Eds.

Skookum Fastenings sent us a note saying that our listing in *Volume 4* has brought not only orders and inquiries, but also interest from several would-be distributors. Write them for their catalog and current distributor list at:

**Skookum Fastenings
2114 Commercial Street
Anacortes, Washington 98221**

Nail Source for the Quick and Dirty Crowd

Your local lumberyard and hardware store sell a nail with a lot of potential uses in low-cost boatbuilding. Zinc-coated, ring-shank nails about 1½ inches long are widely used in installing plasterboard in "drywall" construction and installing asbestos siding on houses. They have excellent holding power and very good corrosion resistance. (Many lobstermen on the coast of Maine use these nails in constructing their traps.—Eds.)

About six years ago I slapped together a camper shell from 1/4" plywood and 2x2 construction spruce. The ply was attached to the outside of the framing with drywall nails left over from some remodeling. I primed the whole thing with Firzite and painted it with latex exterior enamel. It has been outside in the rain and snow ever since, and none of the drywall nails have shown any sign of rust bleeding through the paint, although some of the ply is rotting out. The ring construction makes them grip well, and none have shaken loose in twenty thousand or so miles of highway and byway travel.

—Wallace Venable

45

Glue

John Gardner, Associate Small Craft Curator and Resident Sage of Mystic Seaport, recently discovered, tested, and now applauds the characteristics of Aerolite glue in all applications where resorcinol and epoxy once reigned. A British product developed during WW II for manufacturing Mosquito bombers, this wonderful adhesive has become an industrial standard in furniture and sports equipment manufacturing. The two sources in the U.S. that we've found are both suppliers of aircraft materials. When writing these firms, be sure to ask specifically for the Aerolite information

Aircraft Spruce and Specialty Company
P.O. Box 424
Fullerton, California 92632

Wick's Aircraft Supply
1100 5th Street
Highland, Ill. 62249

End grain gluing is relatively unsatisfactory. This joint:–

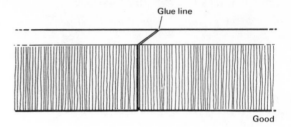

will be much stronger than this one:–

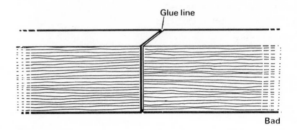

AEROLITE*

The uncomparable glue brought from England for every woodworking job.

Aerolite* is a urea.formaldehyde resin adhesive which was developed during World War II and used in the manufacture of the famous "Mosquito" bombers in Great Britian. In the past 30 years no glue has been found to equal it. Aerolite* is waterproof, insect and mould proof. It has gap-filling properties which make it ideal for use by the amateur. Heavy clamping is unnecessary — good contact is all that is required. Use it for furniture making, aircraft, glider and boat building, the manufacture and repair of skiis, sporting equipment of all types and every other wood gluing application. Acclaimed by industry and hobbyist alike — one test will prove all !

PREPARATION : Mixing container should be glass, tin, porcelain, plastic or iron. Mix any quantity of Aerolite* powder with water in the proportion of four parts powder to one part water by volume (four cups powder to one cup water) or by weight, two parts powder to one part water (4oz. powder to 2 oz. water). Stir until the paste is free from lumps. The use of hot water facilitates the solution and the resin may be used at once. If cold water is used, it is advisable to allow mixture to stand for a few hours before using.

APPLICATION : 1. Resin mixture may be applied with a clean piece of wood, brush or plastic squeeze bottle to one of the surfaces to be joined.
2. The undiluted hardener should be applied by use of clean brush sponge or felt to the other surface.
3. Bring the two pieces together while the hardener coated surface is still damp. Position and assemble. Nail, screw or lightly clamp until set.

Aerolite* liquid (powder mixed with water) and hardener should never be allowed to come into contact except during the gluing process. A separate applicator must be used for each and must never be interchanged.

ASSEMBLY TIME: From the moment first contact is made between the two surfaces, they must be assembled and firmly positioned within 10 minutes.

SETTING TIME: The following table lists the minimum length of time the surfaces must be held in firm contact:

Temperature (°F)	Setting Time, Hours, with GBP (Medium) Hardener	Setting Time, Hours, with GBQ (Fast) Hardener
50	7	5–6
60	3½	2¾
70	2½	1¾
80	1½	1¼
90	1¼	1

Above: Data from Aircraft Spruce and Specialty Co.
Top: Diagrams from CIBA-GEIGY Technical Notes, by the makers of Aerolite.

46

Super Resin

When we heard that there was a resin material that worked as a glue, a laminating resin, or a sealer at temperatures down to 2°C. and would both bond and cure *underwater,* we had to go looking. Found it at:

Industrial Formulators of Canada, Ltd.
3824 Williams St.
Burnaby, B.C. V5C 5P2
Canada

Below: Data and illustration describing Lumiweld from an Alumismiths brochure.

Al U Min E Yum

The cost of aluminum arc-welding can run up to about $3.00 per inch of weld. This is an impressive figure. The cost of Lumiweld is $.05 per inch. This is also an impressive figure. Using an ordinary propane torch and a specially formulated rod, aluminum craft and gear can be either fabricated or repaired with ease. We would be most interested to hear from readers who have tried this system from:

Alumismiths, Inc.
2105 School Drive
Rolling Meadows, Ill. 60008

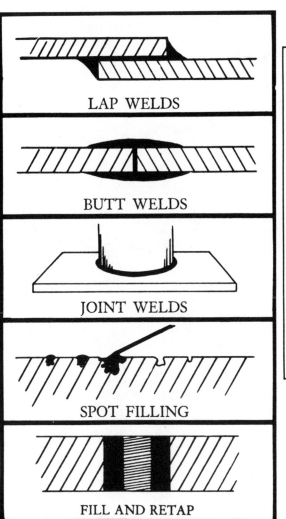

LAP WELDS

BUTT WELDS

JOINT WELDS

SPOT FILLING

FILL AND RETAP

ROCKWELL B. HARDNESS:- (kg load, 1/16 ball)	55 to 60 depending upon cooling rate
ULTIMATE TENSILE STRENGTH:-	Greater than base aluminum, up to 40,000 pounds/sq. in.
ELONGATION	3 to 8% depending upon cooling rate.
COMPRESSIVE STRENGTH:-	55,000 to 78,000 pounds/sq. in.
SHEAR STRENGTH:-	18,000 to 33,000 pounds/sq. in. depending upon joint design
ENDURANCE LIMIT	10^8 cycles at 8,000 pounds/sq. in.
SPECIFIC GRAVITY:-	6.7
THERMAL CONDUCTIVITY:- (70 to 140°C or 158 to 284°F)	.24 cal/sq cm/cm/°C/sec
THERMAL EXPANSION:- (20 to 100°C or 68 to 212°F)	28×10^{-6}°C or 15×10^{-6}°F
CORROSION PENETRATION (New York City)	less than 300×10^{-6} in./year
ELECTRICAL CONDUCTIVITY:-	25% of copper
WORKING TEMPERATURE	730°F or 390°C
SOLIDUS TEMPERATURE	715°F or 380°C
DIMENSIONS OF ROD	1/8 x 18±1/4 inch

So he must build a boat; about which he knew nothing. He began to study. With unswerving purpose he gave himself to the reading of every authority on boat design, he filled himself with lore and facts. He studied catalogues, he looked at craft. And he came to know them.

—Rockwell Kent

Dear Editors:

Brooks Townes (see p. 61, Vol. 3) claims that Arabol is Elmer's glue with a mildew retardant added. I don't believe it. Elmer's glue is soluble in water—no matter how long it has had to dry. I think—and promise to find out if I'm right—that Arabol is a product of milk, most likely a casein. The reason Borden is so tight about information on it—in addition to the fact that it's so cheap—is mostly because the stuff is really simple to make, and/or the technology behind it has all the sophistication of carving soap. I think I know where to look for information and will check it out.

Mark Roeyer
Lawrence, Kansas

Soaking Instead of Steaming

by Walt Simmons

If you are interested in building a traditional wooden boat—a round-bottomed boat—you already know that one process you must come to grips with is steaming. There aren't many times when it is called for in a single boat, but the fact remains that there will be some times when steaming will be the only possible way to twist a plank into position and at the same time relieve as many of its internal strains as possible.

If the boat under consideration is a peapod-type hull, in the very least you will have to steam the hood ends of the garboards (probably the second plank as well), and of course the ribs. The individual processes of steaming and boiling will both serve wherever such shapes are required, but for the person considering the construction or repair of a single boat, both processes require more equipment than is necessary to accomplish the job—not to mention the time and expense required in the construction and tending of either rig.

By far the oldest method employed to render a particular piece of wood limber enough to be worked into position is that of soaking. Soaking the wood to be bent in cold (or, more specifically, unheated) water takes a considerable number of days to accomplish. It does work, however, and many makers of musical instruments are still using this method. Unfortunately, while the instrument makers may have the time, boatbuilders do not. If, however, you should soak the piece to be bent in boiling water, the task can be accomplished in a much shorter span of time—and it then becomes of definite use to boatbuilders.

The general term "steaming" can be defined as the application of moist heat to a piece of wood over a sufficiently long period of time for that piece to become flexible enough to be bent to the required shape. Fine, but if you only need to steam once or twice, why make it any more complicated than it has to be? If you choose to soak the piece in boiling water, all that is necessary is the boiling water itself, and some means by which to hold the boiling water in contact with the piece to be bent.

As an example, I'll use the garboard of a double ender—I know of no more difficult piece to steam. Because it is unhandy at best, I don't much care for boiling the whole plank only to have to carry it to the boat, clamp it into position at the midship molds, and then work the hood ends into position. That can be a considerable amount of work to accomplish in less than the minute that you have to work. Should you use the soaking process, on the other hand, the whole procedure is simplified.

Clamp the garboard in position at the midship molds—there is no steaming required there. I then take the loose hood ends and wrap them each with an old mattress pad of about 3′x4′, making as many turns about the plank as possible. With about 1½ gallons of boiling water, saturate both pads with as much water as they will hold—follow by wrapping each pad with polyethylene to retain as much heat as

Old mattress pad being wrapped around the hood end of a garboard.

The pad wrapped with plastic and secured with rope.

possible. For a cedar garboard with a 7″ hood-end width, 7/16″ thick, I then wait 30 to 45 minutes. At the end of that time, strip off the plastic and pad, and clamp the hood ends into position individually. The beauty of this particular approach is that, although you still have less than a minute to work, the countdown doesn't begin until the wrapping is removed, so you have a full minute for each hood end.

I have also found soaking handy for placing a cutwater when it doesn't make sense to fire up my boiling tank for that one piece. The cutwaters I use vary in thickness from 1/2″ to 2″, and the thicker the piece, the longer the soaking time—as in any steaming process. However, even the 2″ pieces, I have found that using the entire 1½ gallons and waiting 45 minutes is sufficient in all cases.

There are many applications for this soaking process, but primarily it is suited to the steaming of a limited number of pieces without having to resort to other, more involved methods. When used in conjunction with boiling or steaming, soaking with boiling water can save you time and trouble. When working away from a shop (as on a beach), it often proves to be the only feasible alternative: in either instance, it is well worth remembering.

Dinghy Building, by Richard Creagh-Osborne
Adlard Coles, 3 Upper St. James St., London
240 pages, illus., index, list of suppliers, £5.50

Understand that the word "dinghy" to an Englishman means a daysailer of any type and is not necessarily confined to a yacht tender, as is usual in the United States. Also understand that this book is an excellent survey of the most modern methods of building small boats today, both wood and fiberglass. There are chapters on all types of construction—cold-molded, sheet plywood, planked plywood, carvel, strip, lapstrake, bonded plywood, composite, and fiberglass. The chapters on cold-molding and ply-

wood-planked lapstrake are the best we have seen, and the chapter on wooden spar-making, though short, gives one a valuable short-course introduction to the subject. One thing that is lacking is a discussion of Gougeon Brothers' WEST System, which is rapidly catching on as the most revolutionary wooden boat-building technique of the 1970s (for more information on this, see *WEST Manual,* Gougeon Bros., 706 Martin St., Bay City, Mich. 48706, $2.00).

Below: From Dinghy Building.

8.1
How an ultra-light plywood bulkhead and plywood bulkhead knee have been taped on to a fibre-glass shell by means of glass tape and resin. Note also the special plastic screw fixings, which avoid the need for wooden reinforcement behind the thin panel. (Keith Paul, Five-o-Five.)

8.2
The stern end of the exterior jig used for building the O.K. Dinghy by the composite plywood and fibre-glass method. The exterior moulds can be seen set up in their correct relationship, and the battens which were let in at the keel and chine to assist in making the plywood conform to the right shape. Note the well-braced subframe. (Rogers, O.K. Dinghy.)

49

8.3
Extra strutting and reinforcing was necessary at the stem to hold the battens firmly to the correct shape. The stem template can be seen connecting with the first mould, together with jutting out ledges on the upper part to hold the ends of the planks. (Rogers, O.K. Dinghy.)

8.4
The two bottom panels have been placed in the jig and a cramp has been constructed to press them down in the stem area, where there is considerable twisting. Note the additional strut right up in the forefoot to help push the planking downwards against the stem template. (Rogers, O.K. Dinghy.)

Steel-Belted Fiberglass?

If ferrocement and fiberglass constructions were to grow up, get married, and have a baby, the baby's name would be Ferro-Glass. And it is. Aladdin Products of Wiscasset, Maine, offers a free newsletter describing the system or, better, for $5.45 (postage is included) they have a 64-page manual describing the process, use of the new materials and techniques (including an enclosed sample) that have attended the development of this building method. It then shows step-by-step the building of a large sailing yacht using it all. From:

Aladdin Products, Inc.
R.F.D. 2
Wiscasset, Maine 04578

Quantity Supplies

Many yards in the Northeast use Dunbar Marine Specialties for fiberglassing supplies, nonferrous fastenings, and the excellent Gloucester Sea Jacket line of marine paints.

Dunbar Marine Specialties
111B Mill Street (Mill Park)
Springfield, Mass. 01108

A derelict boat used for a building form. The Peapod had a similar stem rod framing except it was carried full length along keel.

Above: From Aladdin's A Revolution in Ferro Construction.
Below: Boxed quote from Aladdin's newsletter.
Bottom, left: From a Dunbar Marine Specialties flyer.

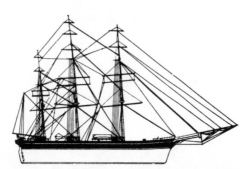

GLOUCESTER PAINTS, INC.

⑮ WORKBOAT UTILITY PAINTS

M V	5 Gal.	1 Gal.
641 Flat White	16.70	17.00
650 Utility White, S. G.	18.70	19.00
652 Nonskid White	18.70	19.00
653 Utility Gray (medium)	16.70	17.00
658 Q.D. Inspection Red (Int'r. Floors)	——	19.00

⑯ CANNERY, DAIRY & SEAFOOD HOLD ENAMELS

	5 Gal.	1 Gal.
850 White (Lead Free)	19.70	20.00
851 Dove Gray "	18.70	19.00
852 Aluminum "	21.70	22.00

50

FERRO-GLAS™
THE STEELBELTED FIBERGLASS™

THE STEEL BELTED FIBERGLASS FERRO-GLAS is the name of a composite structure developed for boat construction. It combines the advantages of fiberglass, wood, sandwich and ferro (steel).

Steel belts of WIRE PLANK brand mesh are used as an inexpensive mold, which is inherently fair. FER-A-LITE type trowelable fiberglass is applied to fill the wire mesh form. Inner and outer glass layers produce a sandwich effect which is tough, light fair, cheap and durable. The ease of handling and versatility of these multi-purpose materials add up to the BEST One-Off building process with a diversity never before available to the boating industry.

The Steel Belted core improves on fiberglass in two ways: impact resistance and excessive flexibility. Hulls are amazingly stiff due to the high modulus of steel, It is quite easy to imagine how the tough steel core could absorb and contain a destroying impact.

This process has evolved as the best yet utilization of the well known WIRE PLANK & FER-A-LITE brand materials. However, we've added an exciting new product, which further simplifies the process...STR-R-ETCH MESH.

STR-R-ETCH MESH is the name of a specialty mesh, which is woven wire cloth that is free forming on the bias. It opens up a whole new concept and makes the existing ideas easier to accomplish. This material works a good deal like WIRE PLANK mesh; in that it will form around a contour in one panel from keel to gunwale without darts. The resulting continuous wire strands in two directions with no overlaps facilitate an incredibly thin shell, which is the key to high strength, for very light weight boats, such as dinghies, Whitehalls and multi-hulls.

The building form is a very simple wood skeleton set up with widely spaced station frames and appropriate size stringers made of clear grain material. The technique is suitable for boats from 8' to 80'.

In short, this system combines the best of fiberglass and ferro construction and eliminates the disadvantages such as molds, wire tying and grinding.

"The original idea was to save on building costs and keep myself out-of-doors"

Wrinkles on Brightwork

Let's rephrase that. A couple of varnish or varnish-like materials have recently appeared at the marketplace with wrinkles to get rid of wrinkles.

Bristol Fashion is a urethane-phenolic varnish mixture formulated so the flowed-on coat will maintain thick coat stability and not require sanding between coats, from:

> **Bristol Marine**
> **420 Jericho Turnpike**
> **Jericho, N.Y. 11753**

Deks Olje is beginning to make news around the country, too. A good record with the fishing fleet of Norway has given this two-part system considerable notice elsewhere, including the U.S. Its reputation is excellent, but, of course, we would like user reports on this and all materials that we list. Deks Olje is distributed by the manufacturers of Penetrol, the old standby marine paint conditioner:

> **The Flood Company**
> **Hudson, Ohio**

By the bye, chilled varnish, which can be used down to 0°C, is still about from various distributors, a current list of which is available from:

> **H.A. Calahan Division**
> **50 Turner Street**
> **Ridgefield, Conn. 06877**

Cartoon above by Darrell McClure.
Quote and photo below from the Flood Company.

Stem-to-stern wood care system!

Deks Olje is a two-part solution to the problem of protecting and maintaining beautiful boating woods against the deteriorating effects of sun, salt, wind and foot traffic. Deks Olje #1 — a highly penetrating oil — leaves a rich matte finish that saturates, seals and stabilizes wood to prevent cracking. Deks Olje #2 — used over Deks Olje #1 — provides a hard, glossy finish that's especially beautiful on teak caprails, skylights, companionway hatches and other wood trim.

Deks Olje #1 can be used alone for the natural, oiled look that many boaters prefer. However, when you cover it with Deks Olje #2, you get a durable, gleaming finish that won't break, blister or craze like other marine coatings after only a few months' exposure.

51

Fiberglass Repairs, by Paul J. Petrick
Cornell Maritime Press, Cambridge, Maryland
74 pages, illus., ring-bound, 1976, $6

If you must have a fiberglass boat, and if you use her with abandon, you'll be making some repairs sooner or later. Six dollars to Cornell for Petrick's book will save you money in the long run.

Below: From Fiberglass Repairs.

Take a piece of plastic wrap, 4" to 6" wide and hold or tape it at the beginning end. Hold the trailing end up away from the wet gel coat to keep from entrapping air. With a clean putty knife using light pressure on the upper surface of the plastic wrap, pull the "bead" of excess gel coat under the plastic film toward the opposite end with a slow steady stroke, letting the trailing edge of the plastic film contact the wet gel coat as the putty knife progresses. A piece of round dowel or pencil can be used instead of the putty knife, if you have trouble "snagging" the thin plastic film. Check thoroughly for entrapped air bubbles through the clear plastic. If they are present, rework or repeat the procedure if necessary. Considering that there is such a minute amount of material involved, several "test runs" can be made over any smooth surface until the technique is perfected.

"I'll Pay the Rent," "My Hero," or Three Notes on Baby Saving

New England Boat Builders has spent the past dozen years developing and refining a system of glass-covering elder boats, including those deemed to be "basket cases." We inquired with the usual objections about adhesion, rot, and weight, and they replied that they had heard of these problems (which showed a nice restraint, we thought) and enclosed a good three-page flyer describing their system and answering the obvious and not-so-obvious questions about placing the old girl in a glass slipper. Write:

**New England Boat Builders, Inc.
Harbor Rd.
Mattapoisett, Mass. 02739**

Do you have one of the old Chris-Craft runabouts, down in keel and deck? Complete restoration services, including hull repairs and refinishing, engine rebuilding or repair, upholstery work, pick-up, and delivery services for them are offered by:

**Chamberlain Automotive & Marine
115 Olive St.
Carterville, Ill. 62918**

Travaco Laboratories, makers and distributors of many well-known wonder drugs for boats, recently introduced Rust-A-Hoy, stuff that dissolves *any* thickness of rust and then phosphates and protects the remaining metal without etching it—only the oxides are removed. We tried some on a glob of rust found in the clamflats. It turned out to be a few links of chain. Almost spooky stuff, from local distributors or:

**Travaco Laboratories, Inc.
345 Eastern Ave.
Chelsea, Mass. 02150**

Who Was That Masked Man?

The filter face mask industry has taken a lesson from the photographic equipment giants who give away cameras and then sell film forever. Make an inexpensive mask and then sell filters forever. Well, since you're going to throw the filled filters away anyway, then why not have the best at a price that is as good or better?

See your doctor and ask him to order a box of O.R. (operating room) masks for you. They cover the whole face from the eyes to the neck, the internal wire allows you to fit the mask to *your own* shape around the nose, reducing the fogging of glasses or goggles. They are engineered to the highest specs, and they will stop anything down to a virus and some of those, too. Also, the hospital interns are right; there is a certain cockiness to having one casually draped around your neck during coffee breaks. Last summer I paid $9.00 for a box of fifty.

WILL OWEN

Three Friends

Our friend Eliot Lamson mentioned the other day that among some Florida yachtsmen it was common practice to make marine undercoating simply by thinning regular surface paint and adding *talcum powder*. Thanks, El.

* * * * * * * * * * * * * * * * * * *

Joel Prins tells us that in the Southeast there are a couple of "new towns" sprung up composed of dozens of people building their own boats out of make-do shelters, communal scrounging, and shared triumphs and miseries. We hear that there are similar communities in California and the Pacific Northwest. If you've the inclination to go crazy in company instead of alone, when next you are doing a coastal trek you might check out the local zoning board for their current "problem." Thanks, Dugon.

* * * * * * * * * * * * * * * * * * *

Velly Engstrom tells us that back in the days when sawmills turned out dimension stock of any interest at all, a man could build a peapod in a week by himself. He knows one guy who built 50 pods in one year. We were too depressed to ask him what the guy built in those other two weeks. Thanks, Goat.

Troglodyte's Corner

We don't know anyone in the wooden boatbuilding business who likes the notion of metrication. It's not simply that 7/16ths, and 1 and an 8th are old familiar friends, it's that small boats and people *go* together: feet, handbreadths, armlengths, real people in man-serving artifacts.

Surely one cannot complain of the freezing point of water being called 0 and the boiling point 100. There is no 32 or 212 of anything to which we can relate. But look at these consummately ridiculous figures on a 16-foot Whitehall rowing boat:

16-foot length equals 4.8768 meters
4′6″ beam equals 1.3716 meters
1′8″ depth equals 50.8 centimeters.
1/2 inch planking equals 1.27 centimeters.
1 ⅛ #8 screws equals 2.8575 centimeters.

The guys building tutus for the Shah's court can go 1/10,000,000th (or whatever) of the ideal distance between the equator and pole all they want; we're going for a row in our 16-foot boat.

Yacht Construction, by K. H. C. Jurd
Adlard Coles, London
160 pages, illus., index, 1970, $12.95

This is not really a boatbuilding book, but a study of construction methods. It should interest designers and would-be boatowners, as it enables the reader to differentiate among good, bad, and indifferent building practices. Since it was written by an Englishman who made no effort to "Americanize" the text, there is some confusion in terminology. For instance, the author speaks of gunmetal fastenings, a term that is meaningless in this country.

On the plus side, there is considerable material on masts and rigging—a subject that is usually neglected in books of this type (we are still looking for a definitive rigging book).

If you are looking for something that will help you understand how a boat is put together, and don't want to wade through a book such as *Boatbuilding* by Chapelle, and are willing to put up with some mystifying English terminology, you might give this book a try.

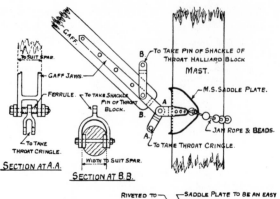

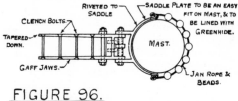

FIGURE 96.

SKETCH OF GAFF JAWS FOR SCHOONER.

The gaff is required to travel up and down the mast, to slew in the transverse direction and to hinge up and down, and to achieve all this an elaborate fitting, commonly referred to as the gaff jaws, is necessary. A good type is sketched in Fig. 96. The plate saddle transmits the thrust of the gaff to the mast, the jan rope and parrel balls prevent the gaff from surging away, the bridle or stirrup for the throat halyard block adjusts itself to all angles of the gaff when hoisting, and the loose links for the throat cringle do the same for the sail.

Above: Quote and illustration from Yacht Construction.

Boatbuilding without Brainstorms, Blisters,
or Bankruptcy, by Charles Green
Cruiser Kits, Ltd.
The Staithe, Bungay
Suffolk, England

54

64 pages, paperbound, illus., $3 cash, $4 check

Not really a book; rather a catalog of plans for a series of kit boats popular in Britain and Europe. The feature of these designs is that they were developed specifically with plywood kit construction in mind. The range is complete, from double-paddle canoes to trimarans, from dinghies to inboard cruisers, from sailing cruisers to motorized catamarans. Some of the designs are so-so; others are downright ugly; none are especially noteworthy. Yet for the kitbuilder, Cruiser Kits offers some interesting services (for a price, of course): practice kits for the rank beginner, 8mm films, photographic albums, and even a "working holiday" service, where you go to their shop during your vacation and build your boat on the premises.

"Pack up your troubles with a Charles Green kit."

Dear Editors:

If any fish factory does not know what to do with fish oil, I would like to recommend an experiment of long ago. Mix two cans of fish oil to one can of any choice paint. The paint lasts nearly seven years near the waterfront—longer inland.

John G. Ammells
Plaistow, NH

Dear Editors,

On page 11 of Volume 3, Mr. John W. Shortall, N.A., in his letter mentioned a book, *Ship and Aircraft Fairing and Development*, by S.S. Rabl. Supposedly it is available in a paperback version. I wrote to the publisher mentioned, Cornell Maritime Press, and they replied that it was out of print.

I have noticed that as I re-read the catalogs there are additional items of information and sources that didn't attract my attention with the first reading. It isn't so much that I missed them the first time around, but rather that my requirements have changed.

Ralph J. Ellis
Columbia, Connecticut

BORING A SHAFT LOG

by Lowell P. Thomas

I got ready to bore a three-foot shaft log the other day, so my first step was to hunt up a lawn chair. I've found that amateur boatbuilding is about 75% sitting and puzzling out how to do things. In this case the problem was how to bore the hole without proper bits. I must have spent a total of about six hours in that lawn chair over the next several days, but no matter how hard I stared at the deadwood and wished, no hole appeared. So I decided to go ahead and try to buy a 1¼-inch auger and have it welded onto a steel rod like Chapelle (*Boatbuilding*, p. 148) and others say you should do. Well, an auger that big is hard to locate, and most of what you do locate are double-twist with two cutters and a screw tip. Bare-foot ship augers just aren't for sale in the average hardware store, even the big ones.

Finally, I found a 1″ barefoot ship and a 1½″ ship with screw lying rusty and unwanted in a store full of shiny spade-type bits and expensive double-twist augers. The price tag on the bigger one was old and dirty and read $4.50; the little one had no tag. Both were about 18 inches long. I figured they'd been lying there since the Great Depression and bought them both for $9.00. The clerk thought the screw had broken off the barefoot auger, but he must have smelled a rat when he saw I still wanted it, so the shifty-eyed bastard charged me the same as for the big one.

When I inquired about having a three-foot rod welded onto the 1½″ bit, I wished I had my own welding outfit. To have the job hired out would cost me considerably more than the two bits together had. Then I got another bright idea. I bought a large spade-type bit, fastened it into the end of a 1¼″ water pipe, made a collar to slip around the pipe and keep the bit centered, and hooked the whole mess up to my half-inch drill. I figured it would be slow, but I didn't realize just how much speed those spade bits need to cut. It didn't work.

I went back to the lawn chair. After another thinking session, I swallowed my pride and began asking other boatbuilders how they solved the problem of boring shaft logs. They weren't much help, since few of them had been crazy enough to build a boat as big as mine, and several thought I had been kind of stupid to have run a 3/8″ bronze rod smack across the area I intended to drill out. A couple even suggested I might break a drill bit when I hit that rod. Well, I just struck them off my list of good friends and went on asking around. Finally Don Heuer, over at the print shop, came up with an intelligent idea.

"Hell," he said, "we bored an eight-foot log in a trawler up in Jersey with a water pipe. We just cut some teeth in the end, bored some holes in the pipe to free the sawdust, and drove it with a six h.p. engine. Went through eight feet in two days turning at about 60 r.p.m."

He looked kind of embarrassed and sorry for me when I mentioned the bronze rod I'd have to cut through, but his idea of the water pipe sounded good, especially since I had a length of pipe the right diameter sitting in my garage. I got the pipe out, figured the direction of rotation for the half-inch drill, cut four teeth in the business end (slanted them and gave two of them a little outgauge and bent two in a little so the pipe wouldn't bind), set up a guide to keep her straight, and started boring. Well, it wasn't all easy coasting, as I hit several bronze screws and at 30 inches I hit that 3/8″ rod. The pipe handled the wood (fir) slowly but steadily, about a half inch a minute, but it didn't bore through the bronze. So I heated a small piece of truck spring orange hot, beat it into shape, sharpened it, tapped it, tempered it in water, and screwed it into the untoothed end of the pipe. That patent cutter went through all the bronze that got in my way and only broke once. I just swapped ends back for the wood part, and was so pleased with the way that pipe finally came through the log centerline that I went on and bored through a 3/4-inch plywood stiffener just for good measure.

It was hard work, and I must have put about two hours running time on the drill over a two-day period. But what a beautiful straight hole she bored. Seems like a pretty good system to me, especially for an amateur with more time than money. The only problem is getting enough power to turn the pipe under a compression load. The more pressure, the faster she'll cut, but too much and of course the drill stalls (and burns up if you load her up too frequently or too long).

I bet some of the *Mariner's Catalog* readers could think up some interesting power take-offs. Like, how about a lawn-mower engine, or a take-off from the rear end of a jacked-up car?

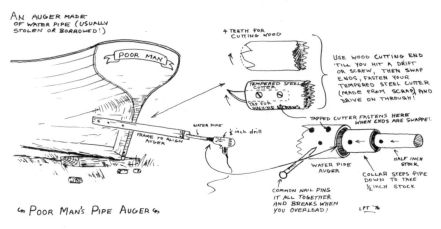

AN AUGER MADE OF WATER PIPE (USUALLY STOLEN OR BORROWED!)

POOR MAN

4 TEETH FOR CUTTING WOOD

USE WOOD CUTTING END 'TILL YOU HIT A DRIFT OR SCREW, THEN SWAP ENDS, FASTEN YOUR TEMPERED STEEL CUTTER (MADE FROM SCRAP) AND DRIVE ON THROUGH!

TEMPERED STEEL CUTTER

TAP FOR MACHINE SCREWS

WATER PIPE

½ inch drill

FRAME TO ALIGN AUGER

TAPPED CUTTER FASTENS HERE WHEN ENDS ARE SWAPPED.

WATER PIPE AUGER

HALF INCH STOCK

COLLAR STEPS PIPE DOWN TO TAKE ½ INCH STOCK

COMMON NAIL PINS IT ALL TOGETHER AND BREAKS WHEN YOU OVERLOAD!

POOR MAN'S PIPE AUGER

LPT '76

Creating Customers

From a practical point of view, being a marine architect specializing in pleasure craft must be a glorious way to starve. Think of it; all those good ideas that you would have in your own boat if there was a shadow of a chance. Your old school portfolio sitting there waiting to bowl over the next visitor—a person no doubt with a bunch of foolish ideas of his own. And then the succession of would-be almost-come-throughers who dally while the overhead piles up. What a good time!

Bruce Roberts International has avoided this syndrome by reversing the order of concern, by starting out not with design ideas, but rather concentrating on the problems facing the would-be customer; namely, how to afford any boat whatsoever.

They sell designs, both their own and others', but their come-on is basic information on building techniques and how to save money by making the boat and gear yourself. They provide hard drawings and specific methods of scrounging materials and making one's own tools. In other words, they not only make designs, they make customers.

They have two books, *Amateur Boatbuilding,* for $7.50, and a shorter, less expensive version, *Build for Less* (the exact price escapes us). Whether you spring for one of their design packages or not, the books offer excellent, well-illustrated surveys of building systems open to the amateur.

Bruce Roberts International
1617 Westcliff Dr.
Newport Beach, Cal. 92660

Boat Plan Catalog

Glen-L Marine Designs, 9152 Rosecrans Blvd., Bellflower, Calif. 90706, has a tremendous (mainly powerboat) catalog for $1. Beautiful little speedboats. Nice bigger boats. *Cheap* plans, and frame kits. A good deal!

—George Buehler

Small Boat Building, by Dave Gannaway
Nautical Publishing Company
Lymington, Hampshire, England
95 pages, illus., index, 1976, £1.95

There's some excellent material in here on making paddles and oars—including the spoon-blade variety—laminating wood, and building a plywood pram. The book is worth purchasing for that information alone. The rest of it? A chapter on how to get afloat, another on buying a secondhand wooden boat (in a book about small boat *building*?), an inadequate chapter on canoes, and more—we would recommend ignoring or, if defacing books bothers you not, tearing out and throwing away.

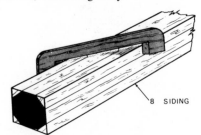

8 SIDING

Top: Rampage, an 18-footer from Glen-L.
Above and below: Spar gauge from Small Boat Building.

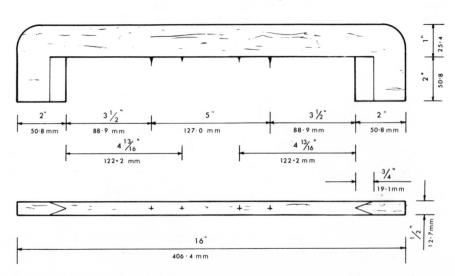

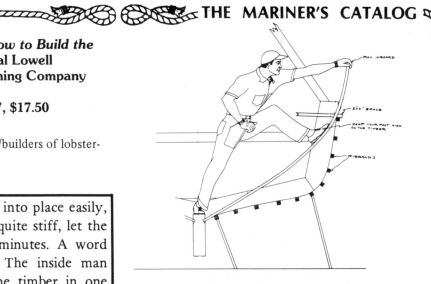

Boatbuilding Down East: How to Build the Maine Lobsterboat, by Royal Lowell
International Marine Publishing Company
Camden, Maine
200 pages, illus., index, 1977, $17.50

One of Maine's leading designer/builders of lobsterboats tells all.

> If the timber bends into place easily, you are all set, but if it is quite stiff, let the others steam another 15 minutes. A word here on bending timbers: The inside man should hold the top of the timber in one hand, with the bottom entered into the box in the keel. He should place his foot quite high on the timber and slide his foot down to the hard turn in the bilge, bending the timber in a big loop at first and then pressing it into the bilge with his foot. The outside man at the side of the boat will also pull with his hands to get the timber out against the ribbands. A good many are broken needlessly by jamming them right into the bilge and hauling in on the top, thus forcing them into a quick bend they can't handle. Remember, keep your foot high on the timber and use a looping and sliding action with your foot. The timber is now clamped into place, and driven down with a sledge hammer until it bottoms in the keel box.

One More Laid to Rest

One of the great hang-ups for beginning boatbuilders is spiling. Actually, it's quite simple once you *understand* it, but gaining that understanding is not that simple. All writers of boatbuilding books and articles take a crack at describing it, but it's only too apparent that not too many readers gain much help from such descriptions. We need to be able to see someone actually spiling—a boatbuilder, preferably. None in your area, I hear you say? I'm terribly sorry, but please don't be put off. There must be a carpet or linoleum layer in your town; go see him. People who install sheet flooring *have* to spile their material. The fellow who installed a single sheet of linoleum in my bathroom was a genius at spiling and pattern making. He did the job in about 2 hours, without seams, and had to contend with the toilet, the bathtub, three pipes from the sink, and two from the radiator. For him, a garboard would be a cinch.

Throw away those dogeared books and magazines. Talk to your carpet layer.

Boxed quote and illustration above from Boatbuilding Down East.

57

A STEAMING BOX.

Wooden Shipbuilding and Small Craft Preservation
The Preservation Press, National Trust for Historic Preservation
740-748 Jackson Place NW
Washington, D.C. 20006
100 pages, illus., biblio., 1976, $5.50

A collection of papers that were presented in 1976 at the Symposium on the American Wooden Ship-building Industry in Bath, Maine, and the Second Annual Museum Conference on Small Craft in New-port News, Virginia. Some of the papers are calls to arms: "We've got a lot of work to do." Others are more practical/historical in nature. We especially enjoyed "Last Days of the Ship Caulking Trade," "19th Century Coastal Lifeboats," and "The Twilight of Commercial Wooden Shipbuilding." The book is illustrated with some excellent photographs, well presented, although quite a few of them have appeared in other publications. Given the resources that must have been at hand, we wish more "never-before-published" photographs could have been included.

Lovers of historical small craft should have this book.

So Just What Is It They Do?

In reply to our query to Caulking Services Ltd., a London, England, company with an intriguing name, we received the following provocative note:

Dear Editors:
We thank you for your letter, but we no longer have any connection with the marine industry.

Yours faithfully,
For Caulking Services Ltd.
J. Cardy, Managing Director

Preservation of a Way of Life

The dream dies hard. The conviction which replaces it is that the vital ingredient which will protect what those vessels represent is the verve or spirit of the next generation. To protect the ships while ignoring the people who will inherit these fine bones would be sheer folly. It follows that the way to protect that spirit is actively to perpetuate the practices to which they testify.

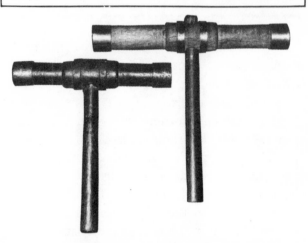

FIGURE 1: *A well-worn black mesquite caulking mallet (left) and a new live oak mallet (right). Both are 20th-century mallets with steel rings and ferrules, a major improvement over the iron ferrules used in the 19th century. (Ellen Newton)*

Above: Boxed quote and caulking mallets from Wooden Shipbuilding and Small Craft Preservation.

Welding Publications

With steel and aluminum boatbuilding becoming more common for small shops, there are some industry publications of importance. The James F. Lincoln Arc Welding Foundation has a library of books on welding.

The James F. Lincoln Arc Welding Foundation
P.O. Box 3035
Cleveland, Ohio 44117

The industry's trade publication is *Welding Design & Fabrication*. They have had articles on ship-building. Qualified subscribers receive the magazine at no charge. (Most anyone can qualify.)

Welding Design & Fabrication
P.O. Box 91368
Cleveland, Ohio 44101

For aluminum, Kaiser Aluminum & Chemical Sales, Inc., Kaiser Center, Oakland, Calif. 94604, has a very complete hardcover manual titled *Welding Kaiser Aluminum*. Here again, the book is (or was a few years ago) free.

—James M. Rudholm

WOOD

Most of the boatstock sources previously listed in the *Mariner's Catalog* have been in the East. To that list we'll add the Clytie Corporation (also discussed in the boatbuilding section), a company that offers virtually every boat wood one could desire, even locust treenails.

Clytie Corp.
60 River Street
Beverly, Mass. 01915

We can thank the *Oregon Commercial Fisheries,* the newsletter of the Sea Grant Marine Advisory Program at Oregon State University, for the list of western boatstock suppliers reproduced in the box below.

To this list we can add:

Spar Lumber Company
1325 Harbor Ave.
P.O. Box 767
Long Beach, Cal. 90801

```
Ehrlich-Harrison Lbr. Co., Seattle, WA  (Mailing address not known)
General Hardwoods Co., 800 Milwaukee Waterway, Tacoma WA  98421
American Forest Products Corp., Building Material Div., PO Box 585, Newark, CA  94560
Macbeath Hardwood Co., 2150 Oakdale Ave., San Francisco, CA  94124
J. E. Higgins Lumber Co., 99 Bayshore Blvd., PO Box 3161, San Francisco, CA  94119
Vance Lumber Co., 14720 Nelson Ave., City of Industry, CA  91744
Simmons Hardwood Lumber Co., 1150 Mines Ave., PO Box 368, Montabello, CA  90640
American Forest Products Corp., Building Material Div., 14103 Park Pl.,
        Cerritos, CA  90701
E. J. Stanton & Son, Inc., 19300 So. Alameda St., Compton, CA  90221
Slattery Hardwood Co. Inc., 11615 Parmelee Ave., Los Angeles, CA  90059
Penberthy Lumber Co.,  5800 So. Boyle Ave., Los Angeles, CA  90058
Stahl Lumber Co. Inc., 3855 E. Washington Blvd., Los Angeles, CA  90025
Saroyan Lumber Co., 30000 Exposition Blvd., Los Angeles, CA  90018
```

Complete Dry Rot Manual
Marine Chem, Suite 303
San Francisco, Calif. 94133
17 pages, 1975, paper booklet, $2.95

"Complete" this booklet is not. The information on defining, preventing, and identifying dry rot is sketchy and best ignored. The value of the booklet is that it tells you how to make your own version of Git-Rot at a considerable saving—$15 will get you the ingredients for a gallon (1975 prices). Anybody priced a gallon of the real thing lately?

We have our reservations about the booklet, however. The information it contains might be worth $2.95, but the booklet as a physical entity is not. If we didn't give a damn, we'd tell you the formula and save you the money; if Marine Chem did give a damn, they'd charge less or give you more or both. (A revised, second edition is in the works, so maybe they will.)

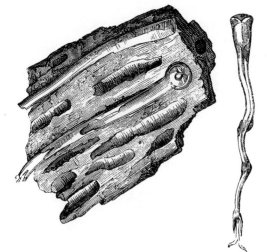

TEREDO, AND HIS PATHWAY IN THE WOOD.

I've read that book seven times, and others like it, and nowhere does it say that boating is inexpensive.

—Fred Brooks

Chain-Saw Maintenance

The need to gain a personal control of our own sources of boatstock remains and grows, and, once this is realized, the relationship that we develop with a chainsaw becomes critical. Quite simply, one has to do it oneself—know how to use them, care for them, and repair them. The work they do is wonderful (even if it's in a neighbor's yard on some vengeance program) and considerable. Inevitably, maintenance is daily and repair perhaps weekly when on a steady working schedule.

Zip-Penn is a very good outfit to have on hand for maintaining your saw over the years. It is a discount house offering chains, bars, noses, and sharpening and maintenance tools of many kinds for all major brands of chainsaws. Zip-Penn has ripping chain for slabbing out that stempiece or keel, chains that will cut soft metals, and chains for bull work through ice or stumping close to the ground.

ZIP-PENN Inc.

Eastern Division
P.O. Box 179
2008 East 33rd St.
Erie, Penna. 16512

Southern Division
P.O. Box 4034
1372C Blountstown Hwy.
Tallahassee, Fla. 32303

West Central Division
P.O. Box 9620
2035 S. Cherokee
Denver, Colo. 80209

Pacific Division
P.O. Box 23159
16436 SW 72nd Ave.
Portland, Ore. 97223

Below: File-in-Joint and Ripping Chain from Zip-Penn catalog

FILE-N-JOINT

Designed for heavy-duty sharpening of chain on the bar. Emery-faced clamps and special chain holding clamps completely eliminate tipping, rear-back and file clatter. Once dial is set for angle clearance and file height, chain continues through accurately without interruption. Adjusts simply to give depth gauges uniform height. Quality engineered for long hard use. All parts replaceable.

G-104B File-N-Joint **$17.85**

RIPPING CHAIN

For speed in making ripping cuts. Ideal with Alaskan Jr. and Mini-Mill. Combines chipper style cutters with cutters re-ground in a scratcher configuration. In 3/8" and .404" pitch in .050", .058" and .063" gauge, and 1/2" pitch in .058" and .063" gauge.

Ripping Chain to fit straight bars with a cutting length of:	Price per Chain with Repair Kit
Up to 16"	$23.00
17" to 20"	$26.00
21" to 24"	$31.50
25" to 28"	$34.00
29" to 32"	$38.00
33" to 36"	$44.00

People who do not own a chainsaw and have never used one invariably regard them as instruments of the devil, deadly devices they wouldn't pick up on a bet, and they see those who do so as lacking a fundamental sense of survival, or sense of any kind. As Shane said, "Shucks ma'am, a gun's (read chainsaw) just a tool like any other tool, just as good er bad as the man behind it." And if a man (read person) buys a good one—a medium-size one at least, not the weightless minis, which are dangerous—studies it, begins slowly, doesn't allow himself (read herself) to become tired, and follows directions, soon a chainsaw becomes as endearing a tool as one has in his (read her) kit. Respect is in order always, but confidence and affection come. It is quite a tool when you think of doing it by hand and realize what your ancestors would have given for one!

60

Cartoon by Darrell McClure.

For getting into the guts of your saw, or the one you borrowed and broke, the Intertec Publishing Corporation has an excellent 312-page book showing blown-up diagrams of every model of every chainsaw made, together with running narratives on the ins, outs, and peculiarities of the machines. The first 36 pages on fundamentals alone make it worth the price.

Chainsaw Service Manual, 5th ed.
Technical Publications Div. (I.P.C.)
1550 N. Topping
Kansas City, Missouri 64120
$7.95

They also offer the *Small Engines Service Manual,* 11th ed., treating in the same way all major brands of utility engines. It's $7.95.

Wood Carving
by William Wheeler and Charles H. Hayward
Drake Publishers, New York
128 pages, index, illus., paperbound, 1972, $4.95

A better title might be *Woodcarving for Cabinetmakers and Furniture Makers,* as this book goes in heavily for carving moldings, frames, edgings, leafage, etc. Yet there are good sections on selecting, handling, and sharpening tools, lettering, and gilding. The material on types of wood for carving is inadequate, especially since the authors are English—they discuss only wood easily available to them.

Below: From Chainsaw Service Manual.

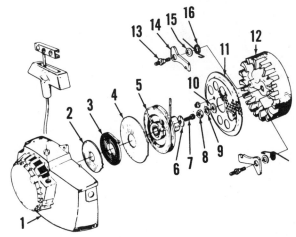

Fig. PN27–Exploded view of recoil starter used on models 360, 361, 400, 400A, 401, 401A, 450, 450A, 451 and 451A.

1. Starter housing
2. Spring plate
3. Rewind spring
4. Spring cover
5. Rope pulley
6. Washer
7. Screw
8. Flywheel nut
9. Lockwasher
10. Washer
11. Flywheel cover
12. Flywheel
13. Stud
14. Starter dog
15. Washer
16. Spring

61

Dear Editors:

This letter is to confirm an item I saw on p. 49, Vol. 3. The man at Quicksilver is right [that interior plywood paneling is many times made with waterproof glue]. I own and operate a Thomaston galley (Bolger design) that I built last year from paneling I bought in a cut-rate place in Portland, Oregon (Mr. Plywood). It cost me $4.97 for a 4' x 7' sheet of 3-ply mahogany stuff, which was 7 mm, I guess. Six sheets did it. Chine, sheer rails are of stair-grade fir, stem from a 2 x 6 red cedar decking plank from my former back porch. The reason I bought 6 sheets was that the center ply—which is the thickest of three—had what looked to be poor-quality lamination areas—small voids running across the sheet. So I cut them out in the laying out—or in noncritical areas, I just forgot about them.

I had seen this stuff and had Bolger's plans for about a year before I got the two things together in my head. I asked about the glue in the paneling and was assured it was interior glue. But—being nuts—I bought one sheet, took it home, soaked a square of it in a bucket of water for what turned out to be two weeks. Nothing—hot dig! Here goes a boat!

Now, gang—here's the kicker. I put the boat together with Elmer's glue, screws, and nails. Yeh. But why not?

After the hull was completed, I glassed the entire outside and all of the interior except the hull sides (just up to and including the chine stringer). Actually, in some areas high up, I just brushed on a coat of polyester resin—a test showed it has good adhesion to this plywood.

I will *never* use fiberglass again. I think it's an utterly horrible material. What the hell do we need it for? The only reason I used it was to stiffen the hull as well as cover up the glue joints. Never, never again.

By the way—if this boat goes as kindly under sail as she does with a 1½ h.p. outboard or with oars, then I may have her for life. I really want to build a schooner (Bolger again).

Mark Roeyer
Lawrence, Kansas

For years, the Belsaw Machinery Company has made various models of their High Speed sawmill. We wanted to list them in Volume 4 but were informed that they had suffered the loss of their factory. Now they are back in production with an improved model, and we would say that any group thinking about cooperating on timber supplies ought to consider this machine. It occurs to us that it could be mounted on wheels and run off the PTO of the tractor or jeep that tows both it and the logs it eats. Its 14-foot limit means butts in your planking, but, then, there's the planking!

**Belsaw Machinery Company
315 Westport Road (Box 593)
Kansas City, Missouri 64141**

Preservation

Unhappily, most of the wood around the water these days is in shoreside structures, not in boats. Building these structures is both labor and capital-intensive, and the days when one could cheaply secure a pile of logs and muster a mess of wharf-rats to replace one's seven-year-old dock and float are gone. Now, if one is going to the expense and trouble, the works should stay there as long as possible, and this means wood *preservation*.

So we explored the field by writing Michael Levi, leader of the Extension Wood Products Section at North Carolina State University, and he sent this helpful note:

Dear Editors:
Copper-chromium-arsenate preservatives (CCA) are excellent multipurpose preservatives. They are applied in a water solution, but react in the wood so that once the wood has been dried, the preservative will not leach out, even when it is re-exposed to continuous wetting. CCA is effective against fungi, insects, and most marine borers. The treated wood is odorless, colored a light green/brown, and can be painted or stained when dry. CCA is specified for treatment of wood in salt water in all areas except where pholads are a severe problem (Florida and Gulf Coast). In those areas a double treatment can be used (CCA followed by creosote pressure treatment). CCA can only be applied by commercial pressure treat-

BELSAW VARIABLE-SPEED POWER FEED

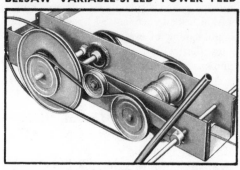

This picture shows the mechanism of the Variable-Speed Power Feed unit supplied with the Model M-14 Sawmill. Recommended for sawing logs of uniform, medium size. Allows you to operate power feed with a minimum of 25 HP. Forward feed variable from 0 to 1-inch each saw revolution. Gigs back at triple speed. Full slipping V-belt feed gets power direct from mandrel. Furnished with M-14 mill, complete with all pulleys, belting, cable, sheaves and attachment bolts.

Above: From a Belsaw flyer describing the M-14 high-speed sawmill for logs up to 18" diameter and 14' length, listed at $1,563.

ment; it will not perform satisfactorily if brushed or sprayed onto the wood.

For suppliers of CCA treated wood, and more information on its use, I suggest you contact:

**American Wood Preservers' Institute
1651 Old Meadow Road
McLean, Virginia 22101**

or

**Society of American Wood Preservers
1501 Wilson Boulevard
Arlington, Virginia 22209**

They are the trade associations that represent the preservation industry.

**Michael P. Levi, Leader
Extension Wood Products Section**

We followed through, and the American Wood Preservers' Institute sent us their directory, a very complete summary of the entire industry, and their publications list, which is loaded with titles to intrigue the troubled marina.

The Society of American Wood Preservers and the Southern Forest Products Association also sent lists of their publications, all worthwhile to the serious inquirer, the former for a list of suppliers and the latter for a use guide on matching treatment to application.

North American Trees, by Richard J. Preston
Iowa State University Press
Ames, Iowa
399 pages, illus., glossary, index,
1976 (3rd ed.), $7.50

Another tree identification book for those who go into the woods for boatstock (we have reviewed others in past *Catalogs*). It's as good as, or better than, most other guides of its type. The one drawback we could find is in the matter of identifying deciduous trees in the winter when the leaves are off. Since the illustrations only show branches, twigs, leaves, flowers, and fruit, but no tree shapes and bark, there are times when you could be out of luck. It's not as bad as all that—many of the illustrations show winter twigs, but if the tree is tall and has no lower branches .... Yet our test of the book in the woods was highly satisfactory: we felt *confident* with our results, and confidence is what you need when you're out there alone.

Right: Longleaf pine, from North American Trees.

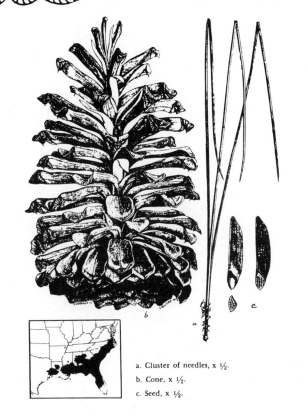

a. Cluster of needles, x ½.
b. Cone, x ½.
c. Seed, x ½.

Dear Editors:

Just a short note to let you know what we are up to. Fred Brooks did put together enough money to hire a lawyer and sue me (see letter on p. 11, MC-4); the case went before a judge in East Orange, N.J., and both of us lost. Seems the judge found the whole argument asinine and forced a reconciliation, without lawyers, in his chambers. The upshot is that I promised Fred that bygones would be bygones if he could prove to me that the Fox Islands Carry Boat was real. So we pooled our resources (all of $76.33) and moved to North Haven, Maine, the home of the boat. We've been here since the fall, and began our digs at the abandoned site of the Shepherd Cove Boat Works. We had just unearthed the partial skeleton of a promising-looking boat (not to mention loose boat nails, a handleless skillet, three Edgeworth Ready-Rubbed Tobacco tins, and the skull of an alley cat), when the frost set in and we had to retire to our "cottage"—a bait shack we rented from the larcenous soul who runs the local fisherman's cooperative. It's the dead of winter now, the worst in the last century, so they say, and we're out of money. We're keeping warm, more or less, by burning driftwood in a barrel stove, and we're eating what Fred can spear through the ice and what I can garner from the Seacoast Mission. Don't even have enough to pay for a ferry-boat ticket to the mainland, or we would drop in on you to pass the time.

I'm worried about Fred. He has spent the last week or so in his bunk reading seed catalogs he borrowed from the schoolteacher down the road, grumbling continually about the cold and the gales, and filling my ears with romantic notions about rows and rows of swiss chard, turnips, cabbages, sweet corn, Big Boy tomatoes, and vine-ripened peas. Even a stack of blue magazines I borrowed off the crew of the mail boat couldn't pull him out of his funk. If spring doesn't come soon, we'll probably come to blows.

Stop in if you can spare the time. I have a few clippings about the fox population problem here on the island at the turn of the century that I found in an old trunk in the cellar of the Fox Islands Odd Fellows Hall.

E.H. Morgan
North Haven, Maine

63

Quick and Dirty Boats —Again?

Wherein Like Real Men We Face a Growing Welter of Rotten Standards and Capitulate.

The poor are those who think poor
—Fred Brooks

Motorboats for the Masses

by Pete Culler

I've just been reading the Coast Guard's latest proposals for safety in gas-propelled motor craft; so complicating, expensive, and nonunderstandable that it's simpler to just stay in bed. When I consider the dire predictions of OSHA, Coast Guard, ecology boys, Woods Hole thinkers, dangers of tobacco, the risks of a square meal, not to say beer, X-rated movies, and the possibility that part of a Sputnik might fall on me, I wonder if it's all worth it, except I would like to stick around to go sailing.

No doubt, to be quick and dirty in the true sense, a boat should be propelled by pole, paddle, oars, and in some cases sticks and a scrap of canvas, with a piece of board for a leeboard, hung by a lanyard from a thole pin. This is keeping it fundamental, as it should be.

However, for some uses, the advantages of a motor can be very necessary. This also ties in with discussions of air-cooled industrial motors in recent *Mariner's Catalogs.* I show some quick and dirty motorboats I have known. The little 8-footer was built and powered in a hurry simply to get her owner to and from work, which she did for a long time with great success. The installation was rudimentary, which was all that was needed. She had no hand throttle, but simply used the governor on the little 3/4-hp engine. Being so short and rockered, she had a built-in clutch—you simply raised the wheel out with your weight when you wanted to (the engine did not race with the governor). The "steering gear" was simply a paddle chopped out of a handy board. Say what you will, the whole thing worked perfectly.

The 13-foot mullet skiff had a lot of charm. She was built by a fisherman-boatbuilder out of what he could get, for times were hard. She was of excellent model and well joined, though the stock in her was scrap of all kinds, including much use of mangrove roots, which were free. She even had a tiny fish well, for she was a great part of her owner's living. The engine was a 1½-hp Briggs—I own one of these of the same vintage now, and it's most reliable. The installation was very fundamental. Due to a changing scene, this little craft made a hundred-mile trip to a place of better employment as a matter of course. She made many a dollar from fish, for her owner was skilled with the throw net and wise in the ways of 'gators and such.

The Bahama boat was a buxom thing, worked daily as shown, and with the big iron Briggs, with an iron crank, was quite a workhorse. Though simple in installation, she had one failing—an outside stuffing box; being deep, and with little range of tide in the area, this was neglected and was no doubt worn, so it was customary to proceed by constant bailing, said bailers nearly all having pin holes in the bottom. She was always so crowded that she carried two "engineers"; one could reach the crank and nothing else, the other could get at the panic buttons.

These craft all had the same thing in common: they were cheap to build or acquire. The Bahama was a

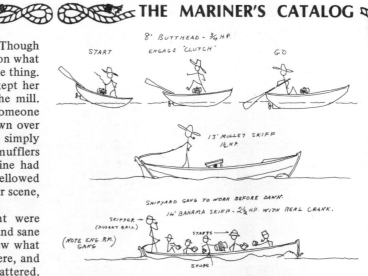

conversion but was picked up for peanuts. Though each installation was slightly different, based on what the owners could cobble up, simplicity was the thing. The fisherman was quite proud of his and kept her well; she had a little open-sided box over the mill. The others ran naked; sometimes, when someone thought to do it, an old coat might be thrown over them. Exhaust pipes were ignored; they simply blatted out through the little squash-shaped mufflers that came with them. However, the big engine had long ago lost whatever she had and simply bellowed into the night. This racket was part of the river scene, and early risers set their watches by it.

Lifejackets and other required equipment were nonexistent. Now, this might not seem safe and sane boating—I say it was, for those doing it knew what they were doing. The Law was busy elsewhere, and these men were doing a job; that's all that mattered.

If these lashups meet the law now, I really don't know; my feeling is, being all in the open, I don't see why not. The same engines power all sorts of things both ashore and afloat. Filling out some state motorboat registration might be interesting—"model, year number, and make of hull." Perhaps 1-X (for experimental)-77 JOE might do.

I show a DIRTY with my notions of about how to go about it. You acquire or build a hull of some sort, guessing about how much hull to engine. How you get the engine—its size, make, and condition—is your business. You may have to buy a shaft unless you

have friends in the business; this may be the big expense after the engine. It must run true. All I had experience with had bronze shafts; no doubt the present-day noncorrosive white metal shafts will do okay. In fresh water, you might get away with plain steel for quite a while. In the above boats the shaft size was the same as the engine shaft size for good reason (see coupling). Some props were scrounged, others made about as shown out of brass and bronze. Don't ask me prop size for each hp, I don't know.

(Continued on next page)

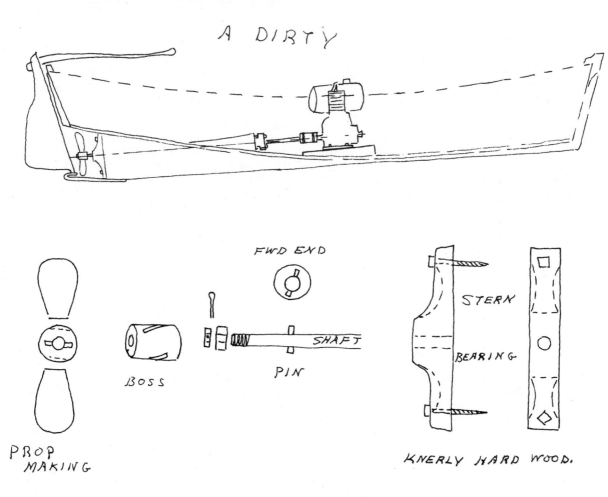

A DIRTY

65

PROP MAKING

BOSS

FWD END

SHAFT

PIN

STERN BEARING

KNERLY HARD WOOD.

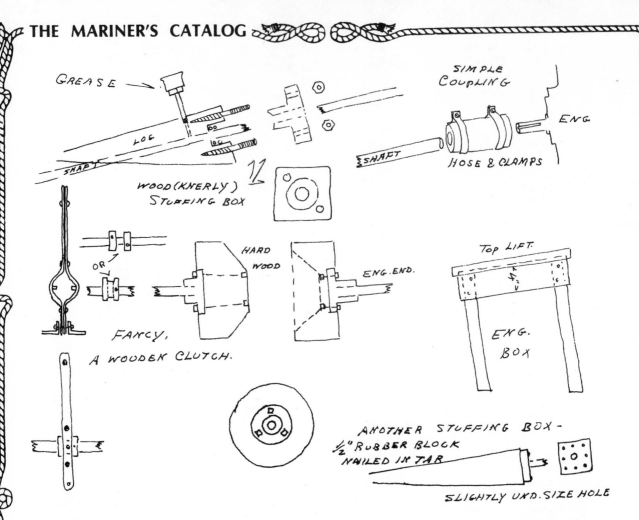

(Continued from preceding page)

Observe and experiment. If it's too big, cut it down. All the rigs I was familiar with were pretty heavily loaded with prop, and the engines seemed to take it.

The propeller boss was usually a piece of big prop shaft bored out by some machinist friend; slots for blades were cut by putting two, or sometimes three blades in a hacksaw frame, depending on the thickness of the prop blades. The blades were brass, or bronze plate if you could scrounge it, about 1/8" thick, and cut and shaped by aping some store-bought prop. Some of the boys got some interesting experimental shapes that worked fine. The blades were brazed in the slots, usually by some garage, or slipped to the welder at his place of work. I think with good fits, silver solder will work quite well here. Silver solder likes good fits.

Note the drive pin in the shaft; it's also a shear pin, so carry some spares. Note the slots in the forward end of the boss; these are a cape chisel job. The nuts and cotter are standard. In the gone and much lamented (here anyhow) magazine called *Steamboats and Modern Steam Launches,* now reprinted and available again through Howell-North in Berkeley, Calif. (1050 Parker St., $12.50), and International Marine, there is some excellent stuff on designing and making your own props, by guess who?—Westy Farmer, of course, worth the price of the reprint many times over. So I need say no more about propellers— except check your rotation. All these little engines I've had to do with are left handed.

The stern bearing (I warned you about an outside stuffing box) is simply swirly grained hardwood. Mount and adjust it for square just like a bought bearing; there should be a gasket behind it. Don't laugh, this is a water-lubricated hardwood bearing like our finest steamships have had. It works. Some groove the bottom of the shaft hole with a keyhole saw, saying it gives water passage and a place for sand to work out; I don't really know if that is true.

The wedge-shaped shaft log has been standard in flat-bottomed boats for years, well bedded and bolted, 'nuf said. The grease cup in it is very good, dirty build or not, and much helps the life of the packing and box, which you note is of wood. Yes, it works. You can make your own hanger bolts by cutting heads off lag screws; a bit of grinding, for the shanks may be a bit oversize, and threading. If this is all too involved, use the alternate rubber block as shown—in shallow boats there is small pressure on the stuffing box. The coupling is simply a stout suction hose and clamps. It's assumed you know, or are willing to learn, how to line up an engine, even with hose. This drive was once common for marine engine water pumps of good size. This is the point of having prop shaft and engine shaft the same size—if you are real hot, you can bush to different sizes.

Engine box should be totally open; these beasts get hot. Make it big enough so you don't have to take it off to start, work throttle, and stop, only remove the lid. An over-riding throttle lever can be rigged right on the engine, just like many lawn mowers, so it overcomes the governor. Some of these little engines run dead slow remarkably well, especially the older, slower models.

The snazzy clutch is for those who just must have one, or are mad tinkerers like myself. These things, in principle, used to be manufactured out of metal, but I doubt if they still are. Acquire, by devious means or otherwise, two couplings that fit the shafts; saw out as round as you can two oak discs fairly thick; lay out with care the location of the couplings and let in by chisel work as shown—you can rough out the female end to make bolting easier. These won't be true. Bolt down the little beast somewhere solid, put on the coupling with disc, making sure it's tight, rig a tool rest, and turn in place so it's true, true as you can get wood, anyhow. This done, do the other, trying to get a fair match to the cones. Set collars, or even a grooved set collar, are not hard to come by; the shift lever I think explains itself—scrap iron, rivets, pins—it should be a slack fit on the collar, plenty of play and grease, as there is no pressure on it once engaged. I can picture some hotshot here friction-loading the thing end, so once engaged, a slight pull-back will have the pins out of contact with the collars—no wear. The very sophisticated may still not see how this works. The prop thrust keeps the thing engaged; simply throttle down, shift in, and give her the gas, the reverse in going to neutral. This unnecessary bit of gear is really a way-out, highly "engineered" contraption, for it is self-takeup for wear, more or less self-aligning, and tends to true up the wood, which always warps somewhat.

Some observations—I've not tinkered with the recent rather higher speed models that have replaced the older engines. As Briggs says, load em; if it's too much, whittle down the prop. You put up with the noise. Don't box 'em in; give 'em air. Don't expect other than modest speed. Those I've played with seemed to go best at very modest wave making, a speed-length ratio of about .90 or 1. The boats and engines were small, and thus the waterline length also. The gas "mileage" was fantastic; a gallon in 8 hours with the little old model 1½s.

I've often wondered about the once-common radial-thrust bearing common on the old make and breaks. None I knew used any on the little Briggs, and the engines seemed to take it. It might be a good idea to use one—cut the hose coupling square and put the radial between it and the motor housing, maybe using some big washers, too; same if you use the clutch and coupling.

While somewhat off the subject of true quick and dirty boats, and knowing the great God of speed still rules most people, fuel consumption be damned. I think I could design a fairly fast, though limited-use boat for these air-cooled engines. Right away you consider a fairly big one, a long, lean, flat-run boat of very good but light construction—with speed you have to start thinking light right off—a hull that could "get away from her wheel." Small diameter, large pitch, interesting prop design; careful lineup; and I doubt if you could drive her through a piece of hose. Now we are getting complicated, expensive, and wasteful, so let's take it slow and be happy.

Note that I've given no fixed dimensions for the boat and motor; you fit what you have to work with into something that operates. Proportion, both for strength and looks, is part of mechanics, even though this is the baling-wire sort. There is no reason why a quick and dirty boat has to be totally horrible to look at, and it must do the job intended for it, or there is no point at all in doing it.

Someone gets the urge to turn out 1-X-77, let us know how she works.

Hello there. I'm driving a 1937 2-door Maine Peapod coupe with four on the floor plus overdrive and flow-through factory-installed air. And you? (Photo by George Putz).

Air-Cooled Engines

Dear Editors:

The discussion between Bill Durham and Mr. Stratton of the Briggs & Straggon engine company is interesting (See MC-2, p. 91, and MC-3, p. 101).

Mr. Durham feels that extensive modifications will be required to derate an engine. Mr. Stratton appears to disagree, suggesting that the maximum throttle setting be established at the low end of the operating range.

I think Mr. Stratton has a point. Maximum torque usually comes in at an rpm level far below the top end, and it's torque that turns the propeller. If you limited the throttle setting to the maximum torque level, you should be able to use a pretty substantial wheel with no chance of overloading it by advancing the throttle where the torque curve begins to fall off. Presumably, any reputable manufacturer would be willing to supply performance charts for its engines.

(That is true; most manufacturers, including B & S, do.—Eds.) I have no accurate idea where maximum torque comes in on Mr. Stratton's air-cooled job, but perhaps his throttle-restriction idea is based on its best torque.

You could arrive at substantially the same result by mechanically derating the engine, as Mr. Durham suggests, but it seems an expensive approach. You'd have to regrind the cam so that it did practically nothing at all and fit a smaller carburetor. This seems a bit much in view of the fact that just the straight marine conversion is going to cost an arm and a leg by itself. Furthermore, messing with the cam and carburation is probably going to affect the torque adversely.

David L. Register
Damariscotta, Maine

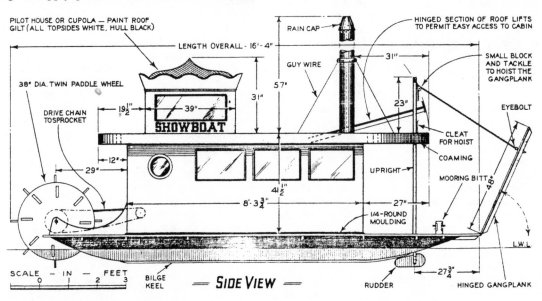

68

Showboat to Seattle

Dear Editors:

I came across the plan of "The Showboat" in an old *How To Build 20 Boats* magazine and thought you might be interested in it. I have always been a sucker for boats like this, which are basically useless except for floating around a lake and looking hip. In the last two years we've been in Seattle we have owned a 21-foot wall-sided cruiser, a 14-foot 3-point hydro with black leather bucket seats from a Pontiac Bonneville, and a 14-foot Bayliner wood double-cockpit ski boat. There is nothing more fun than powering slowly around a lake or bay, drinking beer, and looking at all the boats tied up in marinas.

"The Showboat" is to me especially neat, and some time in the future I want to build it. I would probably put a 50-hp outboard on the back with some sort of deal where the paddles could be lifted out of the water, because I love to roar across a bay at 30 knots, throwing spray, pounding, and making noise.

George Buehler
Seattle, Wash.

Above: Showboat, *a pedal-powered stern-wheeler designed by Douglas Rolfe. From* How to Build 20 Boats *(O.P.)*

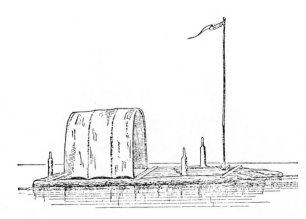

Plastic sheeting and bamboo will do it every time. (Photo by Pat Boyd, courtesy of Practical Boatowner *magazine)*

Nutmegs

Since it is common knowledge that we like to keep up to date on the latest developments in sleazy-boat technology, we were made privy to a letter from Jay Benford to Bruce Roberts, both noted naval architects, and a provocative query to Benford from Slapjack Boatbuilders. We were hesitant to divulge the contents of those letters because the products discussed have yet to be marketed—we assume the delay has been caused by the intense competition among advertising agencies to acquire the accounts—but the parties involved agreed to allow us to reprint these most interesting letters, so they appear forthwith:

The Bruce Roberts (himself)
1617 Westcliff Drive
Newport Beach, Ca. 92660

Dear The:

Knowing how you hate to be left behind on the latest trends in boatbuilding, I thought I'd give you an advance preview of a revolutionary technique we've just developed, and are now seeking a patent for.

The method, which we have named FIBERFOIL, is simplicity itself. It is also ideally suited to the rejuvenation of older boats.

The secret (top) of the system lies in using the widely popular standard foil-backed fiberglass insulating material. The first layer would be stapled onto the old wood hull, foil side to the old wood, and then wetted out with resin and smoothed with rollers. A second layer is applied while the first is still wet, so the staples will go through easily. The second layer will have been wet out on an adjacent table, and is applied with the foil side out, giving an aluminum surface for extra strength and impermeability both inside and out.

The scantlings can be easily varied to suit the size of boats involved by using the 2¼″, or 3½″, or 6″ insulation. According to our laboratory tests, they wet down to 0.563476523% of their original thickness—you can use this figure with some degree of accuracy in making your calculations.

If you would like to be the franchised dealer for the system in the various Commonwealth countries, please let me know, and I will have our negotiators contact you to work out a mutually satisfactory price.

Sincerely,

Jay R. Benford & Assoc., Inc.
Jay R. Benford, President
Chief Naval Architect
Chairman of the Board

Jay R. Benford & Assoc., Inc.
Yacht Designers,
P.O. Box 399
Friday Harbor, Wash. 98250

Dear Mr. Benford:

Slapjack Boatbuilders Inc. has always been progressive with yacht construction methods, having pioneered the *Maple Leaf vertical twig* method as early as 1974. It was with great interest that we received your recent letter concerning your revolutionary FIBERFOIL technique. We too can see the advantages of such a system and would be most willing to become your accredited builders and/or agents for FIBERFOIL.

With our long experience with the VERTICAL TWIG method we can see certain advantages of using a combination of two systems if the FIBERFOIL is used in conjunction. A suggested trade name would be the FIBERTWIG SYSTEM and would consist of twin diagonal applications of foil-backed fiberglass with a central core of our product.

The result would be outstanding strength and ease of application and would largely dispense with the need to construct expensive tooling and molds.

Sample sections of our Maple Leaf vertical twig are currently undergoing exhaustive testing at BOEING, who have expressed considerable interest for use in the prototype B2 bomber now on the drawing boards. The potential of FIBERTWIG is obvious, and we would suggest a joint meeting of our technical staff at the earliest opportunity.

Sincerely,
Jack Slap
President
Slapjack Boatbuilders, Inc.

Builders of the Slapjack Seaslipper Skipjack
"We've been slapping boats together for over 30 years"

69

Books about the Sea for Children

by Marilyn Lutz

With a few classic exceptions, such as *Robinson Crusoe*, the publication of children's books is a recent event in literary history, for until 1850 books deliberately intended for young people were written to preach, exhort, reprimand, and otherwise moralize explicitly. Naturally, children resisted these books, not in any overt sense, but enough to favor other books that gave pleasure and kindled fantasies. The latter books continue to do so, since these choices are classics today—myths, fairy tales, nonsense rhymes, folklore, and romances. Among the latter category, the range of possibilities in the sea story was richly cultivated. Boys ripe for the adventure of running away to a life at sea (a real possibility in the eighteenth and nineteenth centuries when midshipmen began naval life at age twelve) readily enjoyed gripping maritime exploits of early explorers and the intrigues of pirates, or tales of mutiny and shipwreck. Significantly, the romance of the sea is one of the earliest types of literature that children adopted as their own and that is now written specifically with them in mind.

The enormous number of books about the sea for children and "young adults" precludes a comprehensive listing. For present purposes my selection is aimed only at including a few representative examples of various types of books that teach imaginatively, entertain, and reflect seriously some aspect of our relationship to the sea. Spanning 75 years of publication, the titles here include classic romances, historical accounts, fantasies, and science books, among others, that recreate the marine world by conveying a multifaceted view of the real and imagined life of the sea. A balance of fiction and nonfiction cuts across a broad range of subjects, excluding only the war story, which really constitutes a genre of its own anyway, and is one that raises serious questions about its suitability for children, given the tendency to glorify destruction inherent in much of it. The overall quality of individual books (style, art, design, purpose) and uniqueness of their contribution to the field were guiding considerations as well.

In the accompanying bibliographical list, age groups are assigned in accordance with the standard practices of publishers and librarians, although anyone can read sea stories, with guidance necessary only for the very young. (Note: for the uninitiated, ps=preschool.) Such arbitrary divisions (except in the instance of technical material) have only a sketchy relationship to the habits of real readers and should not deter parents from ignoring the signposts if they so choose. Books (with a few exceptions) are available in hardcover and paper editions at local bookstores and generally can be found at a good public library even if they are out of print. For books that are both out of print and unavailable at the library, search in used-book stores, especially those listed in all the volumes of the *Mariner's Catalog* to date.

CLASSIC SEA ADVENTURE

Captains Courageous by Rudyard Kipling. 1896. Ages 9 up.

The Dark Frigate (1923) and *The Mutineers* (1920) by Charles Boardman Hawes. Ages 13 up.

Sea Fever by K.M. Peyton. World Publishing Co., 1963. Ages 12-16.

Treasure Island by Robert Louis Stevenson. 1882. Ages 12 up.

The Tattooed Man by Howard Pease. Doubleday, 1931 (o.p.). Ages 9-14.

MARITIME HISTORY

The Cruise of the 'Cachalot' by Frank T. Bullen. 1898 (o.p.). Ages 14 up.

The Bounty Trilogy: Mutiny on the Bounty, Men Against the Sea, Pitcairn Island by Charles Nordhoff and James Norman Hall. 1932-34. Ages 14 up.

Seabird by Holling C. Holling. Houghton-Mifflin Co., 1948. Ages 9-13.

Two Years Before the Mast by Richard Henry Dana. 1840. Ages 14 up.

TWO MASTERS

Moby Dick or, The Whale by Herman Melville. 1851. Ages 14 up.

The Nigger of the Narcissus (1898) and *Typhoon* (1903) by Joseph Conrad. Ages 14 up.

Books are listed with original dates of publication. Publishers are not indicated for the "classics," of which numerous hardcover and paper editions exist. Libraries or secondhand bookstores are obvious sources for out-of-print titles not listed in current *Books in Print*.

FOLKLORE OF THE SEA

Call It Courage by Armstrong Sperry. Macmillan, 1940. Ages 9-13.

Scarlet Sails by Alexander Green, trans. from Russian by Thomas P. Whitney. Charles Scribner's Sons, 1967 (o.p.). Ages 6-13.

The Selchie's Seed by Shulamith Oppenheim. Bradbury, 1975. Ages 9-13.

The Tower by the Sea by Meindert DeJong. Harper & Row, 1950. Ages ps up.

The Voyage of the Dawn Treader by C.S. Lewis. Macmillan, 1952. Ages ps up.

IMAGINATION AFLOAT

The Sea Egg by L.M. Boston. Harcourt, Brace & World, 1967. Ages 6-10.

Swallows and Amazons by Arthur Ransome. Lippincott, 1931 (o.p.). Ages 8-13.

NAUTICAL PICTURE BOOKS

Burt Dow, Deep-Water Man; a tale of the sea in the classic tradition by Robert McCloskey. Viking, 1963. Ages ps-10.

A Capital Ship or the Walloping Window-Blind (Old English Nonsense Verse) Ill. by Paul Galdone. McGraw-Hill, 1963. Ages ps-8.

Little Tim and the Brave Sea Captain by Edward Ardizzone. Henry Z. Walck, 1955. Ages ps-8. Other titles in the series by Ardizzone: *Tim to the Lighthouse, Tim All Alone, Tim in Danger, Tim and Lucy Go to Sea, Tim to the Rescue.*

Little Toot by Hardie Gramatky. Putnam, 1939. Ages ps-8. Other titles in the series by Gramatky: *Little Toot on the Thames, Little Toot on the Grand Canal, Little Toot Through the Golden Gate.*

Sam, Bangs and Moonshine by Evaline Ness. Holt, Rinehart & Winston, 1966. Ages ps-6.

Seashore Story by Taro Yashima. Viking, 1967. Ages ps-7.

OCEANOGRAPHY

ABC's of the Ocean by Isaac Asimov. Walker & Co., 1970. Ages ps-10.

The Challenge of the Seas by Arthur C. Clarke. Holt, Rinehart & Winston, 1960. Ages 9-13.

A Day and a Night in a Tide Pool by Mary Adrian. Ill. by Genevieve Vaughan-Jackson. Hastings House, 1972. Ages ps-8.

The Gulf Stream by Ruth Brindze. Ill. by Helene Carter. Vanguard, 1945. Ages 9-13. Other titles by Brindze: *The Story of the Trade Winds, The Rise and Fall of the Tides.*

The Land Beneath the Sea by Julian May. Ill. by Leonard Everett Fisher. Holiday, 1971. Ages ps-8.

The Sea Around Us by Rachel Carson. Golden Press, 1958 (special edition adapted for young readers by Anne T. White). Ages 8-13.

The Sea for Sam by W. Maxwell Reed and Wilfrid S. Bronson. Harcourt, Brace & World, 1960 (rev. ed.). Ages 13-18.

Seahorse by Robert A. Morris. Ill. by Arnold Lobel. Harper & Row, 1972. Ages ps-8.

Vessels for Underwater Explorations by Peter Limburg and James B. Sweeney. Crown Publishing Co., 1973. Ages 9-18.

SHIPS AND SHIPBUILDING, BOATS AND BOATING

America Sails the Seas (1962) and *Clipper Ship* (1963) by J.O'Hara Cosgrave. Houghton-Mifflin (o.p.). Ages 8-13.

The Craft of Sail by Jan Adkins. Walker & Co., 1973. Ages 8 up.

Oars, Sails and Steam; a picture book of ships by Edwin Tunis. World Publishing Company, 1952 (o.p.). Ages 9 up.

Ships Through History by Ralph T. Ward. Ill. by Samuel F. Manning. Bobbs-Merrill Co., 1973. Ages 10-14.

(Continued on next page)

71

A NORWEGIAN CHRISTENING PARTY.

(Continued from preceding page)

Immensely popular when first published in 1883, it is easy to understand why Robert Louis Stevenson's *Treasure Island* met with a singular acclaim that remains undiminished nearly a century later. Reading it is pure indulgence in pleasure from the opening chapters, when one is caught up in the magic adventure of buccaneers on the high seas in search of buried treasure, to the tale's climax in which the infamous Long John Silver connives to save the hero Jim Hawkins from the vengeance of the crew, and in so doing insures that he himself will be saved. Stevenson was an inimitable storyteller with an uncanny ability to weave dramatic incidents and unforgettable characters in continuously intensified and rapid action. Equally important, he was master of a powerful narrative technique that tempered the romantic and picturesque with realism effectively to convince and absorb readers into a robust, vigorous adventure. *Treasure Island* represents a milestone in writing for children, for it set a standard in the field for work of technical excellence and imaginative power.

A contemporary of Stevenson, Rudyard Kipling, wrote *Captains Courageous* in 1897 after a decade of literary success acclaimed him as an originator of stories for children. He was an unparalleled storyteller whose vivid imagination, impelling realism, and exacting belief in one's responsibility for a moral universe give spontaneous vitality and universal significance to his work. In *Captains Courageous* Kipling recreates the vigorous individualism of New England fishermen and the way in which their characters are molded by a life at sea. An implicit love and understanding of the men working the Grand Banks in the days before steam-powered trawlers permeates the dramatic story of 15-year-old Harvey Cheyne, a selfish, egotistical, rich boy who finds himself rescued on board Disko Troop's schooner early one season. The story is narrated with authority that commands a classically simple prose style, richly embellished with the fishermen's language.

Following in the tradition of Stevenson and Kipling are myriad writers of sea adventure, some whose work approaches the early originators, others who use

ships and the sea as a microcosmic symbol. Still others create rites-of-passage stories involving a youth who must learn survival among seasoned, often cruel elders in a world circumscribed by the sea and weather. Charles Boardman Hawes wrote exciting, spontaneous, rapidly narrated tales in *The Mutineers* and *The Dark Frigate*, creating anew his plots and characters from actual incidents, narratives, journals, and the yarns of blue-water skippers whose acquaintance he had made. *The Tattooed Man* is the first of a long list of mystery-sea stories by Howard Pease; his simple narrative style, technical skill, and clever plotting make first-class "escape" reading. A contemporary story of boys and men of skill and courage who live by grace of the sea is *Sea Fever*, by the British author K.M. Peyton. The book has dramatic and intense action set on the rugged Essex coast aboard an old fishing smack and a racing yacht.

Maritime History

Two of the best sea narratives ever written are Richard Henry Dana's *Two Years Before the Mast* and Frank Bullen's *The Cruise of the 'Cachalot'*, for they have the distinctive quality of recreating a sense of reality independent of time or place, yet remain actual historical documents of seafaring life. In August, 1834, Dana shipped as an ordinary seaman aboard the brig *Pilgrim* bound from Boston around Cape Horn for California to trade in hides. A Harvard undergraduate who went to sea for reasons of health, he was an intelligent and observant adventurer whose strong, vibrant descriptions and flowing, articulate style give the journal of his voyage a timeless sense of abundant and vigorous life. *Two Years Before the Mast* remains especially distinguished for its accurate and sympathetic account of the common sailor's life and the abuses he suffered. Dana's outrage at the inhuman treatment later aroused public empathy and proved instrumental in encouraging maritime legal reform.

Unlike the educated adventurer Dana, Frank Bullen was a street-Arab *cum* sea urchin who shipped as a cabin boy at age 12 and for the next 15 years sailed the seven seas serving in every capacity but that of master. In 1875, when British and American whaling fleets cruised from the Sea of Okhotsk to the Solander Grounds, pitting skill and courage against the largest living creature in its own element, Bullen (then 18) took a berth on the *Cachalot* and found himself three years at sea on a whaler, notoriously the

(Continued on next page)

worst ships afloat. *The Cruise of the 'Cachalot'* (written in 1898, long after Bullen had given up the sea) records with simplicity and honesty what he actually observed and felt. It is a unique account of life from the forecastle. He fully enlivens the historic whaling industry that brought the species to the brink of extinction and describes the mammal's habits and very human behavior, knowledge to which remarkably little has been added in the last 75 years.

Combining the art of fiction and the art of history, *The Bounty Trilogy* by Charles Nordhoff and James Hall is a superb achievement in historical romance, for it vividly recreates the people, events, and circumstances surrounding the mutiny aboard the English vessel HMS *Bounty* on its return voyage from the South Seas in 1789; the extraordinary maritime feat of Captain Bligh who, set adrift without adequate provisions or arms, sailed 3,600 uncharted sea miles in a 23-foot launch overladen with 18 loyal shipmates; and the dark fate of the mutineers who settled on the mysterious Pitcairn Island, an uncharted dot in the South Pacific. To the actual records of the British Admiralty, court proceedings, and Bligh's wind and weather log of his remarkable voyage, Nordhoff and Hall bring a simplicity, grace, and imagination that transforms the documents into heroic exploits on the high seas.

Holling C. Holling's book, *Seabird*, is an appealing example of historical fiction for children under 10. Seabird is a scrimshaw gull carved by Ezra Brown aboard a Yankee whaler in 1832. Passed down through four generations of Ezra's seafaring family, Seabird watches the harpooning of whales, encircles the globe in clipper ships until steam drives the sails from the sea, and witnesses the dawn of modern ships. The book is an unusual combination of story with technical details in marginal drawings and color illustrations that work well together (particularly the section on whaling) to present a simplified account of American shipping and a feeling for the courage and resourcefulness of seamen.

Two Masters

Jumping from the enjoyment of lightweight historical romance to an appreciation of the psychological conflicts and spiritual quests in the novels of Joseph Conrad and Herman Melville represents a plunge into deeper literary waters, which may or may not be appropriate for children. These are special voyages, however, that should not be overlooked. They are mystical adventures of a symbolic-literary order, and comprehension depends on judicious

timing in introducing them to young readers who are not otherwise likely to tackle them. A discriminate choice is important: Melville's *Moby Dick* and the shorter novels of Conrad, in particular *The Nigger of the Narcissus* and *Typhoon*, are dramatic eye-openers. Both Conrad and Melville went to sea in their youth, later recreating their observations in formidable bodies of literary work. The power and originality of these authors lie in their mastery of language and their ability to describe with unrelenting precision experiences enlarged through the prism of imagination. As novelists they transformed people and events from their seafaring days into meticulously structured narratives animating their moral and philosophical views, which were colored by life as seamen.

Folklore of the Sea

As a child, Armstrong Sperry thrilled to the stories of his seafaring great-grandfather, who had been shipwrecked on the island of Bora Bora in Polynesia. Later in his own travels and working as an ethnologist, Sperry became acquainted with the least-known islands of the South Pacific, learning the culture, language, and music that provides the background for his books. *Call it Courage* is the legend of Mafatu, the boy who went out alone to face the sea, the thing he feared the most, even though he was a son of the great chief of a Polynesian race that worshipped courage and lived off the sea. Mafatu resolves to ride his outrigger canoe on the ocean currents, the paths of the sea that carried the ancient Polynesian navigators from island to island. Sperry relates with unusual skill the story of how Mafatu conquers his fear, meeting the challenges of a violent sea storm and survival on "Motu Tabu," a forbidden island of eaters of men, growing strong and fearless in spirit as days filled with resourcefulness beyond his wildest expectations prove his "Stout Heart." Imagery in the oral tradition and striking line drawings imaginatively enhance the south sea adventure, bringing a rare strength and simplicity to this hero-legend.

Daring sea adventure in a distant timeless world describes C.S. Lewis's *The Voyage of the Dawn Treader*, a series of exploits in the reign of Caspian the Seafarer. Part of the *Chronicles of Narnia* series, this volume can be read independently of the six others. Two North Sea legends: *The Tower by the Sea* by Meindert DeJong is a moving tale in which a wise old woman and her cat save the town from tragedy during a violent storm-tossed night and escape the vengeance of superstitious villagers; and *The Selchie's Seed* by Shulamith Oppenheim is a graceful Scottish legend of sealfolk who, by shedding their skin, assume human form on land. *Scarlet Sails* by Alexander Green is a compelling tale infused with the mysticism of the sea, about a despised and taunted child for whom a prophecy of love from the sea comes true in a vision of a ship rigged in scarlet satin sails.

Imagination Afloat

In Greek mythology, Triton, son of Poseidon and Amphitrite, was a merman who blew a trumpet shell to raise or calm the seas. Subsequently, *triton* became a generic name for half-man, half-fish deities possessing the legendary power of their ancient namesake.

73

(Continued on next page)

(Continued from preceding page)

Lucy Boston captures the enchanting power of this myth in *The Sea Egg*, the dramatic story set on the craggy, sea-ravaged cliffs of the Cornish coast where Toby and Joe are vacationing. In a rare blend of realism and opalescent fancy, she has created a story, remarkable for its alluring atmosphere, in which a mischievous and elusive sprite hatches from an egg-shaped stone in the boys' own special rockpool, and turns their summer into a time of magic. With such a companion inhabiting their secret place (which could only be reached through a natural tunnel in the headland, and only at low tide), the ocean roar ceases to be an awesome force, and, like sea creatures themselves, the boys learn to swim effortlessly and confidently. Throughout, a narrative style of dazzling, polished prose sustains the story's charm and builds rhythm and suspense to a spectacular climax in which Toby and Joe follow the irresistible triton's urgent call to become initiates in a lunar water ritual that seals their bond of faith in the "seaboy" forever.

Arthur Ransome opens the door to a make-believe world of very real adventure in *Swallows and Amazons*, the first of his many extraordinarily well written novels for children. Casting off in *Swallow*, a 14-foot sailing dinghy out of Port Holly Howe, Captain John, Mate Susan, Able Seaman Titty, and Ship's boy Roger set sail for the mysterious Wild Cat Island (somewhere in the English lake district) on an exploration and camping expedition. In a lively story they form an alliance with Peggy and Nancy, owners of the ship *Amazon*, and wage a campaign against the local pirate, Captain Flint in Houseboat Bay, at the same time two thieves make off with his sea chest. The intricate plot builds in dramatic tension until the final moment of reckoning in which the "swallows" and "amazons" recover the stolen treasure on Cormorant Island and weather a violent storm that ends their vacation adventure. Ransome narrates the fantasy nostalgically but creates a real situation with scrupulous technical descriptions, detailing the skills of sailing and techniques of survival. He writes with a child's world view—a world of delight and innocence unhampered by adults except those who extend the adventure by becoming an imaginative part of it. (For a complete list of books by Arthur Ransome, see *Mariner's Catalog*, Vol. 4, p. 91.)

Nautical Picture Books

While the modern picture book can trace its roots to nineteenth-century English book illustration, few among the vast numbers published today can lay claim to the high excellence achieved by the early artists. A notable exception is the work of Edward Ardizzone, whose famous series of books about Tim and his adventures at sea perpetuates the tradition of illustrated children's books that balance fantasy and imagination with pictorial art and a good story. The chronicles of the intrepid, seagoing Tim (*Little Tim and the Brave Sea Captain, Tim All Alone, Tim to the Lighthouse, Tim in Danger, Tim to the Rescue, Tim and Lucy Go to Sea*) are books of strong character combining high adventure, bold exploits, and original pictures of the salty seas and crews. The stories are realistic, yet true to a child's perspective and logic, and are further enriched by Ardizzone's insight into the wonderful, inconsequential details that only children perceive. Simply written with an ear for oral

presentation, each tale comes to life with brightly colored drawings that depict settings, suggest subtleties of mood and moment, animate the characters of Tim and his friends, and give force and presence to the sea.

Visual and verbal wit infuse the comic adventure of *Burt Dow, Deep-Water Man*, a book about a doughty old Maine coast fisherman who puts out to sea in his reliable (but leaky) multicolored dory, the *Tidely-Idely* in the company of his giggling pet gull. Burt's clever resourcefulness and Downeaster attitude are pivotal to this delightful fantasy in which he inadvertently catches a whale. Meanwhile, a gale blows up, and what with the *Tidely-Idely* taking water and the make-or-break engine about to quit, the old salt lights on temporary cover: with an obliging gulp, Burt, boat, and giggling gull land in the dark, damp cavernous tummy of the whale. Burt's ingenuity gets the venture underway again, only to have the lot land smack in the middle of a rainbow-colored school of whales. This tall tale is made more spectacular by the magic colors of Robert McCloskey's painted world—dazzling shades of yellow, pink, green, blue, and magenta spread across poster-style paintings. Its a whale of a book and a hilarious voyage into deep-water art that is singularly satisfying.

Hardie Gramatky's rollicking picture story of a small tugboat, one of a distinguished family of tugs that oversee the bustle of harbor traffic, has endeared the saucy *Little Toot* stories to several generations of young ones. Bold pictures of vigorous activity painted in a sketchy cartoon style match *Little Toot*'s bravado and capture a genuine sense of the waterfront in these daft tales of the infamous tugboat.

There is a plethora of picture books about various aspects of the sea, and about the same number are little more than vehicles for hack commercial artists. Books combining appealing characters in original stories with skillful illustrations particularly worth noting follow. *Sam, Bangs and Moonshine* by Evaline Ness concerns the importance of differentiating reality from moonshine and how confusion leads Samantha unwittingly to put the life of a friend at the mercy of a rising tide. Drawings give the story an abstract ambiance, aptly mirroring the idea of moonshine, which can mean dreams, fantasy, or lies (when you come to think about it). A Japanese myth of ancient Urashima, *Seashore Story* by Taro Yashima, is about a boy who leaves his village on the back of a turtle to seek a timeless, enchanted place beneath the sea, and returns to find the passage of time has taken his people and left him a silver-haired elder. Charles Carryl's old English nonsense verse *A Capital Ship or the Walloping Window-Blind* is put to very funny drawings by Paul Galdone and merits the laughter it is bound to create.

Oceanography

Mapping the ocean floor with echo-sounders is a vital part of the technology that has made oceanography a science of the earth's future as well as of its origins and process of continual change. Maps of the concealed two-thirds of the earth's surface have opened up a new dimension for understanding the planet, visualizing a grand topography of mountain ranges, continental shelves, and the abysmal bottom,

(Continued on next page)

and revealing geologic formation in the deep ocean floor created in vast tectonic plates that grow outward from mid-ocean ridges. Investigations into the nature of the oceanic life that begins with photosynthetic organisms and the wealth of physical and food resources that are keys to survival have transformed an empty ocean wilderness into something we now perceive as a great eco-system.

Teaching children to understand these complicated ideas of science and technology becomes possible with books that translate oceanic information accurately and imaginatively. Two standards in the field are Rachel Carson's *The Sea Around Us* and *The Sea for Sam* by W. Maxwell Reed and Wilfrid Bronson. Originally published in 1935, the revised edition of the latter (already somewhat dated) discusses the origin and physical nature of the ocean and its biology. In a clear and comfortable tone directed at the junior to senior high school level, *The Sea for Sam* describes theories of how the oceans came into being, their depth, currents, the action of waves and tides and what causes them, vast rivers in the ocean, and the composition of sea water. It includes detailed chapters (by Bronson) on the sea plants and animals. Covering about the same material, a special edition of *The Sea Around Us*, adapted for young readers (ages 8-13), features dramatic color photographs of the sea, sky, wildlife, and naturalistic paintings of the primordial formation of the oceans. The text of this vivid one-volume encyclopedia of ocean science is a smooth adaptation of Carson's expert prose and, additionally, includes historical detail absent from other books. The "Mr. Science" approach of *The Challenge of the Sea* by Arthur Clarke makes interesting and informative reading about the underwater frontier and its effect on our future. Clarke details the practical and scientific aspects of the sea while also conveying something of its mystery and the futuristic drama it represents; it is filled with good charts, diagrams, line drawings, and halftones. Three books by Ruth Brindze are fascinating narratives that interweave an historical account with fictional story and precise explanations of physical concepts to define important aspects of oceanography. The books are illustrated simply and gracefully, matching the author's remarkable ability to condense complicated information.

Vessels for Underwater Exploration by Peter Limburg and James Sweeney is a history of the technology that has made possible modern underwater exploration from the early sponge and pearl divers with a net bag, knife, and lungful of air (3000 BC) to the crews on modern research submersibles. The authors trace the story of how scientists have grappled with the problems of pressure, cold, and the unpredictable behavior of the ocean depths to evolve complex technical systems as sophisticated as those used to explore outer space. Over 100 pictures detail the accomplishments (and failures) of daring inventors, private corporations, and government research teams in designing and constructing equipment—boats and bells, submarines, diving gear, sonar, snorkels and aqualungs, research submersibles and habitats—tools to open the ocean's secrets. It includes tables of submersibles and habitats, a glossary, an extensive bibliography, and an index.

For preschool and the early grades, there are some delightful picture books that show a surprisingly imaginative conciseness. Exquisite jewel-like illustrations in pastel blues and browns by Arnold Lobel animate the life cycle story in *Seahorse* by Robert Morris. Dramatic photographs and drawings illustrate two oceanographic terms for each letter of the alphabet in Isaac Asimov's *ABC's of the Ocean*. It is a stimulating ocean primer with lucid, accurate definitions of the underwater world. *A Day and a Night in a Tide Pool* by Adrian May introduces the pool's residents in a simple narrative that shows how creatures interact to maintain a mini ecosystem. *Land Beneath the Sea* by Julian May contains technical descriptions of some difficult concepts of oceanography. The short, concise text parallels visual interpretations by Leonard Fisher printed in sea blues, introduces technology, and explores what the vast terrain of the ocean looks like, how it is formed, and what life exists in the varying depths of the sea.

Ships and Shipbuilding, Boats and Boating

A substantial history, *Ships Through History* by Ralph T. Ward, unravels the story of how sailing ships have influenced the commercial and territorial development of the western world from ancient times to the present. The book looks thoroughly at ship design and the men whose energy and creative power built, sailed, captained, and manned the vessels. Vibrant, skillful illustrations by Samuel F. Manning add visual depth to the text. A glossary and an extensive bibliography complete this well-conceived and well-executed book. Covering the same time span but in a pictorial format is the carefully designed *Oars, Sails and Steam* by Edwin Tunis, a book of elegant pen and ink drawings accompanied by a brief explanatory text and marginal notes defining seagoing terms. A chronological history of ships, it devotes roughly a page to the most important and interesting types of boats that have developed among the seafaring peoples of the world up to 1952. Dated only in this respect, the book is pleasing to look at and one of the more interesting ship histories reviewed.

Approaching from the perspective of American history, John O'Hara Cosgrave traces the design of vessels from the birch-bark canoe to the atomic submarine in *America Sails the Sea* and *Clipper Ships*. Numbered diagrams of all types of ships in various stages of construction and from multiple perspectives (rigging, stern, bow, forward, midship, and after sections), together with illustrated details of gear vital to a sailor and his ship, and drawings creating what it was like to reef the main topsail, for example, give a clear idea of how ships were built, why designs differ, and what purposes they serve. These are information-packed books with well-labeled diagrams, captioned illustrations, and lucid text.

End

75

SEA

CLOTH

Many readers will recall the admiration and sympathy they felt when first they read in Warwick Thompkin's *Fifty South to Fifty South* (W.W. Norton, 1938, o.p.) those passages that described the horrors of living with a weak mainsail that would blow out again and again off the lee shore that was South America. The crew hand-sewed miles of torn canvas. On the other hand, many people cannot and do not sew a stitch, which is not so much horrible as it is dumb. To be able to hand-sew is good. To have to sew a lot by hand is not good. For the stitch in time, we have listed needles, palms, and so on, before and, for the other nine stitches, here are three sewing machines.

Machines

The 132K is Singer's classic heavy-duty machine for general canvas and leather work; the 145A is the long-bed machine for serious sail making and repair, as well as for sewing winter covers, tarps, sleeping bags, jacket kits, and so on. They are sold through local Singer agents or from:

**The Singer Company
321 First Street
Elizabeth, N.J. 07207**

*Above: The Singer 145A.
Left and below: The Singer 132K.*

76

Description of Class

Medium speed, single needle, flat bed, drop feed machine for sitching canvas and leather products.

Features

Rotating Hook mechanism with replaceable Bearing Rings.
Extra large Bobbin Capacity.
Rigid Construction.
Thread Lubricator.
Gear Drive.
Link Take-Up.

General Specifications: Mechanical

Needle Bar Stroke: 2″ (50.8 mm)
Clearance under Presser Foot: ½″ (12.7 mm)

Hand-Sewing Machines

Hand-sewing machines on cruising boats have excited renewed interest since Chay Blyth's recent around-the-world exploits. During 1971-1974 we carried a straight-stitching three-fourths-size Singer hand-sewing machine with us on our Pacific voyage on *Prudence.* It was a great success for all sewing jobs except re-sewing the zigzag-stitched sails.

The machine used by Blyth is the Read "Sail-maker" model, weight packed, hand model 44.0 lbs. and electric model, weight packed 48.4 lbs. The measurements are 20"x8.5"x13.5" in a case. The hand model sells for $173.62 plus duty, plus air freight $85.95 or surface freight $34.29. The electric model sells for $195.97 plus duty, plus air freight $85.95 or surface freight $38.59. These are available from:

J.J. & J. Read Ltd.
327 Shirley Road
Southampton SO1 3HW
England

Singer three-fourths-size hand-sewing models are available from:

Seidel's Sewing Machine Shop
1411 Dorchester Ave.
Dorchester, Massachusetts 02122

at about $49.50 each. (They are also available from local Singer dealers or The Singer Company, address on page 76—Eds.)

However, even better than this, I found Mr. Seidel can supply hand conversion parts (hand crank unit, wheel, clutch washer, etc.) to fit almost all standard makes of electric sewing machines. For less than $25.00, I was able to convert our portable electric Pfaff model 139 zigzag machine to hand sewing in about two hours' time. It performs perfectly.

—Russell G. Williamson

Kits

Sailrite Kits, discussed way back in the first *Catalog,* has added two manuals to its Amateur Sailmaker's Library—*Sail Repair Manual* ($1.50) and *The Amateur Sailmaker's Catalogue* ($1.00), the latter a listing of kits, books, tools, and generally the works for the sailor with an itchy palm. (Their other publications are described in the *Mariner's Catalog, Volume 1,* p. 157.)

Sailrite Kits
2010 Lincoln Blvd.
Venice, California 90291
(Note new address)

TECHNICAL DETAILS
Electric Model 1000 sts per min
SIZE:- 20" × 8½" × 13½" IN CASE

Link take-up.

Neutral two-tone grey.

Built-in anti-glare needle light.

Forward and reverse sewing.

Dial stitch length regulator.

Automatic bobbin winder.

Scaled tension adjustment.

Drop feed for darning.

Imprinted seam guide.

Hinged presser foot and thread cutter.

Complete with two-tone base and cover with accessories compartment in solid mahogany type wood.

This machine is made of cast iron with mild steel working parts cadmium or chrome plated for rust resistance.

Above: Data from a J.J. & J. Read flyer concerning the Sailmaker model.

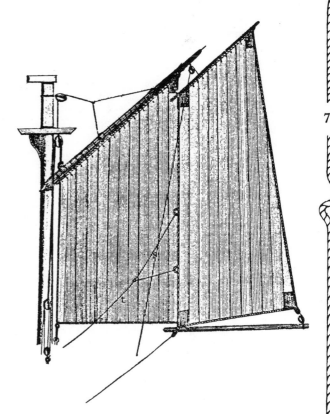

77

An Excellent Traditional Sailmaker

E.W. Smith is the owner of a family loft and the maker of many cotton and occasionally flax sails. He makes sails for everything from sprit- to square-rigs, and he's made the sails for most of my designs. Some modern, young sailmakers can't do it; classic boats stump them.

E.W. Smith, Sailmaker
Union Wharf
Fairhaven, Mass.

—Pete Culler

Altering a Mainsail from Slides to Grooves

A frequent modification is to alter a mainsail from slides to grooves. This entails rather more than might at first appear: the luff rope must be removed from around the top of the headboard and left with the bare end cut off at the top, so that it can be fed into the groove. In addition, the headboard will have to be reduced in size, so that there is a narrow space between the board and the luff rope; this is to allow room for the jaws of the groove. It is neither practical nor strong enough to add a small extra strip at this point (fig. 41).

Similar treatment will have to be given to the clew. It is a matter of luck whether there will be enough room between the existing clew eye and the rope, for the former to clear the upper edge of the boom groove (fig. 42).

The Care and Repair of Sails
by Jeremy Howard-Williams
W.W. Norton Co., N.Y.
139 pages, illus., index, 1976, $9.95

Surprisingly enough, the books on sail repair are few and far between. This one, written by an experienced Englishman, is as good as anything you will ever see and has the cruising sailor in mind. Just look at these chapter titles: sailcloth, care of sails in use, examination for repairs, typical repairs, alterations to size, sail repair equipment, hand work—and there is even more. Well worth the purchase price.

Some Prices on Cotton Duck

Dear Editors:

I contacted the Denison Cotton Mills [Box 1099, Denison, Texas 75020] and received samples and quotes on their single filling cotton duck. They have 8, 10, 12, and 15 oz. duck in grades "A" and "B", 36″ and 48″ wide by 100-yd. rolls. "A" grade is slightly lighter in color at an 8% cost increase. I received samples on 12 and 15 oz. material, 12 oz. "B" 36″ was $1.21/yd. and 15-oz. "B" 36″ $1.48/yd. in 100-yd. rolls. Price per pound is slightly less in wider/heavier ducks.

James M. Rudholm
Kingsburg, California

. . . and then Bart Hauthaway pointed out to us that permanent-press bedsheets, composed of half synthetic and half cotton threads make perfect sailcloth material for canoes and other small craft at a very modest cost. One of those Eureka! ideas, isn't it?

Quote at left and illustration below from The Care and Repair of Sails.

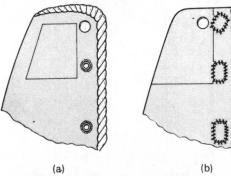

(a)   (b)

41. Altering a Headboard from Slides to Grooves. *When a sail is fitted with slides as in (a), the luff rope is usually carried round the top of the headboard, which must be made narrower so that there will be room for the sail to go inside the groove. The rope must be stopped at the top, and the eyelets taken out and patched.*

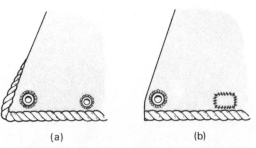

(a)   (b)

42. Altering a Clew from Slides to Grooves. *The foot rope has to be stopped off at the leech, so that it can feed into the groove. Patch the slide holes and pray that there will be enough room for the groove between the eye and the rope, so that you will not have to take out the clew eye, patch the hole and then work another eye about an inch higher in the sail.*

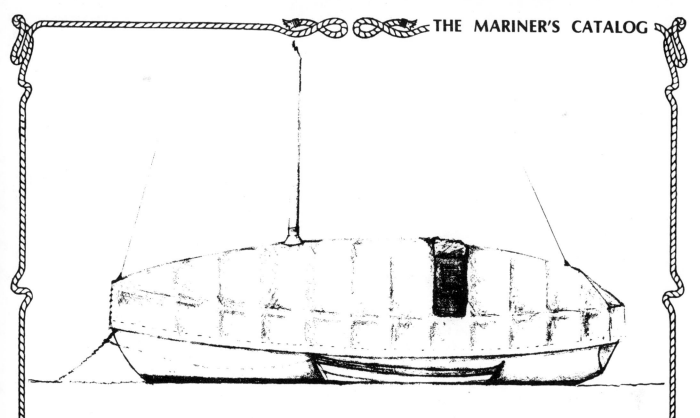

A WINTER COVER

by Maynard Bray

For the past 20-odd years, I have been thrashing around with winter covers for boats stored outdoors. They have been made of tarpaper, plastic, canvas, and various other materials, most of which had one thing in common: low cost.

Most all of these winter covering schemes had some disadvantage, and I think that boats stored inside sheds come out better in the spring, generally speaking. So if you can arrange it, by all means get your boat inside before the dew begins to freeze and Jack Frost starts lifting the paint and varnish that you worked so hard on last spring. This is good, but expensive, advice. Because of the high cost of inside storage, most owners end up with their boats outside and have to dream up some kind of cover, usually to be put up in a northwest gale and a −10° F. chill factor.

Either tarpaper or plastic, properly vented and carefully put together, will make an adequate cover. But care is hard to exercise in those cold fall days, and besides, both of these materials are pretty well worn out after a season, making their purchase and disposal an annual event. A reusable, fitted canvas cover, in spite of its higher first cost, is easier to put on, better once in place, and probably costs no more in the long run. I think it is the next best thing to a storage shed.

The cover I will try to describe has worked out well over the last few years on several boats, both afloat and ashore. It is basically the old standby of fitted canvas over a wood framework, but there is a good reason for the shape and proportion of its parts, which I will explain.

The frames are put together solidly, with the idea of staying that way (i.e., they do not come apart for

(Continued on next page)

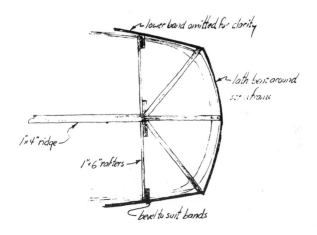

PLAN

PROFILE

79

(Continued from preceding page)

storage), and are made high enough so the snow will slide off and you will have enough room to get around on deck underneath them. If the peak pieces are of 2"x6" or 2"x8" and the rafters are bolted to them, there is no need for collar ties, so you can work under this frame quite easily. The vertical sides are also a way of getting more room, and for a boat with lifelines they are a must anyhow. The side pieces are from the same 2" stock as the peak, although I've found that nails can be used here to attach the rafters, rather than bolts. The width of these side pieces not only gives them a good connection to the rafters but also allows their lower ends to be shaped as shown in the sketch. A length of 1" x 3" furring nailed on the outboard edge of each side piece completes the frame by acting as a support for the fore-and-aft bands.

In laying out the frames, you first decide what height you want for the sides and what pitch you want for the rafters and hold these factors constant for all the frames. The boat's beam at each frame station will give you the rest of the layout, and the result should be a nice, fair curve of the ridge as it runs from bow to stern. I have found that 30 inches is a good spacing for the frames, but you may want to modify this to accommodate the deck layout of the boat or the length of the fore-and-aft bands.

There are five fore-and-aft bands, and they tie the whole thing together. All have to be put up and taken down annually, so it is important not to overfasten them. One 5d box nail will usually do for each connection of the ridge and the upper bands, while galvanized bolts work well for the lower bands. You will probably have one or two butts in all of these bands, and I have found that it is perfectly okay to center the butts in the three upper bands on the peak and side pieces if they are lightly nailed and you are careful about removing them in the spring. Locate the butts in the lower bands halfway between the frames and use a butt block to connect the pieces.

The forward and aft endings for the cover frame will depend on the particular boat, but for a boat without bow and stern pulpits, a 4" x 4" upright in the bow, beveled to take the bands, and three half-frames at the stern will do quite well. The rafters for the half-frames should be put on the flat, however, so they can be nailed to the aftermost peak piece.

As for materials, stay away from western fir and redwood, as they splinter and split too easily. Use spruce for the 2 by's and pine for the rafters and bands if you can. Although I haven't always done it, I think it is a good idea to tie the frame down to the hull in a few places so it can't blow away.

Once the frame is up, you can measure for the cover. Your sailmaker will tell you what he wants for measurements, or he might prefer to do it himself. Be sure to have him put reinforcing patches in way of all frame members, because there is a surprising amount of chafe at these points. Tell him also where you want the access door and where the docklines lead, if she is to be afloat. I see no need to put vents in unless the material is tarred and can't breathe. I've had these covers on through the summer and with the built-in opening around the rail, have never found it unusually hot under them.

In the Mystic (Connecticut) area, I have always had Roy Burdick make my covers. He is the sailmaker for Bailey and Staub (New London) and is a whiz at making them. I'd recommend him without reservation.

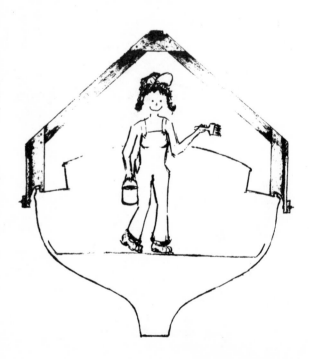

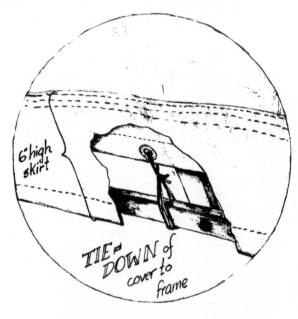

6" high skirt

TIE-DOWN of cover to frame

The formula is this—purchase a rather cheap grade of derby, hang it in the forecastle when the ship is being fumigated for bedbugs; if it comes out too green, don't hang it so close to the sulphur candles next time.

—L. Francis Herreshoff
on making your hat look salty.

Coat of Many Pockets

Marine scientists, photographers, beachcombers, and their friends, look at this coat! Some years ago a company in Massachusetts was happily making coats for people who work in big walk-in freezer lockers, a coat with good fill for warmth, yet enormous capacity and versatility for taking this and that cut for orders. A photographer from the Boston *Globe* discovered the coat one day, and the *rush* was on. Today, many photographers and TV cameramen in the Boston area sport one, and for good reason. No better coat for the equipment-laden has ever been offered. Look first at the outside pockets. All four are the same size, big, their genius being that the uppers can be totally explored by the hand on the same side. Both arms have sleeve "meter" pockets; I carry a meter in one and a Swiss Army knife in the other. Inside the coat are four more pockets, the uppers a large eight inches square and partially tucked into the lowers, which are great, yawning, cavernous sixteen-inches-square monsters. They will swallow telephoto Nikons like anchovies, whole press cameras (open!), and even tripods. Walk into a store wearing one slightly open and the house detectives will press in around you, their faces ashen with suspicion, foreboding, and greed. The coats have a warm collarhood, are well-filled, and long—the ultimate beachcomber's *America*'s Cupper's gadget-freaker's jacket. $44 per, navy or black. Send chest, height, waist, and sleeve measurements to:

**Outlast Uniform Company
6 Hancock St.
Chelsea, Mass. 02150**

Eine Wetterschutz und Rettungsjacke, Maat

Another superior jacket is the KD-matic 700 made in Germany. Very fancy, very expensive, this jacket has well-placed zippered handpockets, flapped sleeve pockets, a built-in life belt, and built-in heavily reinforced lifting eyes. It's made of bright polyurethanecoated cotton, "breathing material" so-called; a very, very, good heavy-weather jacket. It's the top of the line for this company, which makes other jackets and flotation collars as well.

**KD-matic
2000 Hamburg 50
Buttstrasse 4
West Germany**

81

Left, top: Outlast Uniform's freezer-locker coat.
Left, bottom: The KD-matic 700.

Sail Books

In rounding up publishers of nautical books in the 3rd volume of the *Mariner's Catalog* (p. 113), we inadvertently left out Sail Books, which is the book-publishing arm of *Sail* magazine. As you would expect, they specialize in books about sailing, primarily in the modern, high-performance category. Titles include *The Best of Sail Trim* ($7.95); *This is Sailing* ($12.55); *This is Basic Sailboat Cruising* ($12.55); *The Ditty Bag Book* ($7.95); *A Cruising Guide to the Lesser Antilles* ($18.50); and *The Care and Repair of Sails* ($9.95).

Sail Books
Editorial Office
38 Commercial Wharf
Boston, Mass.

Sail Books
Order Department
126 Blaine Avenue
Marion, Ohio 43302

Below: A sweet young miss ready to do battle with a ferocious trout in her Insulata Body Heater.

Flags

Yachtsmen who intend to go foreign or charter abroad will want to display a courtesy flag. A U.S. importer of standard-size (30 x 45 cm) courtesy flags at $8 to $10 each is:

ERKEI International Studios
P.O. Box 2174
Union Center Station
Union, N.J. 07883

Fashionless Warmth

Halfway between a sweatsuit and a wetsuit are the Body Heaters, manufactured by:

Insulatawear Ltd
127 Old Street
Clevedon, Avon BS21 6BW
England

Clothing Kits

Country Ways offers outdoor clothing and equipment kits of several sorts, most of them using Polar-Guard, a polyester fill that is rapidly replacing down in most applications, certainly all those where the article will be used in wet or damp environments. Kits for jackets, vests, sleeping bags, and blankets are offered, the latter making good boat sense for their ability to maintain loft even when wet.

**Country Ways, Inc.
3500 Highway 101 South
Minnetonka, Minn. 55343**

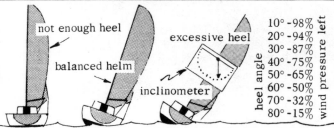

Many sailboats are designed to have a neutral balanced helm between 7° to 15°. In lighter wind with less heel sailing upwind, boat becomes cranky producing downwind helm. When heel increases beyond ideal angle, underwater shape of hull, pg. 132, wants to force it to go up into irons if compensation isn't made. drag — rudder

With too much heel comes a little tiller pressure.... which exerts tremendous rudder pressure, the only way the boat out of balance can fight back. Rudder beyond 5° produces tremendous drag due to water density being over 800 TIMES that of air. This drag reduces boat speed and pointing ability, as well as producing very strong & unnecessary pressure on rudder and its fittings.

When forces are in balance you can trim sails and hull so the boat sails itself. Crew of 60' 10 meter 'Branta' prefer tiller to wheel. They watch tiller continually trimming sails for neutral helm. If rudder were lost 'Branta' could sail triangular course relying on sail choice and hull trim. Turns would naturally be wider around buoys without rudder to provide rapid change of course.

Sailing Primers

A number of readers have written us asking why we haven't recommended sailing primers. We've always answered that we have no special bias against them, it's just that we assumed that anyone who would buy the *Mariner's Catalog* would have already learned how to sail. Apparently not, and we're sorry we haven't paid attention sooner.

So, our favorite how-to-sail pocket manual:

Royce's Sailing Illustrated
**by Patrick M. Royce
Royce Publications
Box 1967, Newport Beach, Calif. 92663
300 pages, illus., glossary, paperbound, 1974
(6th ed.), $5.50**

Windsurfing, by Uwe Mares and Reinhart Winkler
**David McKay Co., New York
92 pages, illus., index, paperbound, 1976, $5.95**

We don't even pretend to give a fig about windsurfing (even if we did, the incredibly cold waters of Penobscot Bay are hardly the place to engage in the sport), but our mission to report on the sources of unique data impels at least a mention of this only-book-of-its-kind. Consider it done.

Left: From Royce's Sailing Illustrated.
Below: From Windsurfing.

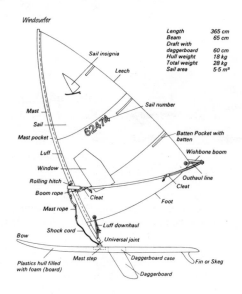

83

Royce understands beginners. He knows what they are up against and makes every effort—without an ounce of patronization—to make things clear, simple, and concise. The book *is* a little busy, with sketches, diagrams, and tables all over the place, but once you get used to the layout, you're home free.

Another good beginner's book is:

Hand, Reef and Steer, by Richard Henderson
**Henry Regnery Co., Chicago
95 pages, illus., index, 1965, $7.95**

Not as upbeat as Royce but still head and shoulders above the rest of the competition.

Here's to You, Bill Adams

It goes without saying that the measure of a great sea story writer is the ability to bring home to the reader the realities and truths about life at sea. The writers who have been given the appellation "great" have, for the most part, deserved it—the test of time sees to it. But for some reason, there are many writers who have done their damnedest, who have written what can only be considered great works, yet have failed to achieve the recognition that is rightly theirs. Why this is so is an unfathomable mystery. After all, don't we all know that cream rises to the top?

Until a short time ago, I never heard of Bill Adams. I just finished going through a number of respected bibliographies of sea literature and found him hardly mentioned. I have asked around among acquaintances who have made it a fetish to read as many sea stories as they possibly can find and discovered nary a one who knew anything about him. Yet I have just put down a book by Bill Adams that, in my opinion, has to be the peak of a genre—the life of a deepwater, Cape Horn sailor.

Bill Adams' story is a familiar one: the young boy who grows up next to the sea, thinking only about running away to a deepwater sailing ship, signing on to find the work backbreaking and the living conditions abominable, repelled by the maggots in the biscuits and the slime in the drinking water, yet finding the joys and strengths gained from being a sailorman far superior to anything to be found on land. Then whatever makes his story different from the others?—the same thing that makes *Tom Sawyer* different from all the other thousands of tales about boyhood. It's all in the telling.

Bill Adams tells his story in a way that makes you think twice about those tired clichés about fighting the raging sea, wallowing in the Horse Latitudes, and suffering under the tyranny of a surly first mate. He makes you think about the terrible conditions aboard merchant squareriggers, makes you feel guilty about ever imagining that to drive around Cape Horn in a towering iron bark would be somehow romantic, but makes you understand why he, and many others like him—given the reality of the situation—*volunteered* to do it. His tale, which is essentially his autobiography, is so well written that you are swept up into his life, rising when he rose, falling when he fell. There is a rhythm to *Ships and Women* that is easily recognized in truly great literature, a rhythm that carries the narrative and brings the reader along naturally. You never feel rushed to reach the end of the story, yet you know full well that there is something unique and something shattering to be discovered when you turn the last page.

Richard Henry Dana, Felix Riesenberg, David Bone, Frank Bullen, Alan Villiers, Rex Clemens—they're all great writers of the sea. They can't hold a candle to Bill Adams.

—PHS

Ships and Women takes up the major part of *Ships and Memories*, an anthology of Adams' writings recently published in England. The price of the volume is steep by anyone's standards, but the book is immaculately produced and edited and contains 153 striking ship photographs and a number of well-done pen-and-ink sketches.

***Ships and Memories* by Bill Adams
Teredo Books Ltd.
Brighton, Sussex, England
449 pages, illus., 1975, £14.80**

ENGINES

Crank It

Ladies and gentlemen, the handpowered outboard, from:

Finn Machine Products Co.
P.O. Box 396
Lithia Springs, Georgia 30057

wholesale from the factory, $59.95
retail is in the $75.00 range

85

Seagull-type outboard fans may find some thought in the Whitehead 6 or 12 outboard motors. They are made in Italy by a large armaments firm founded by an Italian and an Englishman named Whitehead who, by the way, was the guy who invented the torpedo. The name of the firm has eluded us, but its English distributor is Navigair. These machines offer a choice of three shaft lengths—16, 21, and 27 inches—two reduction ratios—3.5:1 and 2:1—and their complementary propellers. The prices vary with options. The "6" is in the £300-£400 range; the "12" around £525, plus shipping.

Navigair Ltd.
St. Andrews Buildings
High Street, Hamble
Southampton SO3 5JE
England

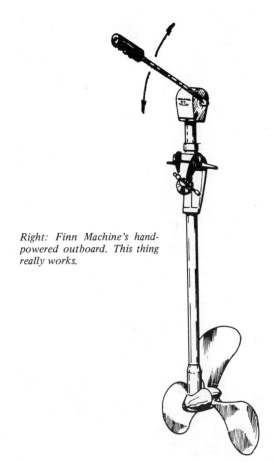

Right: Finn Machine's hand-powered outboard. This thing really works.

Kero Outboard

The mention of a Japanese (Yamaha) outboard motor that burns kerosene caught our attention in a Dutch trade journal. We searched around and discovered that Yamaha outboards in this country are both manufactured and distributed by the Brunswick Corporation and sold under the name Mariner outboards. Here's what they told us about the kero outboard: "You expressed interest in the Yamaha Enduro 15AK, which burns both gasoline and kerosene. We do not offer this model in the U.S. at this time. It was our opinion that there wasn't sufficient demand to warrant importing the engine."

Whataya going to do? To be sure, kero has some objectionable features, a bit greasy and smelly, but it's not explosive and has other uses around a boat; it's a solvent, lamp oil, preservative, lubricant, etc. And it packs more nautical miles in it than gas both by volume and bucks. Dagnabit! If you feel like bugging Brunswick about the Enduro 15 AK, write:

**Mariner International Company
1939 Pioneer Road
Fond du Lac, Wisconsin 54935**

Foreign Power

Imp and Sprite by Brit, 5 and 10 hp, £450 to £550, depending on installation packages.

**Brit Engineering Co., Ltd.
Bridport
Dorset, England**

Above: The Brit Imp 5 hp 4-stroke gasoline engine. Left: The Watermota Sea Cub Mark II 7 hp diesel. It has a single cylinder with a four-stroke cycle.

Fascinated by any power package that includes adjustable, reversing wheels, we inquired of Watermota about their well-known Shrimp engines and were pleasantly surprised to discover that they also offer a diesel at the same power (7 hp) and an extensive line of both gas and diesel engines in larger sizes up to around 100 hp.

**Watermota Ltd.
Abbotskerswell
Newton Abbot
Devon TQ12 5NF, England**

The robust Solé 9-hp diesel is manufactured in Spain and distributed by Beacon at $1,425, FOB New York:

**Beacon Plastic and Metal Products, Inc.
50 Park Avenue
New York, N.Y. 10016**

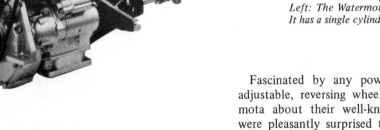

Left: The Sole 9 hp 4-stroke diesel.

Deutz manufactures great, hairy, monster diesels that drive the industrial world in many capacities. Way, way down at the bottom of their line are the FL411D single-cylinder and FL912-series two- to six-cylinder diesels that are *air-cooled*. We also couldn't take our eyes off their 6,400-hp 16-cylinder RBV16M, because there is something kind of beautiful about it.

Deutz Diesel Corp.
90 Alpha Plaza
Box 546
Hicksville, N.Y. 11802

Single and two-cylinder in-line engines.
Series FL 411 D and FL 912 engines are locally equipped for marine duty. Their indifference to spray and splash water, their easy starting also under adverse conditions and ability to run regardless of whether or not the hull is in the water make these engines especially suited for powering open fishing boats and workboats.
Ocean-going vessels utilize these engines not only for life boats, but also for emergency generating sets and for harbour sets.

Top: The incredible 16-cylinder Deutz 6400 hp diesel, just what you need for fooling around in the bay.
Quote above and photo left: The Deutz Fl 411 single-cylinder diesel.

Folding Prop

Martec has developed an elliptical folding propeller with its greatest area on the inside, away from the power-robbing disturbances at the blade tip. To give you an idea of cost, a 16-inch wheel with a pitch of between 6 and 14 inches for a one-inch shaft lists at $328.

Martec Engineering Corp.
2257 Gaylord St.
Long Beach, Calif. 90813

Martec Engineering, originators of the modern streamlined folding propeller, present the Mark III.

New ELIPTEC (pat. pend.) blade makes improvements in power performance due to this revolutionary break through in engineering design. Martec now offers bigger, stronger props with less drag.

The Mark III with its smaller cross section and increased effective prop disc is more efficient than any previous folding prop.

The Mark III exclusive ELIPTEC (pat. pend.) shape puts blade area where it is needed for greater efficiency and power.

Reverse the Mark III and all the old myths about folding props are exploded The ELIPTEC (pat. pend.) design provides fixed blade reverse.

Cut drag! Martec's **new** Mark III is the world's most advanced folding prop.

Above: Quote from a Martec brochure.

87

"It's just forethought, me lad—let 'em drop the H-bomb, they won't catch me in a gas shortage again!"

The Cone Propeller

People with large-displacement craft in very shallow waters will generally be disappointed with the performance of jet-drive units. They work well on light, planing hulls because, like all jets, they feed on their own velocity; the faster the faster, as it were. Displacement hulls just can't get out of their own way enough to make the jet units go.

It was for displacement hulls in thin soup that Donald V. Hotchkiss developed the Cone Propeller, designed to suck a really large volume of water from the stream along the bilges and to slough it aft and out a tunnel in either the run or the stern. Many configurations are possible, apparently, and interested persons should write:

**Donald V. Hotchkiss
4 Tolstoi Rd.
Parkstone, Poole
Dorset BH14 OQJ, England**

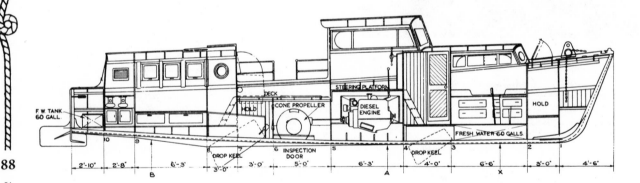

Steam Power

We mentioned the Semple Engine Company as makers of fine steam engines and boilers in the *Mariner's Catalog, Volume 2*. Semple has a new address now, so while listing that, we thought we would show you a little something from their new catalog. They sell complete engines, complete boilers, complete power units (engine, boiler pumps, accessories, etc.), and engine kits, which consist of castings and detailed drawings.

**Semple Engine Company
Box 6805
St. Louis, Missouri 63144**

Above: a 47' launch with a Hotchkiss Cone Propeller installed.
Left: The Semple 34-DW 5 hp standard steam engine. This is a double-acting unit with hand wheel reverse and a feed water injector.

A Horsepower is a Horsepower . . .

Dear Editors:

Regarding a few letters in the *Mariner's Catalog, Volume 2*: A horsepower is a horsepower—technically the ability to lift 550 pounds the distance of one foot in one second. Yes, some manufacturers may rate their engines at a continuous output and others may advertise a "short-term" horsepower rating, and some may or may not include the typical loads of water-pumps, alternators, etc. Usually, one can figure this out by reading their *complete* literature. Despite these variables, though, I would like to straighten out some of your readers on other points:

1. You can't get something for nothing.

2. On a modern, reasonably efficient engine, you get about 12 hp per gallon per hour of gasoline (4-cycle engine) and a *maximum* of 21 hp per gallon per hour of diesel fuel.

3. If anyone can better those figures in a reliable design, they could retire early.

If your Stoutfella diesel is burning two gph, you are producing about 40 hp, plus or minus a couple for state-of-tune. If your Gulpalot V-8 gas engine is using 8 gph, it is delivering about 96 hp. The one exception to this rule is small diesels (5 to 15 hp)—they only develop about 15 to 17 hp per gph, and 2-cycle outboards only about 8 hp per gph. If anyone can better these figures, please send me your plans: but you better have Patent Pending!

One thing further that may be of interest. One horsepower typically develops about 450 watts, but automotive alternators are notoriously inefficient, consuming about one horsepower for 250 watts output (approximately 17 amps at 14v). And an automotive air-conditioning compressor, such as used in marine holding-plate systems, consumes about 6 to 8 hp during clutch-engaged periods.

Stephen Crow
Fort Lauderdale, Florida

A Horsepower is More than a Horsepower?

Dear Mr. Putz:

I've just been leafing through the first *Mariner's Catalog* and noticed your squib on Seagull outboards on page 142—specifically, the statement that the 5½-h.p. Seagull is equivalent to nearly 20 domestic h.p. It sort of brought me up short. How can this be? The *Boat Owners Buyers Guide* gives the specs for this motor as 5½ h.p. at 4,500 r.p.m., based on a bore of 2.24″, a stroke of 1.57″, and a displacement of 6.1 cu. in. These data compare closely with those of domestic outboards of comparable power, so I have to wonder what Seagull advertising means by the word "equivalent." Certainly, if you arranged a tug-of-war between a Seagull 5½ and, say, an OMC 18, it would be strictly no contest. The OMC 18 would develop much greater thrust, notwithstanding its smaller, quicker propeller.

David L. Register
Damariscotta, Maine

Dear Mr. Register:

Seagulls can do more work, lots more work, than their domestic displacement brethren. They do not push anything faster, but certainly more surely, steadily, and consistently in more adverse conditions. A few years ago, I worked a season with a herring gang here, most of the time standing and taxiing in a really terrible 14-foot punt built of one-inch stuff soaked up and jungle-bottomed. Things were okay during the summer with a small Johnson, six or seven hp, but in the fall, the machine just wasn't up to it at all, not only unable to push the craft through the 2-foot chop of the East Side, but also unable to keep the craft on course. The Seagull 5½, a borrowed oily thing, didn't even cough; just put the boat where pointed and at the speed indexed. The balance of that season I tended to be a lot wetter, but the boys on the sardine carrier didn't get to laugh as much.

So how does one say it?

George Putz
Vinalhaven, Maine

Dear Mr. Putz:

Thrust is what pushes a boat, and thrust depends on how much water the propeller is pushing aft and how fast it's pushing it. The Seagull, with its large, slow-turning wheel, moves a lot of water, but moves it slowly. On the other hand, the Johnson, with its small, fast-turning wheel, moves a smaller volume of water at greater velocity. That the boat moves is an example of Newton's Law, and because the Seagull moves so much more water than the Johnson, the Seagull has the greater thrust.

Your first combination of the Johnson and the heavy, soaked-up punt with its grassy bottom was a real mismatch. That little propeller was doing its damnedest to throw a small volume of water at high velocity. Though its diameter was small, its pitch and blade area were so great that it was biting off more than it could chew. Overloaded by the weight of water it was attacking, it slowed the powerhead, which operated at less than full r.p.m. and hence less than full horsepower. There was just too much weight to move.

When you clamped on the Seagull, however, things began looking up. Its 4:1 reduction afforded much greater propeller torque but still managed to turn that big wheel at about 1,000 r.p.m. When you can turn a Seagull wheel at 1,000 r.p.m., you're going to move a hell of a lot of the Old Briny, and that's where you got your thrust. You didn't move fast, but you MOVED. Here the motor's greater thrust was equal to the load.

You could have used the Seagull on a 14′ aluminum skiff, and it would have chugged along with typical British restraint at maybe eight knots. The light load wouldn't have come close to absorbing the motor's thrust, but the slow-turning wheel and the drag of that club-like lower unit would have severely limited the speed. Replace the Seagull with the Johnson, however, and you're off. Here the little high-speed propeller would be easily equal to the light load.

David L. Register
Damariscotta, Maine

89

In 1883 Frank W. Ofeldt of Newark, New Jersey, had taken out a patent on a "naphtha engine." Because it offered a market for a by-product of petroleum distillation, the oil interests are said to have encouraged this experiment. As developed by the Gas Engine and Power Company of Morris Heights on the Harlem River (later Gas Engine & Power Company and Charles L. Seabury, Consolidated), Ofeldt's invention was essentially a three cylinder steam engine which vaporized naphtha instead of water. "My invention," he declared, "relates to the known processes for obtaining a motive power by working a liquefiable vapor expansively, then conveying it to a condenser for liquefaction, and thence returning it automatically . . . without loss of fluid, to a device for reconverting it into readiness for use again."[10] By diverting a small portion of the naphtha vapor into flame under the boiler, he completed the cycle without resorting to any external source of heat. That was the only consumption of the fluid; the rest continued in circulation through repeated vaporization and condensation. There was no external exhaust.

90

The World Water Speed Record
by Leo Villa and Kevin Desmond
Batsford Ltd., 4 Fitzhardinge St.
London, England
206 pages, illus., index, biblio., 1976, £4.75

The day after the first person put mechanical power in a boat, there were undoubtedly schemes to make that boat go faster. Those schemes haven't ended yet, fuel crises notwithstanding. That's perfectly all right with us . . . just as long as some speedboat out of control doesn't cut us in half when we're out in the bay fishing in a skiff.

For a history of man's attempt to make powered craft (sail and oar excepted) go faster, this book has much to commend it. We must confess that we never had an interest before in knowing who was the first to drive a prop-driven hydroplane at 200 mph, but after reading this book, we're not particularly sorry we found out.

The Naphtha Launch, by Kenneth Durant
Adirondack Museum
Blue Mountain Lake, N.Y. 12812
31 pages, illus., biblio., paperbound, 1976, $3

Steam and sail weren't the only small-boat power sources killed by the advent of gasoline engines at the turn of the century. The short-lived naphtha power-plant went by the boards as well. This short booklet tells about the development and demise of the naphtha launch, which was invented to avoid the disadvantages of steam launches and was marketed to replace the necessary oar power of Adirondack guide-boats. The text is short but informative (those who have read Durant's *Guideboat Days and Ways,* reviewed in MC-2, p. 41, will know what we mean), and the footnotes and bibliography will lead serious students of naphtha power in the right direction.

The Adirondack Museum, the publisher of this booklet, also has enlarged plans of the boats that appear in the back of their book *Rushton and His Times in American Canoeing* (see review in MC-1, p. 15). These plans measure 22½" x 17¾" and cover the following craft:

John Blanchard Guideboat, 13' x 27⅞", $2.00
Rushton Sailing Canoe, *Princess* Model, 14'3" x 32", $1.00
Rushton Guideboat, *Saranac Laker* 16' x 39", $1.00
Rushton Canoe *Cayu,* Canadian *Ugo* Model, 15' x 30", $1.00
Rushton Canoe *Sairy Gamp,* 9' x 26", $1.00
Rushton Sailing Craft *Wanderer,* 17' x 42", $1.00
Rushton Sailing Canoe *Nomad,* 16' x 32", $1.00
Rushton Canoe *Wee Lassie,* 10'5¾" x 27", $1.00

Left and top: Boxed quote and illustration from The Naptha Launch.
Below: Gar Wood's Miss America X, *with four Packard engines for a total of 6400 hp and 125 mph.*

Engine Repair Manuals

Unless you're that rare beast—the complete mechanic—you can't work on your engine without some type of manual, even if you only use it for ordering spare parts. The best one you can get is the factory manual written by the manufacturer specifically for your engine. These are sometimes difficult to come by, especially if your engine model is old or obsolete, but a letter to the manufacturer will provide information on availability and price.

Repair manuals for antique engines are an entirely different problem. You'll probably get no satisfaction from the original manufacturer, even if the company is still in business, and no publishing company today that we know of is reprinting antique engine manuals (if you do know of any, please tell us). Your best approach is to advertise your needs in the classified section of appropriate boating magazines, check used-book stores, especially those we have listed in the *Mariner's Catalog*, and spread the word. In some sections of the country, there is an antique engine buff under every other rock; they can provide help.

There are books available from some publishers that cover the principles of operation, repair, and maintenance of a number of marine engines of recent vintage. These books are not as complete as most factory repair manuals, though many draw on the latter for their data, and for experienced mechanics might be too rudimentary to be of much use. But if you want to do your own minor work, and understand the basics of the more major jobs, you will find these books most worthwhile. So here's an annotated listing of those we were able to find:

Clymer Publications
222 N. Virgil Ave.
Los Angeles, Calif. 90004

British Seagull Service-Repair Handbook. Covers 40 Featherweight, 40 Plus, Century 100, Century 100 Plus, Century, Century Plus, Silver Century, Silver Century Plus. 1975, $8.

Stern-Drive Service-Repair Handbook. Covers OMC, Mercruiser, Volvo, Dieseldrive, Berkley, Jacuzzi. 1975, $9.

Sailboat Auxiliary Engine Maintenance. Covers Chrysler, Ford, Pisces, Universal, Perkins, Volvo-Penta, Westerbeke, and Yanmar. 1975, $9.

Johnson Service-Repair Handbook. Covers models up to 33 hp from 1965 to 1975, $8.

Evinrude Service-Repair Handbook. Covers models from 1.5 hp to 33 hp from 1965 to 1975, $8.

Mercury Service-Repair Handbook. Covers models from 3.9 hp to 40 hp from 1964 to 1975, $8.

Abos Marine Publications
1014 Wyandotte St.
Kansas City, Missouri 64105

Evinrude 1½-40 hp Outboard Motor Service Manual. Covers models from 1956 to 1975, $4.95.

Evinrude 50-135 hp Outboard Motor Service Manual. Covers models from 1958 to 1975, $4.95.

Johnson 1½ to 40 hp Outboard Motor Service Manual. Covers models from 1956 to 1975, $4.95.

Johnson 50 to 135 hp Outboard Motor Service Manual. Covers models from 1958 to 1975, $4.95.

Mercury Outboard Motor Service Manual. Covers 3.9 hp to 150 hp models from 1955 to 1975, $4.95.

Contemporary Books
180 North Michigan Ave.
Chicago, Ill. 60601

Glenn's Outboard Motor Tune-up and Repair Series, by Harold T. Glenn
    Johnson 1&2 Cylinder, 1974, $7.75
    Johnson 3&4 Cylinder, 1974, $7.75
    Evinrude 3&4 Cylinder, 1974, $7.75
    Evinrude 1&2 Cylinder, 1974, $7.75
    Chrysler 1&2 Cylinder, 1974, $7.75

    Chrysler 3&4 Cylinder, 1974, $7.75
Glenn's Outboard Motor Mercury Tune-up and Repair, by Harold T. Glenn, 1974, $8.50.

Voyaging Under Power, by Robert P. Beebe
Seven Seas Press, New York
256 pages, illus., index, 1975, $12.50

Bob Beebe is a retired Captain, USN, who has made a life study of naval architecture.

As navigating officer aboard the aircraft carrier *Saratoga,* he began dreaming of seeing the world in his own power cruiser, and devoted years of study to the problem of crossing oceans safely at reasonable speed and in comfort, freed from the vagaries of wind.

He has put all this into his book, *Voyaging Under Power,* after having designed his own boat, *Passagemaker,* having her built by Thorneycroft in the Orient, and then "shaking down" in a mere 6,000-mile voyage that brought him into port without mishap across the Indian Ocean, the Mediterranean, and wide seas beyond, making his landfall through fog at the breakwater entry.

Obviously, Bob Beebe has "been there." His book, becoming known among yachtsmen as "VUP," is of incalculable value to any skipper who cons his own cruiser from port to port, for ship's husbands who like to KNOW what their boats can do and how to measure it, and for naval architects, especially, who are faced with the task of designing long-range power vessels.

Beebe's subject is fascinating, but his exposition, to me, is even more so. He has a brilliant way of making complex problems very simple, and he writes concisely in well organized channels.

All of the logic that goes into designing a good water machine is clearly laid out and well explained.

Many of Beebe's own boats are displayed in line and photo, as well as the work of some well-known yacht designers who have helped round out the book with examples of their planning and with their thinking on the subject.

I wouldn't trade my copy for fifty bucks, and it is my conviction that this book will be the classic on the subject for a long time to come. If you don't have it, get it, and you'll have a solid new friend in the book and in its author, who has done a peach of a job.

—**Weston Farmer**

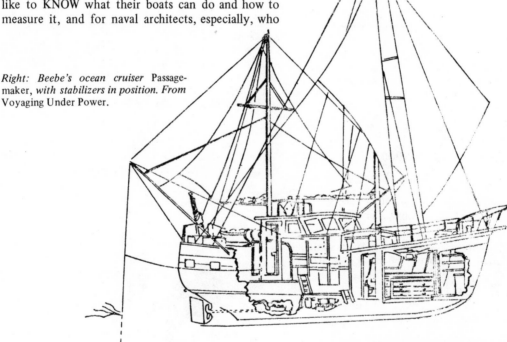

Right: Beebe's ocean cruiser Passage-maker, *with stabilizers in position. From* Voyaging Under Power.

92

Let not a book lead you into the temptation of feeling experienced; only by building boats, having boats built, and going out in boats can experience be got. However, a book shows the way.

—**William Atkin**

The Slotted-Tombstone Dory

Adapting dories for power is a problem that has been dear to my heart for many years. Actually, I don't think there is much of a problem, notwithstanding the pundit who years ago decreed that dories and outboards couldn't be emulsified. There's a way to do it without the well, which, though well intentioned, turns out to be an abomination.

Years ago, I had a tiny sixteen-foot Banks dory. After messing with a variety of propulsion units that

(Continued on next page)

(Continued from preceding page)

all proved unsatisfactory, I finally in desperation dropped a little three-horse Evinrude through a slot cut in the tombstone, and everything came up oranges on the slot machine. With one person at the con, another in the bow (and sometimes a third amidships), she punched right down in the water where she belonged. There's nothing like a little bottom on a boat. The lesson was well learned: a dory is designed as a displacement hull, but until you get her down in the water, she isn't. She's cranky as hell and, especially in the small sizes, virtually uncontrollable under too much power. On the other hand, load her up with ballast and/or people, and you're off.

Looking back on the transitory succession of watercraft I've owned since, I can say without hesitation that this little Banks, with her three-horse kicker, was the cheapest and best boat of them all.

The point is, obviously, that if successful powering can be accomplished with a little Banks, it can be done with a big one—indeed, any one, but the bigger the better. Dories don't have too much interior space for their length. Tuck the ballast to her (nice, flat stones from our beloved Maine coast), a low-power, long-shaft motor, remote controls rigged to a console forward, plus such niceties as the right propeller, single-lever control, and so forth—all this will keep the weight out of the stern and offset the hull's tendency to squat under power. She'll ride nearly level, well down in the water with several persons aboard, and take you just about anywhere you'd want to go—not quickly and not too economically either—but then you can't have everything. And, naturally, you could build a nice motor compartment into the stern to quiet the motor . . .

But an outboard is really a lousy form of propulsion for a real displacement hull like a well-ballasted dory. On the other hand, outboards are handy as hell in many ways and much less expensive than inboards. It looks as if we'll just have to use them and make the best of it. Actually, the new sailboat kickers are slight improvements, as they tend to have better reduction gears and slower propellers, and the propellers themselves are better designed for heavy hulls. You'll gain a little but not too much. The Michigan Wheel people put out some low-pitch options that are interesting, or you could just get a larger motor and run it at about two-thirds throttle. The dory will go just so fast anyway.

Tiller extensions in dories are impossible. You want to get as far from the motor as possible for better trim, and this practically puts you astride the gunwale on a turn to starboard. It can be done, but it's makeshift and unprofessional. This is the reason for the remote controls, which give you a leg-up in a dory—indeed, they're a necessity. The OMC remotes start with the 6-horse motors, and I'd guess somewhere around there with the Mercs. Six horsepower will push quite a good-size dory in good shape. Try to stay away from the motor manufacturers' remote controls. They're designed for mounting under the gunwale with the lines leading directly aft. Mounting them on a console results in another abomination—again, workable but makeshift. A console requires either a binnacle or a side-mount shift, and these are available (at least, they have been) from such manufacturers as Morse, Marmac, or Teleflex. The cables drop down vertically from the fixture and can be neatly tailed off under the floorboards and through the limber-holes aft to the motor.

—David L. Register

Spare Him

Dear Editors:

HELP!

Your nice story about me and Acadia engines appeared in the *Mariner's Catalog* some time after I had stopped handling them for several reasons. After the catalog was published, the inquiries built up. I would reply to them and, for a while, would send them up to Acadia. During the past year or so, I have just replied to each inquiry, suggesting that they write to Acadia. As far as I know, the factory has built only a few two-cycles each year, so that the price has probably skyrocketed, so I doubt if they have sold any. Instead, they are just converting Chevrolet and Oldsmobile engines, using conversion castings from the U.S.

I thought the inquiries would die down, but I still get six or eight a month, from everywhere from Maine to Hawaii and Alaska; even one from Japan, so the replies take time and stamps.

Walter Hadley
Jamestown, R.I.

So lay off him. If you want details about make-and-break 2-cycle marine engines, write to:

Acadia Engines
Bridgewater, Nova Scotia
Canada

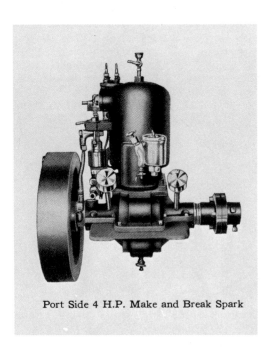

Port Side 4 H.P. Make and Break Spark

Above: The Acadia 4 hp make and break.

93

Cruising in comfort . . . and it hasn't cost me a cent for upkeep

More Used-Book Dealers

We ran our first selection of dealers in used nautical books in the first *Mariner's Catalog*. All volumes since then have had completely new listings, even though we were convinced that we would run out of sources after the second volume. It was with a heavy heart that we began research on this subject for the present volume—we were convinced the well had gone dry. Yet it hadn't. More new sources not only came to light, but also those that did proved themselves to be pretty impressive.

Seadragon Maritime
2212 Olson Court
Marlow Heights, Maryland 20031

Specializes in naval, shipping, and government publications. Besides books has paper memorabilia, such as certificates of discharge, passenger lists, and stationery. Also has back issues of some magazines. Catalog, on request, is lightly annotated.

Carl Apollonio
3885 Prudence Drive
Sarasota, Florida 33580

Has titles covering ships and the sea, polar exploration, fishing, and naval history. Prices are moderate to high. Annotation confined to indications of physical condition of books. Catalog on request.

Nautica Booksellers
Box 132
Dartmouth, Nova Scotia, Canada

One of the most impressive collections we've seen, with fairly reasonable prices. Covers naval, merchant, yachting, piracy, law, whaling, voyages, diving, sciences, professional, and arctic subjects. Catalog, updated at least quarterly, has good annotation as to content and condition.

Francis Edwards Ltd.
83 Marylebone High St.
London, England

Carries rare books and manuscripts on naval and maritime history, shipbuilding, seamanship, navigation, exploration, voyages, and military history. Catalog (ask for "Naval, Maritime and Military History") is extremely well annotated, with details about authors, editions, condition, contents. Prices are very high, primarily because they are featuring rare, collector's volumes.

Norman Kerr, Bookseller
Cartmel
Grange-Over-Sands, England

Listed previously, but no longer has a catalog. Send your wants, giving as much detail as possible. Covers all naval and maritime subjects, including fiction.

McLaren Books
Ardenconnel Cottage
Church Road Rhu
Dunbartonshire, Scotland

Carries books on all naval and maritime subjects, with special emphasis on Scotland. Plans to expand collection and issue 5 or 6 catalogs per year. Brief annotation, moderate prices.

Arthur J. Peterson
1948 South 50
East Orem, Utah 84057

"I do not deal in books. I do deal in, and stock, marine picture post cards, mainly of ocean liners, ocean freighters, and naval ships, but really of most anything in ships. I normally sell at retail on an approval basis."

(Continued on next page)

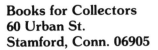

Books for Collectors
60 Urban St.
Stamford, Conn. 06905

Carries the following subjects: Antarctic, Arctic, naval and maritime history, yachting, modelling, cruising, whaling. Catalog (ask for "Maritime Books") is annotated only by condition of books.

G.L. Green
104 Pitshanger Lane
Ealing, London
England

Mostly naval and shipping titles, with a special selection of nautical postcards. Booklist is well annotated by content and condition of books. Prices moderate to high.

H.A. Reichenberg
Route de la Heitera 22
CH-1700 Fribourg
Switzerland

Features naval history, merchant shipping, naval air, etc. Many German titles. Prices are in Swiss francs, catalog is 2 Sw.Fr.; correspondence must include International Reply Coupon.

Robert F. Lucas
Box 63
Blandford, Mass. 01008

Mostly whaling titles, with some general maritime history. Catalog annotates books as to condition. Prices are fair.

Back Issues of Magazines

We were looking for back issues of various boating magazines and came across the P. & H. Bliss Company, which has an extensive list of periodicals, reprints, and government publications covering all subjects.

P. & H. Bliss Co.
Middletown, Conn. 06457

Dear Editors:

We deal with individuals, as well as libraries both large and small, but we must have a list of exact titles and issues wanted. We do not look for specific articles that appeared in various publications.

Our business is all conducted by mail; we are not a store.

Harry W. Dickerson
P. & H. Bliss Co.
Middletown, Conn. 06457

Two Reference Books

No comments on nautical books can ever be complete; it's hopeless trying to keep up with everything. But there are a couple of titles that I feel ought to be in the *Catalog*:

One is a reprint published by David and Charles, Newton Abbot, England, and North Pomfret, Vermont: *Last Days of Mast and Sail*, by Alan Moore (An "Essay in Nautical Comparative Anatomy" originally published in 1925) $12.50. As a person interested in nautical terminology across language boundaries and through the ages, I found more insight into unexplained phenomena in this book than in any other single publication. The other is quite recent: *The Oxford Companion to Ships and the Sea*, by Peter Kemp (Editor), Oxford University Press, 1976. 972pp., $35. (See review elsewhere in this *Catalog*.—Eds.)

—Karl Freudenstein

95

Dear Editors:

Don't know if you've noticed, but *Motor Boating & Sailing* magazine has turned, the last six months or so, into the best goddamn boating magazine in this country. Period. In a previous *Mariner's Catalog*, you described *Rudder* as being "grand," and had no adjective at all for *MB & S*. You might consider steering people toward *MB & S*.

George Buehler
Seattle, Washington

Brigantine at left and dghaisa above from Last Days of Mast and Sail.

German Nautical Publishers

by Karl Freudenstein

Drawing from Hamburger Rundbrief.

Verlag Horst Hamecher
Goethestrasse 74
D-3500 Kassel
Germany

Horst Hamecher is a publisher who has produced a considerable number of reprints, mostly in the fields of local and regional history, Americana (cf. Friderici's 1907 book on American Indian shipping and boatbuilding!), and nautical subjects. Their reprint of Ulffers' 1872 *Manual of Seamanship* (*Handbuch der Seemannschaft*) is considered a German classic which has been unavailable for a long time except for a partial reproduction of the illustrations. German nautical etymology is not covered elsewhere in any way comparable to Kluge's 1911 *Seemannssprache*.

Hamecher is also a used-book dealer. Furthermore, he is the author of the book on *Preussen* published by Verlag Egon Heinemann (*The Mariner's Catalog, Vol. 4*, p. 166).

Hamburger Rundbrief (Hamburg Newsletter
for Collectors of Ship Miniature Models)
Publisher/Editor: R. K. Lochner
An der Alster 26
D-2000 Hamburg 1
Germany

Published bimonthly in German. All back issues available. Correspondence in English welcome. Data sheets contain complete ship history plus press report reproductions.

Christian Schmidt's Verlag
Sauerbruchstrasse 10
D-8000 Munchen 70
Germany

A publisher who specializes in ship model information, distributing German and foreign books on maritime (primarily naval) subjects, and has initiated a *Maritime Reprints* series.

Koehler's Verlagsgesellschaft
Steintorwall 17
4900 Herford
Germany

Publishers of books on nautical and naval subjects, both fiction and nonfiction. They have a special series, "Koehler's maritime mini-library". *Sails from Downeast* (*Segel aus Downeast*) should be of special interest to readers from New England, if they can read German; this is not a translation of an American original. Also noteworthy is the German Society for Nautical and Naval History, whose publication *Schiff Und Zeit* is also published by Koehler's.

Verlag Gerhard Stalling
Ammergaustrasse 72-78
2900 Oldenburg
Germany

A publisher with various fields of activity, including a maritime division (Stalling Maritim). Quite a few of their books are translations of foreign publications. A series of publications of the German Maritime Museum and a paperback series, *Bluewater Sailors* (publications of the German Sports Sailing Institute).

Verlag Die Brigantine
Hamburg
Germany

Publishes primarily maritime fiction (all novels by Hans Leip, author of the text of that WW II song "Lili Marleen") and historical/biographical items. A gem: the reprint of a 1809 primer on marine subjects for children: *Gallerice Der Schiffahrt*.

BLV Verlagsgesellschaft
Munchen
Germany

Mainly nonfiction publishers, with a special interest in contemporary sports sailing authors: a special sailing division whose titles include *Denk's Sailing Dictionary* (German only), a very useful and handy paperback; and a large-format handbook on sailing co-edited by the same author.

Arbeitskreis Historischer Schiffbau
Postfach 176
D-6501 Heidesheim
Germany

An association of historical ship model buffs; they published several reprints of pertinent older books (including the illustrations part of Ulffers, cf. above), unfortunately out of print. Also, a bulletin on nautical history subjects and maritime museums with historical models. Title: *Das Logbuch*.

[Other German publishers, as well as additional foreign-language publishers, can be found in MC-4, p. 112. —Eds.]

96

Find It Fast

We all know that the boating press publishes many good articles, especially the how-to variety, which might not do you much good when you read them but would be of use later when you really need them. We know some packrats of information who clip out the good material and file it for future reference; we know others who clip it and forget where they put it; we know still others who save their magazines without clipping them and are constantly muttering, "Now, what issue was that article on making baggy-wrinkle in?"

What we really need is a comprehensive index of boating magazines, so that if we have the magazines, or access to them (big-city libraries, perhaps), we can look up our interests and pinpoint articles on them. Finally, we have one:

International Nautical Index Quarterly
2632 North Forgeus Ave.
Tucson, Arizona 85716
Subscriptions: 1 year $10, 2 years $18,
3 years $24

INI indexes most of the major nautical magazines and many of the minor ones. The index is broken down into categories and most of the categories are on practical subjects.

Northwest Publications

One book I would have liked to have seen in the "Women of the Sea" section (MC-4, p. 134) is *The Curve of Time* (Gray's Pub. Co., Sydney, B.C., Canada, $1.95). And I think the enclosed photocopies will give an idea of the content. It is a book especially meaningful for me, as I've been along the San Juan, Gulf Islands, B.C., coast on a couple of trips. Cruised with a friend who lives in that area aboard his 40-foot Dunlin. A fine, no-tinsel craft built in 1920 and powered by a beautiful 45-h.p., three-cylinder Atlas diesel.

Other NW publications of interest to some might be:

Raincoast Chronicles
Box 119
Madeira Park, B.C. VON 2H9
Canada

I find all issues first rate, and, while they don't always cover maritime areas, the publication is strictly coastal oriented.

Also:

The Puget Sound Maritime Historical Society
2161 E. Hamlin Street
Seattle, Washington
$10/yr.

Good organization, and puts out *The Sea Chest*. Well-done publication with pictures. Just the thing for anyone interested in this area.

—Bart Kister

Dear Editors:

You mentioned the Slocum Society in the *Mariner's Catalog*, but with no address. The secretary is: Richard Gordon McCloskey, 9206 N.E. 180th Street, Bothell, Washington 98011. Dues are $10 (U.S.) or £5.70 (U.K.) per year.

Mike Hardcastle
Atherstone, Warks, England

SHIP'S GEAR

Testing

A truly excellent new magazine has appeared in this field, *Geartest*. It is a British quarterly and expensive ($18/yr.), but the expense is understandable the minute you open to any page; no advertising, of course, and the work they put into their evaluations is just fantastic. The two issues we received cover depth sounders, heads, bearing compasses, and radar reflectors, and a thorough reading makes one trust their conclusions. Candor!

Geartest
c/o Kenneth Mason Publications, Ltd.
13-14 Homewell
Hevant, Hants, England
$18/yr.

Boxed quote below from Geartest *prospectus.*

A Straight-shooting Newsletter

Dear Editors:

Please include a plug on the *Telltale Compass*, 18418 South Old River Drive, Lake Oswego, Oregon 97034. If you have a gripe about anything in the marine industry, they will print it—I guess you know it, but so many who need it don't know about it.

George G. Lee
Memphis, Tenn.

We reviewed the *Telltale Compass* in the first *Mariner's Catalog* (p. 175), but think enough of that publication to recommend it again. The newsletter accepts no advertising, so a year's subscription (12 issues) is steep—$20—but what you get in return is honest information on marine products and services from people who know what they are talking about.
—Eds.

The appraisals are based on visual inspection, shore test, sea test, and, where applicable, simulation test (including wind tunnel) and test to destruction.

We are particularly concerned with reliability and total maintenance costs throughout the useful life of gear: the cost per season spread over the useful life is more important than the initial cost. Such information is not easily acquired by individuals but hopefully our collective efforts will save the *Geartest* subscriber many times the value of his annual subscription.

What are the journal's aims? Apart from *Geartest's* primary aim which is to provide subscribers with practical comment and, treating them as discerning consumers, supply sufficient technical and costing information for them to make their own assessments in accordance with their own particular needs (in addition to any best buy recommendations), manufacturers will benefit from practical, experienced observations on their own equipment with recommendations for improvement where applicable, resulting in generally higher standards and improved sales.

English Fittings

A.N. Wallis and Company are English factors offering a wide range of fittings for yachts and small craft, including deck fittings, door and hatch furniture, lights, pumps, valves, hatches, windows, sterngear, ventilators, masts, marine bearings, trimtabs, steering pedestals, seats, davits, anchors, boathooks, screen wipers, rudders, propeller brackets, deck coverings, sheet winches, toilets—most of this is of contemporary yacht type. They have cast and machined nonferrous alloys for 25 years.

A.N. Wallis and Company
Greasly Street, Bulwell
Nottingham, England

—John Leather

Dutch Fittings

W.H. Den Ouden is a Dutch company producing a wide range of modern fittings and equipment under the trademark "Vetus." This includes the "smallest hydraulic steering gear in the whole world" for craft up to 32 feet long. Den Ouden's list also includes bollards, anchors, portlights, anti-slip deck coverings, hand and electric anchor windlasses, deck hatches, metal-framed windows, water pressure pumps, rubber tanks, toilets, stainless steel fuel tanks, ventilators, stanchions, cleats, seats, plastic imitation wood decking (I can hardly bear to write that one), davits, plastic fenders, bow rollers, valves, searchlights, navigation lights, cabin lights, clear-view screens, gas detectors, depth sounders, switch panels, anemometers, propellers, sterngear, flexible couplings, exhaust systems, and control levers.

Their distributor in the U.S. is :

W.H. Den Ouden (USA) Inc.
P.O. Box 8712
Baltimore, Maryland 21240

Above: The Viking centerboard winch.

Low-Cost Sailboat Winches

Somehow or other the *Catalog* seems to have missed the Viking winch. These English winches are available to suit a wide range of small boat applications. Thomas Foulkes had some on display at the Annapolis Sailboat Show a few years ago, and I was so taken by the line I would have bought four or five, only we didn't have a boat to install them on at the time.

Viking Winches
Southend Engineering
Leigh-on-Sea, Essex
England

As I remember them, they were of light-alloy construction, with most surfaces in their "as cast" condition, or perhaps tumble-polished. No chrome or gears. Just an honest, simple collection of line-handling equipment at very low prices. The 27-foot economy cruiser in my mental plan file has a Viking deck winch with gypsy to help haul in the 30-fathom chain rode.

—Wallace Venable

Below: Den Ouden's MT 30, said to be the smallest hydraulic steering system in the world.

Type MT 30 (30 mkg/210 ft. lbs.) for boats up to 10 metres (32 ft.) (depending on rudder torque).

	MT 30
Max. torque	30 mkg (210 ft. lbs.)
Number of pistons	5
Theor. rev. of steering wheel from SB to PS	3.8
Stroke of cylinder	150 mm (5⅞")
Max. pressure	40 kg/cm² (570 lbs. sq. inch)
Volume of cylinder	81 cm³ (4.9 cubic inch)
Total rudder angle	70°
Length of tiller arm	129 mm (5⅛")
Weight of pump	3.1 kg (6.8 lbs.)
Weight of cylinder	1.8 kg (4 lbs.)
Dimensions of tube	8 x 6 mm

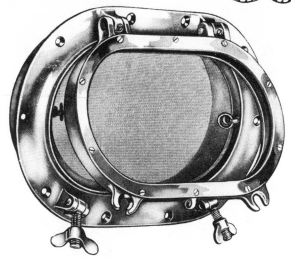

Galley or Pantry Pump

Top: Rostand's heavy-type improved portlight, available in cast bronze or aluminum—plain, polished, or chromed.
Above: Briggs Marine's galley pump.
Bottom: Surflock's bronze-manganese rail-mounted oarlocks.

Oarlocks

Surflock is a one-off group making what is certainly the most sturdy oarlock available, at $21.50 a pair. The locks have been used for years on lifeguard surfboats.

Surflock Associates
914 Poe Place
South Plainfield, N.J. 07080

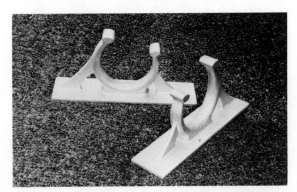

Bronze, for Those Who Care Enough

Because the manufacture of bronze hardware is so generally rare, we like to list all makers as they become known to us.

Rostand is the country's largest factor of bronze portlights in several models—all the sure-enough thing. They also are well known for their bells.

The Rostand Co.
Milford, Conn. 06460

Dear Editors:

After your request in *Mariner's Catalog, Volume 3,* on ship's bells, I could hardly wait to see the response in *Volume 4.* What a disappointment—only one English manufacturer, so I must put my "two cents" in.

I purchased my 6-inch bell, made of "Bell Metal," from the Rostand Manufacturing Company of Milford, Connecticut. They will chromeplate them and make them to Navy spec #23B2; what else could you want? I am very pleased with mine. Just think, there are some things that are still made in the U.S.A.

Paul J. Adams
Lambertville, New Jersey

Pacific Bronze Company makes many nonferrous fittings, most of them of heavy section for working craft: stuffing boxes, hawse pipes, ports, bitts, cleats, rails, and so on.

Pacific Bronze Company, Ltd.
1615 Franklin St.
Vancouver, B.C. V5L 1P5
Canada

Briggs Marine, an Australian firm, is another general bronze-casting outfit with a very broad range of items:

Briggs Marine Products
60 Shafton St.
Huntingdale 3166
Victoria, Australia

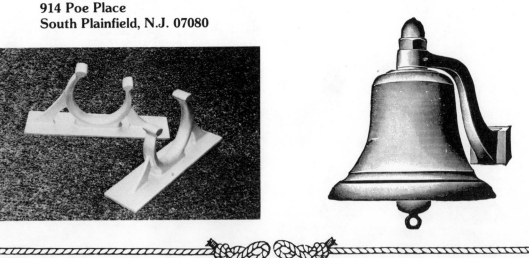

Blocks

Teak blocks from:

> **Troy Bros.**
> **P.O. Box 71**
> **239 Seal Beach Blvd.**
> **Seal Beach, Cal. 90740**

Water-trap Vents

Though dorade vents are time-proven and no problem to build, some may want to give Martec "Dri-Vents" a try, from:

> **Martec**
> **2257 Gaylord St.**
> **Long Beach, Cal. 90813**

Seaworthy Flush Hatches

With the use of General Electric's *Lexan*, which is far stronger than Plexiglass, flush or near-flush large glazed hatches are not only pleasant, but seaworthy. Many production builders install them routinely, from:

> **Bomar, Inc.**
> **Box 162**
> **979 Post Rd. East**
> **Westport, Conn. 06880**

THE FRAME

The cast aluminum alloy frame is made of Almag - 35 having a tensile strength of 44,000 lbs. p.s.i. This aluminum meets U.S. Army specs for lightweight armor and aircraft landing gear. Yet, it is 10% lighter than pure aluminum. Almag - 35 has the highest non-corrosion level of any known aluminum casting alloy.

We strongly feel that only Almag-35 cast aluminum should be used for boats. While other alloys are cheaper, they do tend to pit and corrode over a period of time. Bomar castings will stand the test of time.

THE HATCH COVER
WE GUARANTEE THE HATCH COVER
TO BE UNBREAKABLE!

The cover is a LEXAN sheet made by General Electric. The LEXAN used in all Bomar Hatches has the strength of more than 5" of Plexiglass. To insure privacy below deck, the LEXAN is tinted to a dark smoke color that lets in 80% of the available light, allows you to look out with ease, yet is nearly impossible to see through from the outside.

Boxed quote above from Bomar catalog; hatch at right is Bomar's No. 170 with a 1" spigot intended to cover the headliner of a fiberglass boat.

Above: Teak blocks from Troy Bros., with sheaves of bronze and Micarta.
Below: The Martec Dri-Vent in flexible polyvinyl chloride.

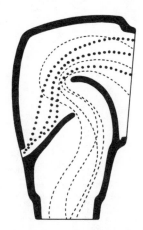

HOW DOES IT WORK?

The cross section shows two baffles which effectively trap any water entering the vent and channel it out the two drain holes in the back. Solid water instantly collapses the flexible outer baffle to keep the unit from being flooded.

101

H & L CUSTOM LAMINATED TILLERS

Professionally laminated with alternating 1/4" strips of Dibetou Mahogany and Ash for strength and beauty. Finished tillers are varnished with four coats of marine varnish. Unfinished tillers are completely shaped and sanded, ready for varnish or oil. Delivery is approx. 10 days. Prices listed below are for unfinished tillers. **If you would like a varnished tiller, please add $5.50.**

Available for the following boats:

Part #	Boat	PRICE	Part#	Boat	PRICE
100	Catalina 22	$14.40			
101	Cal 20 & Cal 21	16.20	1147	Yankee 30	20.70
103	Col. 22 & Cor. 23	14.40	1148	Yankee Dolphin	14.40
104	Cal 34	19.80	1149	Catalina 27	14.40
105	Cal 25	16.20	1150	Aquarius 21	14.40
106	Cal 28	16.20	1151	Islander 30 Mk II	17.95
109	Ericson 32	17.95	1152	Cal 27	17.95
110	Sabot	6.30	1153	Pearson 30	17.95
111	Sabot, with Extension	9.50	1156	Cal 39	21.60
112	Coronado 25	14.40	1157	Ericson 27	17.10
113	Omega-Super Satellite	14.40	1159	Balboa 20	14.40
114	Lido 14 w/ Extension	16.20	1160	Balboa 26	14.40
115	Catalina-Victory	13.50	1161	Pearson Electra	15.30
116	Ranger 26 & 29	14.40	1162	Pearson Ariel	16.20
117	Cal 24	14.40	1163	Pearson 26	16.20
118	Cal 33	20.70	1164	Pearson 33	18.90
119	Cal 36	20.70	1165	Pearson 33 Commander	17.95
120	Newport 20, 27, & 30	14.40	1169	Columbia 30	20.70
121	Coronado 15	7.75	1172	Clipper 21	16.20
122	Columbia 28	14.40	1173	Santana 26	16.20
124	Cal 2/30	20.70	1174	Clipper 26	17.10
126	Ericson 30	18.90	1178	Easterly 30	14.40
127	Cal 40	21.60	1179	Chance 30-30	17.10
128	Venture 17	22.50	1181	Ranger 1 Ton	21.60
129	Venture 21,22,222,& 24	22.50	1182	Easterly-Luders 16	17.10
130	Santana 22 & 27, Col.26	14.40	1183	O'Day 26	15.30
131	Coronado 30	16.20	1185	O'Day 22	15.30
132	Santana 21	17.10	1187	Rawson 30	17.95
133	Ericson 26 & 23	14.40	1192	Cal 3/30	16.20
134	Ericson 35	21.60	1193	Tartan 27	15.20
136	Aquarius 23	14.40	1194	Tartan 30	16.20
137	Ranger 33	18.90	1195	Tartan 34	16.20
139	Cal 29	17.10	1196	Catalina 30	16.20
1140	Lido 14, No Extension	10.90	1197	Lancer 25	14.40
1142	Ericson 29	17.95	1199	Islander-30-II	17.10
1143	Columbia 36	17.95	1200	Clipper 30	15.30
1144	Coronado 27	14.40	1203	Islander 28	17.10
1145	Cal 2/24	14.40	1211	Pearson 26 (1976)	15.30
1146	Columbia 34 Mk II	20.70	1212	Pearson 28	15.30

Add $5.50 for varnished tiller.

Above: From Sailing Equipment Warehouse's catalog

No Tears, But Cheap

We get scads of stuff from all over the industry: leaflets, flyers, catalogs, letters, and phillippics, and, or course, we don't use much of it. Stash it somewhere and that's that. One list we get is from Sea and Save Company, and truly their prices are often extremely low. The merchandise may not bring tears to your eyes, but, by gum, it is cheap!

Sea and Save Co.
P.O. Box 1335
Lexington, Mass. 02173

Right: Sea and Save's outboard motor bracket, rated at 20 hp, listing regularly at $49.95, to you for $28.95 (as of mid-1977). Sea and Save also promises free freight.

Builder's Choice

The Sailing Equipment Warehouse has always paid especially close attention to people building and fitting-out their own boats. They have their own catalog now, and she's a gooder.

Sailing Equipment Warehouse
Box 2575
Olympia, Wash. 98507
Catalog, $2.00

LFH's Pump

L. Francis Herreshoff continued his prodigious outpouring of designs and ideas to the very end of his life. Few yachtsmen will not be familiar with at least some of the Skipper's great yachts, but considerable number do not realize that when the gentleman designed a craft, it was from the keel to the truck and usually included every fitting to be placed aboard. Sometimes he built the fittings himself. There was no aspect of experience on the water to which he did not give his thorough attention.

His very efficient yet inexpensive design for a bilge pump is an example and, happily, still available from:

Herreshoff Bilge Pump
The Castle
Marblehead, Mass. 01945

Also available is a boat's syringe built on the same basic design as the pump but, instead of lifting the water through a large orifice at the bottom and ejecting it out the top, it draws the water through a small tube and holds it for ejecting back out the same way—an excellent solution to the problem of water in small spaces on a boat, such as between closely spaced frames and floors with clogged limberholes, through fixed gratings, etc. It doubles as a most effective fire extinguisher with a long, precise reach, an awesome water pistol, and, we suppose, an engine oil extractor.

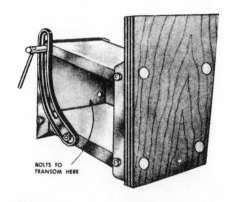

BOLTS TO
TRANSOM HERE

Wipers

A reader recently impressed on us the expense and impracticality of centrifugal rain shields on most pleasure craft and countered by saying that very strong wiper systems are used successfully all the time on locomotives, big trucks, tugboats, and so on, Air-Push being a very common one. They are manufactured by Sprague, which also makes automatic lubrication systems.

Sprague Devices, Inc.
500 Huron Street
Michigan City, Indiana 46360

Dear Editors:

As most people concerned with boats have probably found out, Army surplus cartridge boxes provide an excellent container for any rustable items. Well, for the seagoing photographer, better protection than most is provided by these boxes because of their watertightness.

It is quite simple to convert a cartridge box into a camera case by using the Styrofoam packing that comes with new cameras. I find I have room for two lenses, one camera body, six rolls of film, and several large filters. If the rubber gasket around the lid of the box is not perfect, try a little Vaseline or silicone sealant.

John H. Betts
Champaign, Illinois

Ships' Figureheads, by Peter Norton
Barre Pubs., Barre, Mass.
144 pages, illus., biblio., index, 1976, $10

Along with binnacles, engine telegraphs, bells, belaying pins, and half-models, ships' figureheads are one of the modern era's premier collectibles. For those of us who don't have the economic muscle to get our own, or who lack the weak aesthetics to buy a plaster or fiberglass reproduction, the only chances to study their beauty are to go to museums or read books. This book gives us both—a readable treatise on the history and development of figureheads and the added bonus of a list of museums around the world noted for their figurehead collections, not to mention a sizable bibliography to add to your future reading pleasure.

Above: Cartoon by Darrell McClure.
Below: From Shipcarvers of North America.

Another well-known book on the subject, back in print in a quality paperback edition is:

Shipcarvers of North America
by M.V. Brewington
Dover Pubs., New York
173 pages, illus., biblio., index, 1962, $3

As the title indicates, Brewington doesn't confine the coverage to figureheads alone, but describes other types of ship carvings as well and gives short biographies of outstanding carvers.

Traditional craft aren't complete without proper decorative touches. Both Norton and Brewington point the way toward an understanding of what is appropriate for your dream ship.

103

Gronicles, for Better or Worse

We knew that our discovery of first-rate gronicles, as reported in the *Mariner's Catalog, Volume 4* (p. 79), would arouse some comment, but we weren't prepared for the intensity of it all. Our first indication of that came with a telephone call from a worker at the Electric Boat Company in Groton, Conn., who evidently had a sum of money riding on the outcome of the conversation. We don't know whether he won or lost; all we heard was a long, drawn-out, "Well I'll be damned."

We ask you to enjoy the following in the spirit in which they were received and sent:

Dear Editors:
. . . all right, wise-guys, what's a gronicle?

Kent B. Power
Boise, Idaho

We dug deeply into our past experience and sent this reply:

Dear Mr. Power:
In response to your recent query about gronicles: they have a multitude of uses and come in a variety of shapes. We once saw a friend open up a very complex camera that had been inadvertently soaked in water. In it he found square gronicles, round ones, a very interesting oblate spheroid one, and a multitude of your common, garden-variety rectangular types (all with clewnets, of course). The same fellow reached down under the hood of our malfunctioning car and ripped out a chipped gronicle from the starting mechanism. Once it was replaced, we had no difficulty starting the car.

The Editors
Mariner's Catalog

Then we received a letter from a fellow who quibbled with our definition of "first-class":

Dear Editors:
I would draw your attention to a possible error in the *Mariner's Catalog, Vol. 4.* I believe that you have called out a smidgen too much antimony for the traditional alloy used in first-class gronicles. I tried to verify this by phoning the supplier, but, unfortunately, the telephone company seems to have misplaced Belleville, North Dakota.

Murray L. Lesser
Yorktown Heights, N.Y.

Murray wasn't the only one who couldn't locate Belleville, North Dakota:

Dear Editors:
Having received your *Mariner's Catalog, Volume 4,* I was delighted to see listed on page 79 a supplier of first-rate gronicles.
Currently, I am attempting to fill my garage with every piece of hardware I will need for the Tahiti ketch I intend to be building within the year.

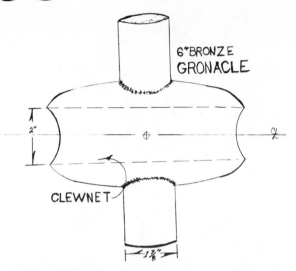

Needless to say, a matched pair of gronacles (I believe you misspelled it in your handsome book) are essential—if hard to come by—pieces of hardware.

I wrote the Acme Foundry and Machine Shop in Belleville, N.D., but our postal service failed to raise them.

Still, I need that pair of gronacles, and at this point I will settle for even second-rate gronacles. Enclosed is a drawing of what I need in case you know of a fine metals foundry that could make them up for me. I'm sure there are many others around the coasts who could use them as well.

Chad Thomas III
Sarasota, Florida

We found Mr. Thomas's letter interesting, yet provocative. Our reply:

Dear Mr. Thomas:
For heaven's sake, don't settle for second-rate gronicles* if you plan to spend any time at sea. Other readers have indicated that Acme Foundry and Machine Shop is not answering their mail, so we are searching for a new source—one reader suggested a place in Rhode Island, but we misplaced the reference some time back when we were forced to straighten up our office after the fire marshal's inspection team declared it a hazard. We haven't been able to find anything since.

Keep a stiff upper lip.

The Editors
Mariner's Catalog

*You are mistaken about the correct spelling of gronicles. Yes, there is such a thing as a gronacle, but it has no marine application. Rather, it is an animal husbandry term. Dudley Kirhener's *Advanced Terminology for Dairy Farmers* indicates that the word originated as "groin-acle." We'll leave the rest of the definition and the use of the article to your imagination.

AT SEA

Art above by Buck Smith.

I remember that passage from the Shannon to the Solent more pleasurably and more vividly than any previous and many subsequent ones, chiefly, I think, because I was now going to sea not yachting but sailing a ship upon her lawful occasions. Indeed, all my happiest memories of the sea refer to voyages undertaken with some object, other than the search for pleasure. I believe pleasure-seekers generally remain such to the end of time. I found my pleasures incidentally to the more or less legitimate business of carrying a fishery inspector round the West Coast of Ireland, myself to New Zealand and back, or contraband of war to Dublin; but most particularly to the quite illegitimate one (from the yachting point of view) of carrying a trading ketch that had been sold to the Falkland Islands out to her owners. A voyage with an object has another great attraction for me; one really has more freedom when one is under orders. He who is nobody's servant is everybody's servant, and when in the middle of a good run some passenger wants to go ashore for letters, you can't refuse her, unless you can give a definite reason for it.

—Conor O'Brien
From Three Yachts (1928)

Roll, Pitch, Yaw, Lurch, and Shiver Also Barf

105

Seasickness is a Big Drag and, when prolonged, dangerous. It is caused by neural overloading when the brain tries to fully interpret "information" coming from the semicircular canals of the inner ear. The orientation of the fluids in these canals provides us with our sense of external orientation and balance. When too much of this information is contradictory, as it is bound to be when we are bounced through three dimensions at once, either we must develop an ability to censor some of this information (and get our sealegs) or we'll overload and become ill, usually with complications created by anxiety, fatigue, and embarrassment.

The drugs usually administered to control motion sickness are the so-called H1-antagonists, mildly depressive antihistamines that reduce responses to information from the inner ear in much the same way as other antihistamines reduce responses to information in the sinuses or throat when we have a cold or hay fever. There are two families of over-the-counter

(Continued on next page)

(Continued from preceding page)

motion-sickness drugs, the ethanolamines, of which the familiar Benadryl and Dramamine are members, and the piperazines, of which meclizine (Bonine) is an example. Generally, they prevent symptoms with equal effectiveness, except that the latter works two to three times longer but has a greater possibility of producing side effects, drowsiness or nervousness being the most common. People who anticipate the need for heavy artillery can get on prescription a combination of Scopolamine and weightier H1 blocker, such as Promethezine, to be taken together. Frankly, our advice is to take a nice long nap as soon as possible and let your subconscious figure it all out. Nibble on some bland crackers on rising, and you've got it licked by the middle of your first watch. [We would like to thank Gordon Paine, physician and surgeon at Penobscot Bay Medical Center, Rockport, Maine, for the information above.]

Medical Kit

Crews on cruisers and working vessels that get off-soundings for any length of time should provide themselves with as good a medical kit as they can. The most complete that we've found is one used by many of the commercial fleets in the Pacific and offered by Emergency Medical Systems in San Diego.

Emergency Medical Systems
3340 Kemper St.
San Diego, Cal. 92110

Boxed quote below from an Emergency Medical Systems flyer.

> Marine Medical Service is: a complete standardized pharmacy containing prescriptioned drugs, a detailed medical manual which is coordinated with the pharmacy, special medical equipment and supplies, a 24 hour physician counsel, and replacement of used or outdated drugs which can be sent to you anywhere in the world.
>
> This Marine Medical Service Kit for the <u>non-commercial yacht</u> is priced at $450.00 for the basic kit, plus a service fee of $150.00 per year. The service fee covers the physician on call 24 hours a day via any radio telephone, and replacement of all medical supplies in the kit once a year. This type service requires a contract to be signed before receiving the pharmacy kit. Also, you must remember that this kit, because of the nature of its contents, is to be used <u>only</u> outside the three mile limit.

The V-Bunk Bag

"Mate, send the guilty ones forward. They're confined to quarters until further notice. We'll get to the bottom of this, or my name isn't. . . ."

R.V. Enterprises
1012 N. Jantzen Drive
Portland, Oregon 97217

Right: The V-bunk Bag by R.V. Enterprises. Price is $60.

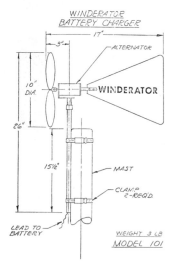

Above: The business end of a Winderator.
Below: Boxed quote and illustration from a Ponsharden Marine Services brochure. Sail rig, which attaches to the transom, is said to be suitable for boats from 8 to 15 feet and can be fitted in 10 minutes. It would be an understatement to say that we would like to try one out.

Wind-Power Generator

A lot once in a while is expensive. A little constantly is less expensive. Winderators in four sizes, 18" to 36", 1½ amps to 6 amps at 20 mph, $125 to $199, from:

Sun Water, Inc.
P.O. Box 732
Northridge, Calif. 91328

Is It, or Isn't It?

Either the Katainen Outboard Sail is an outrageous shuck, or it is the most ingenious nautical development since the Viking longboat. We have thought through the relevant physics a couple of times and have not found a reason why it shouldn't work. It is made in Finland. Somewhere in the U.S. ("yoohoo!") there is a distributor, but we haven't been able to find him. The British distributor is listed here, but using them will require a U.K. pickup location. Perhaps the Canadian distributor would be the best bet. (And if you should try one out, do let us know the results.)

107

Ponsharden Marine Services
Ponsharden Shipyard
Falmouth, Cornwall, England

Haines-MacIntosh Enterprises
Box 1064, Station Q
Toronto, Ontario, Canada

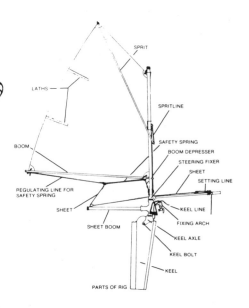

Technical data

Sprit sail 3.5 m². Constructed of aluminium, mast and boom eloxidised, mar-ply-keel, gross weight is approximately 12 kg. The boat is steered with a tiller, which controls the angle between keel and boat. The steering motion automatically gives the keel the correct angle of incidence. The sail is controlled by means of a sheet running to the tiller. The adjustable springing affects the sheet. The depth of the "rearboard" is controlled by a rope. The sail, mast and the boom make up an entity easily detachable from the rest of the structure. The device can easily be packed into a small space. Detailed instructions accompany every outboard sail unit.

Folding Transportation

There are a number of folding bicycles and motor scooters made, and we were going to do a survey of them. However, workmanship seems uneven at best, and the powered ones are plain suicidal. The one outstanding exception is the Bickerton line of folding bikes. Nicely made, easy to erect and fold down, and smartly sporty in use, from:

Bickerton Bicycles Ltd.
84 Brook St.
London W1Y 1YG, England

Below: The Bickerton portable bicycle.
Right: Safariland's Kel-lite, said to be the last flash-light you'll ever have to buy. Now there's a promise . . .

108

Flashlights

If all the flashlights we've ever owned were placed end to end, the true shape of space could finally be demonstrated. Wanting mightily to discover if a good one existed, we looked in every nook and cranny, and, naturally, the cops have them, and the ones they use are made in Texas and distributed through places like Safariland. Be sure to ask about flashlights specifically. Otherwise, you'll get a knockout catalog of leather goods and devices.

Safariland
1941 S. Walker Ave.
Monrovia, Cal. 91016

And because of its unmatched durability, all Kel-lites are guaranteed for life. Unless you lose it, your Kel-lite will be repaired or replaced if anything goes wrong. It's offered in 27 models from 2 to 7 cells, small, medium or large head. So look for a flashlight that suits your needs—for now, and ten years from now. With Kel-lite, you'll find they're one and the same.

D-Cell Medium Head Kel-lites:

		PRICE:
D-MKL-7	7 D-Cell	$24.95
D-MKL-6	6 D-Cell	$23.95
D-MKL-5	5 D-Cell	$22.95
D-MKL-4	4 D-Cell	$21.95
D-MKL-3	3 D-Cell	$20.95
D-MKL-2	2 D-Cell	$19.95

Enduring Padlocks

Like flashlights, padlocks become a regular purchase. The conventional ferrous ones at sea and alongshore become ever more raunchy, staining the hasps, companionway doors, and hatch covers, finally keeping your key if allowed admission in the first place. Solid or laminated brass ones are available from:

Master Lock Company
Milwaukee, Wisconsin 53210

Left: Master's 16-D solid brass padlock with a case-hardened steel shackle.

Ye Olde Curiositie Shoppe

Either my watch has stopped or this man is dead.
—Groucho (feeling for a pulse)

When one thinks of the kind of production that has to take place for cheap watches to be as cheap as they are, one can be reminded of the stories about how deep in flies or alligators we'd be if all the eggs hatched. We aren't only concerned about how they are able to do it—build watches that actually tell time at these prices—but what happens to them all. Is there an abysmal deep somewhere where the stratified ooze is composed of countless watches? Recent months have brought these to attention:

**The Seven Seas Watch
Nautical Clock Company
P.O. Box 253
Bristol, Conn. 06010**

**Great White Shark Watch
Foreign Exchange Company
P.O. Box 20403
Chicago, Illinois 60620**

Wholesale Near-Kitsch

You walk into a ricky-ticky-tacky boater's shop (oy!) and spread out before you is a quarter-acre of the not-to-be-believed. Look more closely, however, and some of it maybe ain't too bad; not at retail, you understand, but if you could come up with a pitch to get things wholesale—a friend with a shop or letterhead, perhaps—finestkind maybe. We found some interesting stuff at Marspec, wholesale.

**Marspec, Inc.
235 Commercial Street
Box 636
Provincetown, Mass. 02657**

CANDLE SCONCE IN GIMBALS

Old fashioned style.

Very heavy, highly polished, solid brass construction. Sold complete with candle on spring arrangement and frosted chimney. Quality workmanship. Individually boxed.

$11.00 each

An Import

Above: From a Marspec catalog issued in late 1976.
Right: The Ghost Clipper, a 5' kite from Land's End. The kite comes in a kit and is priced at $29.95.

Above: From a Nautical Clock Company brochure. We wanted to show you the Great White Shark Watch, but we're running out of space and you know what it looks like anyway.

Nice kite from:

**Land's End Inc.
P.O. Box 66244
Chicago, Illinois 60666**

109

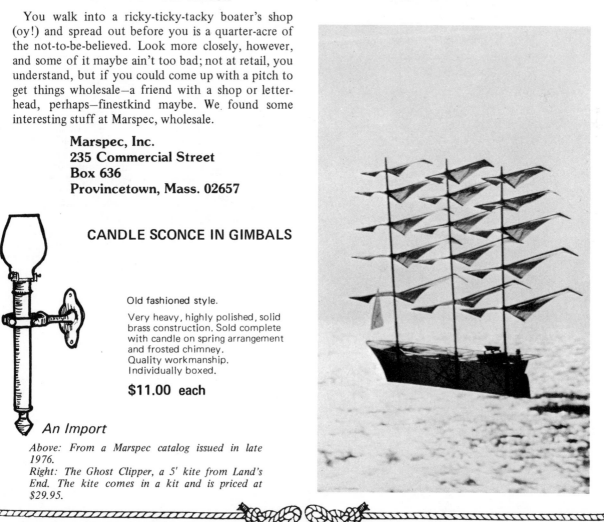

Above: A.G.A. Correa's Logical Log—8½" x 11", 200 pages, rag paper, sail cloth cover, $16.50. Right: St. Elmo's Medal from Management Services Center.

St. Elmo's Fire

How about a 2½-inch-diameter cast-bronze St. Elmo's at $21.95, shipping included? From:

**Management Services Center
P.O. Box 615
392 Boston Post Road
Orange, Conn. 06477**

110

WIB

Women In Boating is a journal published four times a year at $4.00/ year by the Women In Boating Association, membership being $14.00, including the subscription.

**Women In Boating
P.O. Box 40
Williamsville, N.Y. 14221**

Log with Class

A classy logbook, the *Logical Log*, from:

**A.G.A. Correa
Rum Cove
Westport Island, Maine 04578**

Dear Editors:

Well, here's letter #4 from a female (see MC-4, "Woman of the Sea," p. 134, and "Breeches Buoy," p. 137). I think one of the reasons you don't get too many of them is that we don't like being singled out. After all, we're human beings first, females second, and sailors by choice and hard work. And from my experience, those of us who are out there running our boats and doing boat things are at least as capable as the men, except perhaps when it comes to horsing in anchors and furling very large sails. Most of the stuff written about women is so incredibly fatuous that I think we'd rather be ignored and accepted than have such ridiculous attention drawn to us. When people can stop regarding various endeavors and lifestyles as specifically masculine and specifically feminine, we will all have come a long way.

At the risk of sounding peckish and grouchy, a few more comments about women at sea: I'm afraid I do rather resent being picked out as a female who sails. After all, it's perfectly obvious that I'm a female. And it all sounds so much like "see, even cripples can do it," or, "see, so simple even a child can do it." Or, almost anything you want to say that draws attention, not to a person doing a successful job, but to a person who isn't really supposed to be there but manages to get there somehow by overcoming great limitations and handicaps. There are some fields of endeavor in which distinctions of gender are totally irrelevant; competence has nothing to do with sexual distinctions, unless one is going to start discussing the differing abilities of girl children to verbalize well and boy children to "visualize spatially" well, etc., ad nauseam.

Milanne Rehor
Yacht *Hippopotamus*
Coconut Grove, Florida

Tierra del Fuego
by Rae Natalie Prosser de Goodall
Ediciones Shanamaiim
Casilla de Correo 41, Ushuaia
Tierra del Fuego, Argentina
253 pages, illus., biblio., 1975 (2nd ed.),
paperbound, $6

We introduce this book for those romantics among us who find the idea of exploring the Straits of Magellan/Cape Horn area irresistible. Our fascination with Tierra del Fuego goes back a long way—to when we first read of the exploits of Drake, Magellan, Darwin, and Slocum. It was recently whetted by a re-reading of Rockwell Kent's *Voyaging* (out of print but well worth seeking out in a used-book store).

This is a bilingual—Spanish and English—guide to all aspects of the Argentine part of Tierra del Fuego. It was written more as a tourist guide than as a cruising guide, but the background it gives about the island, the directions, the descriptions of official agencies, flora and fauna, sources of services, and the historical data—all of it taken together is of immense value to the vagabond sailor. And you would be suprised how many boats are going that way. The publisher also offers a beautiful geographical map of Tierra del Fuego at $2, and a flora and fauna map at $3; no mention was made of postage, but we suggest that you add an amount for it—your postmaster can give you an estimate.

If you are interested in a history of the voyages of exploration and discovery in the Tierra del Fuego area, covering the earliest times to the 1930s, look up *Cape Horn* by Felix Riesenberg. The book is out of print but can be found in many larger libraries and in used-book stores.

Canal de Beagle

AL ESTE DE USHUAIA

ISLAS BRIDGES. Las islas frente a Ushuaia fueron llamadas islas Bridges por el capitán Martial, de la expedición Romanche, en 1882. Cada isla representa uno de los entonces jóvenes hijos del pastor Thomas Bridges: Despard, Lucas, Willie, Alice y Bertha. Más al sur están las islas Lawrence, Whaits y Cole, también en memoria de los antiguos misioneros.

Los lobos de mar (o de un pelo) llegan a veces a estas islas; pero la mayoría se ve en la ISLA DE LOS LOBOS, más al este, cerca del faro. Es una de las pocas loberías que quedan en la Tierra del Fuego.

El FARO LES ECLAIREURS marca la entrada de la zona de Ushuaia, y es el sitio donde naufragó en 1930 el **Monte Cervantes.**

VIAJES POR LANCHA. Aunque al presente no hay lanchas especiales turísticas, a veces se pueden hacer viajes por lancha a los siguientes lugares:
 -- Isla de los Lobos y otras islas cercanas;
 — Lapataia e isla Redonda;

Beagle Channel

EAST OF USHUAIA

BRIDGES ISLANDS. The islands in front of Ushuaia were named the Bridges Islands by Capt. Martial, of the Romanche Expedition, in 1882. Each island represents one of the then young children of Rev. Thomas Bridges: Despard, Lucas, Willie, Alice and Bertha. Farther south are the Lawrence, Whaits and Cole Islands, also named for early missionaries.

Southern sea lions (locally called *seals*) are found at times on these islands, but it is much easier to see them on ISLA DE LOS LOBOS (Seal Island), farther east near the lighthouse. It is one of the few breeding sites left in Tierra del Fuego.

Faro Islas Eclaireurs   Eclaireurs Lighthouse

Above: From Tierra del Fuego.

Shackleton's Boat Journey, by F.A. Worsley
W.W. Norton, New York
220 pages, illus., 1977, $8.95

Everyone has a candidate for the greatest small-boat voyage of all time. Here's ours. Worsley was the captain of Sir Ernest Shackleton's Antarctic exploration ship *Endurance*. In 1915, the ship became stuck in the ice in the Weddell Sea and nine months later she was crushed and sank. The crew of 28 men took to the boats (2 of them), and, despite cold, gales, monumental seas, cramped conditions, and incredible hardships, made it to Elephant Island and eventually to a whaling station on South Georgia Island. There have been boat journeys of greater length, both in time and distance, but none to equal this one against enormous odds.

Ah, ah, Mr. Aberneathy. Crush that impulse!

Seasteading

Having successfully negotiated their first trial year, the folks at *Wind Vane* have given themselves a go-ahead for another year of publication. *Wind Vane, the Bulletin of Seasteading or Self-Sufficiency Afloat,* is a new magazine by, of, and for the growing number of people who have decided to try living aboard their craft on the world's waters, not in marinas. Food, getting and saving cash, dealing with that breed of shoreside yahoo who instinctively can't stand others who have taken life by the tiller, maintenance, and other subjects are covered regularly. This is a nice little journal that shows promise, and we wish them the best of luck.

Wind Vane
241 West 35th Street
National City, Calif. 92050
$5/yr.

Right: From Ocean Wanderers.
Cartoon at top by Darrell McClure.

***Ocean Wanderers (Migratory Birds of the World),* by R.M. Lockley**
Stackpole Books, Harrisburg, Penn., 1973
$15.00

Penguins, albatrosses, fulmars, shearwaters and petrels, tropic and frigate birds, gannets and boobies, skuas, gulls, terns, auks and phalaropes; their origins, navigation, feeding, and breeding in large and well-illustrated book.

112

Marine Loos

Blakes of Gosport, England, have been in the marine loo business longer than most others except the man who first took a padsaw to the poop rail of a sailing ship. The Blake Baby is almost an institution in British yachts, but the range now includes the Eclipse S, for larger craft with more pretentious bathrooms (fatter owners?); the Victory type, recommended for larger yachts or where the installation is considerably below the waterline; and the Baby Minor, with width restricted and where space is at a premium (your boat and mine). These come with oval or round pans (some dark subtlety here), and prices range from a commercial-finish Baby, round pan at £123.43, to the De Luxe Finish 3 colored pan, chrome-plated fittings at £208.98. Good values for items that are notably long lasting in service.

**Blake and Sons (Gosport) Limited
P.O. Box 15, Sunbeam Works
Gosport, Hampshire
England**

—John Leather

Marine Sciences

Our famous, most popular BABY marine toilet

IDEAL FOR SMALL TO MEDIUM SIZE YACHTS

Without a doubt, our most popular model. Suitable for small production craft where a long and reliable life is essential.
SPECIFICATION All metal parts: high quality non-ferrous. Pan: vitreous china. Valves: neoprene & natural rubber Seat and Cover: heavyweight Celmac plastic. Weight: approx. 45 lbs (20 kilos). Available in all finishes (see back page). Inlet for ¾" (19 mm) discharge for 1½" (38 mm) bore pipe. Supplied with pumps in the right, left or bow positions. **Seacocks:** use our "Y" or Popular Seacocks (see back page).

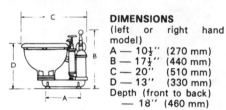

DIMENSIONS
(left or right hand model)
A — 10½" (270 mm)
B — 17½" (440 mm)
C — 20" (510 mm)
D — 13" (330 mm)
Depth (front to back)
— 18" (460 mm)

Above: From a Blake and Sons catalog.

113

Appropriate and heady vituperation from a qualified and experienced oceanographer-marine biologist:

Dear Editors:

It is my impression that the Marine Sciences section of *Volume 4* is directed to the interested layman. This would encompass not only individuals seeking to enhance their own understanding of the marine environment but also secondary school teachers or members of environmental groups wishing to establish or improve educational projects. In most of these situations, financial resources would be very limited so that funds would have to be allocated prudently. Money wasted on poor equipment could thus ensure the mediocrity of an entire program.

My major criticism is directed at your recommendations of scientific instruments. I've handled most types of oceanographic gear at sea and also seen the "junk tools" of oceanography at work when guest groups were invited aboard the research vessel YP-654 at the Naval Academy. The LaMotte kit depicted on page 171 and described by you as "A-1" equipment for the serious investigator simply emphasizes your inexperience as an oceanographer. In my opinion, this gear is not worth the shipping cost. I should add that the LaMotte equipment is not unusual but only typical of a whole family of "low-priced" gear sold by a variety of companies. Also, it should be noted that my opinion *does not apply to the LaMotte chemical kits.*

It would have been more in keeping with the philosophy of the *Mariner's Catalog* to advocate good oceanographic gear (which is expensive) or to offer suggestions for improvising equipment. Sir John Murray, when urging a young Henry Bigelow to investigate the Gulf of Maine, suggested he "make some tow nets out of your wife's old bobinet window curtains." I've had midshipmen build special-purpose plankton nets from nylon stockings rather than use the very expensive meter-nets aboard YP-654. The homemade nets worked effectively, the students

(Continued on next page)

(Continued from preceding page)

learned about net design and had fun collecting the stockings.

I will illustrate my point by considering the gear you recommend on page 171. Rather than expending limited funds on junk, the researcher or teacher would do much better to improvise. The homemade equipment would be superior, the $150 could be put to better use, and the investigators would understand their scientific capabilities.

Improvising a sounding lead and calibrating a nylon line is not difficult. A thermometer in a small water bucket would prove much more effective than the one shown. A plankton net constructed from a stocking will provide fine qualitative samples. The "bottom dredge" illustrated is a grab, and grabs of that size and weight simply are not effective under most conditions. A weighted bucket would prove to be a superior benthic sampler in most instances. The water sampler is the most difficult item to produce, but with a couple of hours of effort with plastic tubing, appropriate stoppers, and shock cord or surgical tubing, even an amateur could achieve success. The final result is homemade equipment equal to and often superior to the LaMotte kit. The $150 saved can be applied to books, slides, etc., or put toward a single piece of real oceanographic equipment required for further studies.

The approach I have described seems consistent with the philosophy you have advocated for gradually acquiring quality hand tools. This commonsense attitude applies to all tools, whether for wordworking or science.

Your choice of ecology textbooks could be debated, but certainly a range of appropriate texts could have been presented for readers of different levels. It would also seem particularly important to your readers to include a selection of regional and/or topical field guides. You have not included (except in the Science extract) any companies manufacturing real oceanographic gear, yet you waste valuable space with an illustration of the Alpine Model 200, which has its uses but probably has little potential application for your average reader. Alpine is a fine company and apparently they were nice to you on the phone, but there are many other sources of information and assistance available and more appropriate for your readers. On page 174 you cite sources for purchasing fossils, yet you suggest not a single book to aid in identifying fossils which the reader might discover. This is rather ironic, considering that the essay on that page urges the reader to get into the field and observe his environment.

James F. Clark
Chestnut Hill, Mass.

Above: Section from Sable Island Graveyard of the Atlantic.

Marine Art

If you like nautical graphics, things to hang on your wall, few could raise more eyebrows, interest, pathos, and conversation than *Sable Island Graveyard of the Atlantic* (known wrecks since *1800*AD). 21 by 36 inches, this dropped-out-white line art on deep navy blue chart was made by the lighthouse keeper on Sable Island in the 1930s and has now been updated to include more than 300 wrecks. It is published and distributed by:

> **The Book Room Ltd.**
> **1664-1666 Granville Street**
> **Halifax, N.S.**
> **Canada**
> **$4.25 each, including postage**

Ring's End Landing, Darien, 1900, *by John Stobart. Carried both by Maritime Heritage Prints and Sportsman's Edge.*

Two marine art catalogs (Sportsman's Edge includes sporting and wildlife art as well) that are in themselves worth the purchase price because of the quality of their material and reproduction are:

Maritime Heritage Prints, by John Stobart
Suite 502
1055 Thomas Jefferson St. N.W.
Washington, D.C. 20007
$5 (brochure about catalog is free)

and

Sportsman's Edge, Ltd.
136 East 74th Street
New York, N.Y. 10021
$10

For those interested, there's a round-up of present-day marine artists in the Winter 1977 issue of *Sea History* magazine. The article contains color and black-and-white reproductions of the artists discussed, who include among others: C.G. Evers, George Campbell, Frank Braynard, Kipp Soldwedel, John Stobart, and Oswald Brett. We all have favorites who were not included, but it's a nice start, anyway.

Sea History
National Maritime Historical Society
2 Fulton Street
Brooklyn, N.Y. 11201
Annual subscription is $10; single issue $1.50

115

Houseboat waiting out the tide on a beach in Norfolk, England. (John Topham Picture Library).

Above: Captain Ahab, from The Prints of Rockwell Kent.

The Illustrations of Rockwell Kent
by Fridolph Johnson and John F.H. Gorton
Dover Publications, N.Y.
130 pages, paperbound, 1976, $3.50

We freely admit to being fans of Rockwell Kent's work. Those who are with us will appreciate this book, especially in light of the last one on Kent we recommended in *Volume 4* of the *Mariner's Catalog* (*The Prints of Rockwell Kent*, by Dan Burne Jones, University of Chicago Press)—it cost $32.50, though we don't mean that it's not a good book or that it's not worth the high price. But this volume covers some of the same ground and includes many great marine illustrations from such books as *N by E, Voyaging, Moby Dick, A Treasury of Sea Stories*, and *Rockwell Kent's Greenland Journal*. There are in all 231 illustrations (perhaps one-quarter marine-oriented) that appeared in books, magazines, and advertising art. We might add, too, that the introduction—the only real text in this essentially picture book—is a well-worth-reading biography of the artist.

We've said it before and we'll say it again—Dover Publications puts out some of the best books at the best prices you'll ever see. Their list is wide-ranging and includes a series of well-nigh-indispensable craft books. Send for their catalog listing hundreds of titles:

Dover Publications
180 Varick St.
New York, N.Y. 10014

More Freighter Travel

We thought we had discovered all the guidebooks on freighter travel last year (see MC-4, page 89). Not so. We missed:

Ford's Freighter Travel Guide
Semi-annual (March and September)
from
Ford's
Box 505, 22859 Hatteras St.
Woodland Hills, California 91364
Subscription is $8.50 per year

Each issue has articles and tips for travelers, and listings of travel agents who handle freighter trips, passenger-carrying freighter lines, foreign government tourist offices, ports of call, and more. Information is specific and includes up-to-date rates.

Below: Boxed quote from Ford's Freighter Travel Guide. *The Mediterranean cruises described are on Hellenic Lines Ltd ships.*

116

From New York, sailings twice monthly on modern Greek freighters carrying up to 12 passengers. Outside double cabins with private facilities. There is a dining room and social room for passengers only. Standard ports of call: **Piraeus, Salonica, Beirut, and Constanza,** returning to **New Orleans, Houston and New York.** Vessels remain at each port of call 2 to 3 days. Passengers use the vessel as their hotel while in port. Cruise averages 65 to 75 days. Passengers over 65 years of age must submit doctor's certificate.

Cruise Fares: $1600 per passenger (Sept. 1 to April 30); $1800 (May 1 to Aug. 31). One-way fares on request. Passengers may also embark at **New Orleans or Houston.**

British Canal Boat Rentals

Thinking about renting a canal boat in Britain but intimidated by transatlantic paperwork? Wallace Venable of Bargain Boating has just the service for you:

Bargain Boating
Boat and Yacht Charter Agents
Route 1, Box 229A
Morgantown, W. Virginia 26505
(free brochure on request)

Dear Editors:

Your request for information on British canal cruising got us to reminiscing, which in turn led to thoughts of going back. The end result was that we spent a week on the Norfolk Broads in May on a wooden, gaff-rigged sloop, and then went to Scotland, where we spent the first week of June sailing a heavy 25-foot fiberglass cruiser between the Highlands and Islands.

I think I mentioned in my last letter that I felt someone should make it easier to hire boats in Britain. We are going just that. While over there I visited with Blakes (Norfolk Broads Holidays) Limited and with Arden Yachts. Both expressed interest in increasing American business. Bargain Boating is the outcome of my talks.

We can supply boats on the English and Scottish canals, the Norfolk Broads, Thames River, River Shannon in Ireland, French canals, and the West Coast of Scotland. It would be very helpful if inquirers mentioned the waterways, boat size/type, and dates of trip in which they are most interested.

Wallace Venable
Bargain Boating

A Canal and Waterways Armchair Book
by John Gagg
David & Charles, North Pomfret, Vt.
144 pages, illus., 1975, $10.95

A sequel to *The Canalers Bedside Book*, which I haven't seen, but would like to, this book makes a pleasant digression from weightier reading matter. I left it lying around the house, and, while waiting for the glue to dry during a building project, or when resting my eyes between chapters of *Shoreline Erosion and Landslides in the Great Lakes*, I'd read a section. John Gagg roams from subject to subject, randomly, without a thesis, without polemics—bollards, bottled gas, Anton's Gowt, canal cowboys, hand-spikes, Pudding Green, shear-pins, tidal locks, tractors, waterfalls. An Englishman, Gagg is talking about British canals.

Good fun.

Legging

This curious activity is regarded by most people as a thing of the past, which disappeared when canal boats were motorised. But in one place at least it still goes on, the newly-reopened Dudley tunnel (qv).

Legging was the method used to propel boats through tunnels which had no towpath for a horse. He went off over the top, and leggers lay on boards on the boat and walked along the tunnel sides. In narrow tunnels the boards could lie across the boat, but when a narrow boat went through a broad tunnel such as those on the Grand Union, the legging-boards had to be extended outwards from the boat sides so that the leggers' feet could reach the tunnel walls. This must have been not only a strenuous but also precarious occupation, since a fall into the water in a pitch-black tunnel would make rescue very difficult.

Nowadays occasional enthusiasts try legging for fun (there was once a 'sponsored leg' through Blisworth tunnel for charity), and occasionally a breakdown in a tunnel may lead to some unexpected legging and poling on the roof. But the legging necessary in Dudley tunnel is due to the fact that boats are not allowed to use their engines because of ventilation problems.

Boxed quote on left and sketch at top from A Canal and Waterways Armchair Book.

Dear Editors:

In the *Mariner's Catalog, Volume 2*, there was a little insert about Cairns, Australia, and how there should be quite a few boats there left in storage, etc., by people who had become discouraged and had taken the easy way home. Well, I immediately wrote to the harbormaster there and finally a letter came from him. But no boats were there, never had any, except some old steel fish boats that couldn't be taken out of the country. The man who wrote to me was real nice. But I had the wind all out of my expectant sails!! Just thought you'd like to know—not a complaint, just a little observation.

**Jim Portwood
Kenai, Alaska**

Parable Beach—A Primer in Coastal Zone Economics
by J.W. Devanney, G. Ashe, B. Parkhurst
The MIT Press, Cambridge, Mass., 1976

Anyone currently or prospectively involved in coastal development for any reason, from any point of view, *ought* to read this book. Planners, government officials, bankers, investors, and their kin and direct enemies *must* read it.

The book takes a parable town on a parable coast (the terrain looks a lot like parts of the Middle Atlantic seaboard), describes the town and its people thoroughly, outlines a proposed complex of development (with options), and then dives into the economic subsystems and the consequences of all the options of all the operants. It is not a text, not a manual, not an eco-activist's trouble-shooting guide, not an investor's bible. There are no dos and don'ts, only whats, hows, and whys. It is the anatomy, physiology, and internal medicine of the coastal body politic.

Boxed quote below from Parable Beach.

```
The Parable Beach Boatowners' Account
Banks decided, in his first cut at the problem, to ignore
any changes in the real income of the Parable Beach residents
who would make use of the Paragon Park marina.  He now de-
cides to go back and actually work out this account.  As we
shall see, this analysis will allow us to illustrate several
interesting points.
     The proposed marina will handle 500 boats.  At present,
dock space in the Parable Beach area is quite limited--no
more than fifty boats.  As a result, the available dock space
commands premium rates:  twenty dollars per boat-foot for
the summer six months.  Only ten Parablites keep their boats
on this expensive space.  Several hundred Parablites own
boats, almost all of which are presently on moorings for
which they pay fifty dollars per season to the town harbor-
master.
     The developers estimate that in order to fill the marina,
the rate will have to drop to ten dollars per boat-foot, at
which point they can still make a handsome profit.  Banks
estimates that at ten dollars per foot, 100 Parablites,
whose boats average thirty feet in length, will abandon
their moorings and take space at the marina, paying $30,000
a year for the privilege.  The question, then, is:  does
this outlay represent a change in Parable Beach real income?
     Whenever a significant change in either the price or
quantity of a good is implied by one of the alternatives
under analysis, it's a good idea to sketch the demand curve
for that good or service.
```

Marine Policy
**IPC Business Limited
205 East 42nd St.
New York, N.Y. 10017
$78/yr. (four issues)**

An intelligent publication that looks in depth at maritime issues. Aimed at professionals in business and government. All important problems are covered clearly, replacing clichés with facts and fragile arguments with sound ones.

Journal of a Voyage to Nowhere
by Charles Fenn
W.W. Norton, N.Y., 1971
$5.95

Ostensibly a book about a writer who is wrecked off the southwest coast of India and marooned for months on a small atoll, the story in fact is about a man's reflections on life's important issues: birth, copulation, and death; loneliness; and how we imagine and bungle our respective ways through this odd and wondrous experience.

Boxed quote from Journal of a Voyage to Nowhere; *illustration at right from* Secrets of the Deep.

Secrets of the Deep
by Stephen Spotte (drawings by Gordy Allen)
Charles Scribner's Sons, N.Y., 1976
$7.95

A silly title for an otherwise interesting book on selected biological topics; schooling, protective mechanisms, relationships of mutual dependence, toxins, chemical and luminescent phenomena, and so on, simply described with good examples. The drawings are very good.

Clearly, no man can be happy if he suffers from anxiety. And one way to avoid anxiety is to retain one's independence. To my way of thinking, a basic rule is not to work for other people; or at least to work for them as little as possible. This has nothing to do with working in co-operation *with* other people; on the contrary, such co-operation is a most desirable attribute of higher development. A man who has not learned how to co-operate with his fellows can hardly have achieved harmony within himself. I am speaking essentially of working *for* other people: that paid employment which nine out of ten of us are engaged in, and which makes us subject to the whims of others; whims that necessarily endanger our harmony. It is true that a completely harmonious man would be harmonious even in a concentration camp. But such perfection is denied the majority. And the safest thing is not to expose ourselves to

> The insolence of office, and the spurns
> That patient merit of the unworthy takes . . .

Not that our employers are actually insolent or unworthy, while we ourselves are to be accredited with 'patient merit'. In our employers' place we should act as they do. As in so many instances, the individual is the prey of the system.

Spike mackerel schooling

119

"Do you ever sometimes kinda wish we hadn't started?"

FOR THE BRIDGE AND QUARTERDECK

Not to serve two masters is as impossible as it is moral. No doubt some fanatics will go to their rich reward, but they will leave behind some exhausted friends and will have missed that wonderful tilt on the path to adulthood, the achievement of a balanced view.

A look at the bridge of some power cruisers would have one think that they went somewhere on occasion: wintertime scientific expeditions to the Antarctic, and so forth (yawn). On the other hand, watching the effect that small radar units, RT, RDF, CB, Loran, fathometers, and recorders have had on

the lives of fishermen and their families is genuinely impressive. One wants one's friends who work five hours out to have them, and the best that they can afford, too.

A compass, a chronometer, a portable radio, a log, a leadline, and a chart are aboard, and their use understood and practiced (add sextant and tables for outside—oh, yeah, a pencil and straightedge). As the logician says, these are both *necessary* and *sufficient*. Beyond these we are grappling for a balanced view, and we are each alone at it.

Electronics for All

Kelvin Hughes outfits with electronics everything that floats. Their many catalogs bristle with freighters, big trawlers, and supertankers. Indeed, they have situation-display packages that cost much more than your wildest dreamboat. But they also have classy tough stuff that you may wish to consider, like a repeating towed log, suitable for larger powercraft, or an exquisite quartz chronometer. It will help to be specific when writing them.

Kelvin Hughes
New North Road
Hainault, Ilford
Essex 1G6 2UR
England

Left: The Mercer quartz crystal chronometer with a mean rate of 0.01 second. From the Kelvin Hughes catalog.

Make Your Own

More attuned to the *Mariner's Catalog*'s general purposes, the General Time Corporation offers an extremely inexpensive quartz movement suitable for making your own ship's chronometer, the model GT-600 for $16.50. This movement is rated at plus or minus 1/2 second per day! There are many General Time Service centers around the country. For the closest one, write:

General Time Corp.
3500 North Greenfield Rd.
P.O. Box 4067
Mesa, Arizona 85201

Packaged Navigation

Mason Marine of Great Britain has put together an interesting "Navigator Kit" composed of a practical, inexpensive sextant (not meant to be compared with the best instruments) with an azimuth attachment and a unique grid calculator that would seem to take the numbers fear out of the aesthete who would go aroving. Captain Namo's Navigator, from:

Mason Marine, Ltd.
Britannic Buildings
Foregate Street
Worcester WR1 1EE
England

Right: General Time's GT-600.
Boxed quote below from a Mason catalog. Captain Namo's Navigator sells for £29, plus postage and packaging; with a Seafarer "Special" Azimuth Sextant, price is £59 plus p & p.

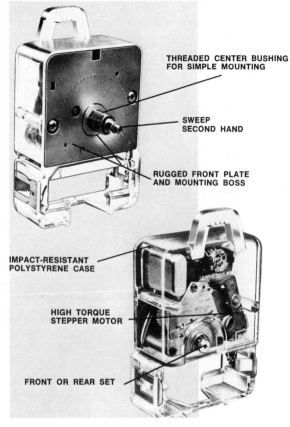

THREADED CENTER BUSHING FOR SIMPLE MOUNTING

SWEEP SECOND HAND

RUGGED FRONT PLATE AND MOUNTING BOSS

IMPACT-RESISTANT POLYSTYRENE CASE

HIGH TORQUE STEPPER MOTOR

FRONT OR REAR SET

The GT-600 combines advanced solid-state integrated circuit electronics with the latest in quartz crystal movements. 4,194,304 oscillations per second produce a precise input to a unique powerful stepper motor. Pulsing twice per second, this motor drives the clock hands with unexcelled reliability and an accuracy of plus or minus one half second per day.

CAPTAIN NAMO'S NAVIGATOR
CODE NAME 'NAMO'

Captain Namo's Navigator is a precision grid calculator approximately 39.6 cm. in dia. The Calculator consists of a transparent dial marked with a cursor rotating over a precision grid. A moveable marker is used by the Navigator at the various points or intersections and then turned according to the related problem, the answer being read directly off the grid from the cursor and marker point.

A detailed, simple to use, Instructional Manual on the complete System is provided with the Navigator which includes sets of working examples enabling you to acquire the necessary knowledge in the comfort of your home.

Captain Namo's Navigator measures approximately 50 cm square, is laminated, framed on an attractive wooden base to withstand continuous use and comes complete with detailed Instruction Manual, Sights Data Pad and Marker enclosed in a Document Case, the whole contained in a Waterproof Plastic Protective Case.

The Navigating Device forms a unique system of Navigation allowing the user to quickly and accurately obtain, without the knowledge or use of trigonometry, a fix or position, thus enabling him to find, maintain and correct his position and course.

The system is based upon the reduction of spherical trigonometry problems by means of an ingenious, yet simple to operate, grid calculator or sights reduction calculator.

Once the system has been learned it can be applied to many of the requirements of the ocean-going seafarer.

The Navigator is used primarily to determine the following:

1. Latitude and Longitude (including ex-Meridians).
2. Azimuth, Altitude and Amplitudes.
3. Hour Angle and Declination.
4. Identification of Stars.
5. Great Circle Sailing (Courses and Distances).

The keen Navigator will find that with further study and application other related celestial problems may also be solved. The user should be able to provide the following basic data requirements:

1. Altitude (by Sextant).
2. Azimuth (Azimuth Sextant, Compass Bearing or Calculated Azimuth).
3. Declination (from a Nautical Almanac).
4. G.H.A. (from a Nautical Almanac).
5. G.M.T. (accurately obtained from watch or chronometer).

Hip-Pocket Magic

But grids notwithstanding, the computer age is upon us; in fact, is *us*. As you so well know, we can take or leave the modern world. But if you take our little calculator, we'll blow your head off.

Two pocket calculators with powerful marine-related programming have appeared: the Tamaya-made "Astro-Navigator" distributed by Nautech, and the SR-52 by Texas Instruments, the word "powerful" for which is an understatement.

Nautech
445 N. Sacramento Blvd.
Chicago, Illinois 60612

Texas Instruments, Inc.
Special Systems Dept.
P.O. Box 1210
Richardson, Texas 75080

Imagine you are sailing from Norfolk, Virginia to Bishop Rock, England when you receive word of a dangerous storm:

The storm is approaching in a direction of 010° (true) at a speed of 23 knots. Plotting the coordinates of your vessel and the storm you determine that it is 385 miles from you at a true bearing of 150°. You are capable of making 13 knots through the water. What course will provide for maximum storm avoidance? How long will it take the storm to reach the point closest to your boat? How far away will it be at that point?

You pick up your SR-52 and with a few keystrokes enter the speed of your boat, the speed and course of the storm's advance, and the initial true bearing and distance to the storm from your boat. Now push the A' key: The SR-52 automatically gives you 314.4° as optimum course to steer. Push the B' key: The storm will be at its closest point in 5.2703 hours. Push the C' key: The storm center will be 370.8 miles from your boat at its closest point.

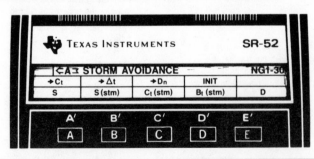

122

Note on Electronic Calculators

The worry (there always has to be one) is greater than that for the use of calculators in schools. If you can't pencil and paper it and the unit is lost, broken, or the batteries go, *bon voyage.*

—Eds.

Boxed quote above: From a Texas Instruments flyer. The SR-52 has a library of 40 prerecorded program cards covering a wide variety of problems. Price as of early 1977 is $345.
Top of page: Nautech's NC-2 Navigation Calculator, with 9 internal navigation programs. Early 1977 price is $199.95.

Build-Your-Own Electronics

Most everyone knows about Heathkit, but their list of offerings grows so continuously and so fast that being reminded about them doesn't hurt. Marine-related kits include depth sounders, foghorn-hailers, vapor detectors, RDFs, weather stations, RC model control devices, and digital-readout everythings. Distributors are nationwide, so check the Yellow Pages and ask your nearest one for a current catalog. The equipment is very good, you save bucks by building yourself, and you get the luxury of not being intimidated by black boxes.

**Heathkit
Schlumberger Products Corp.
P.O. Box 167
St. Joseph, Missouri 49085**

Black Boxes

Speaking of black boxes, the National Weather Service will soon be finished with their early warning system and, for between $25 and $70, you can purchase a black box that will automatically give you warning of severe weather headed for your area. Meanwhile, by triggering it yourself, you can get an updated weather report for all stations in your region, including all marine-related data. One source of five models is:

**Weatheralert
639 South Dearborn
Chicago, Ill. 60605**

Boxed specs and binocular above are from the Charles Frank binocular catalog.

A magnificent binocular with an outstanding light passing capacity which makes it ideal for use under poorest light conditions. The rubber encased body is designed to protect the binocular against shock and impact and adverse weather conditions. The roof prism system, which was first adopted by Hensoldt and latterly by Zeiss and Leitz, enables the binocular to be made flatter and slimmer whilst the height remains unchanged. As it is rubber protected, a carrying case is not provided.

Specification:

Magnification: 8×.   Diameter of Object Glass: 56 mm.   Exit Pupil. 7 mm.   Field of View: 6·5°   Weight: 46 ozs.   Height: 9½″ Width: 6″   Price...£58·50.

Instruments

We've found an exciting source of high-quality instruments in Charles Frank, Ltd. of Glasgow. They are a supplier for the needs of surveyors, cartographers, and the like, but we're especially interested in their optics. They also have good prices on compasses and clocks, in spite of Sterling's chronic instability.

**Charles Frank, Ltd.
144 Ingram Street
Glasgow G1 1EH
Scotland**

123

Above: The Maximum tell-tale, which has printing on both sides of the card, allowing it to double as a regular compass. 1976 price was $98.
Below: A selection of compasses and binnacles from Sestrel.

Tell-Tale

When going through the recent marine press, probably you, too, have seen that fellow tucked up under the carlings asleep, a tell-tale overhead. Maximum makes some most interesting instruments, their tell-tale polyaxial compass most particularly.

Maximum, Inc.
42 South Avenue
Natick, Mass. 01760

A Classy Outfit

If we were to fit out a traditionally styled cruising boat today, it is very likely that Sestrel would get an order from us. We like their old-style binnacles and for-truly tell-tales.

Home Office

Henry Browne & Son, Ltd.
Sestrel House
Loxford Road
Barking, Essex 1G11 8PE
England

U.S. importer

Fleet Marine Supply
1820 N.E. 146th Street
N. Miami, Florida 33181

Hold It

Of the several small hand-bearing compasses available, the "Mini-Compass" by Offshore Instruments of England seems to us to be the most practical. It's tough, small, works well, and people who own them like them.

Offshore Instruments, Ltd.
41 Birmingham Road
Cowes, Isle of Wight
England

	89544	88865	88866	88882 88883 88884	90583

CROUCH Box Compass In polished hardwood box with slide lid. For commercial fishing craft, and small yachts. Card as Langton below

Cat. No.	Card dia.	Bowl dia.	Box dimensions	Weight
89544	4 in	5 in	7¾ x 7¾ x 5⅛ in	5¾ lb
	101 mm	127 mm	197 x 197 x 130 mm	2·607 kg
88865	5 in	6 in	8½ x 8½ x 5½ in	9¾ lb
	127 mm	152 mm	216 x 216 x 139 mm	4·421 kg
88866	6 in	7 in	9⅞ x 9⅞ x 5½ in	14¾ lb
	152 mm	177 mm	251 x 251 x 139 mm	6·689 kg

LANGTON Binnacle With removable top to facilitate the taking of bearings.

Cat. No.	Card dia.	Bowl dia.	Flange dia.	Weight
88882	4 in 101 mm	5 in 127 mm	8¾ in 222 mm	9¼ lb 4·195 kg
88883	5 in 127 mm	6 in 152 mm	10 in 254 mm	12½ lb 5·669 kg
88884	6 in 152 mm	7 in 177 mm	11½ in 292 mm	16 lb 7·257 kg

Card Style: 0-360° and ¼ points.
Lighting: Combined oil and electric lamp.
Bowl liquid filled, brass construction.
Finish Polished Brass.
Ring Sights (Details on application)

LIFEBOAT Binnacle Compass Meets D.T.I. requirements for Lifeboats.

Cat. No.	Bowl dia.	Card dia.	Flange dia.	Height	Weight
90583	5 in	4 in	8¾ in	8 in	7 lb
	127 mm	101 mm	222 mm	203 mm	3·175 kg

Card Style: ½ points notation.
Approved "BRYTLIT" illumination. No oil lamp housing.

LIFEBOAT Binnacle Compass Meets marine specifications of most foreign Govts.

Cat. No.	Bowl dia.	Card dia.	Flange dia.	Height	Weight
88880	5 in	4 in	8¾ in	8 in	7 lb
	127 mm	101 mm	222 mm	203 mm	3·175 kg
89742	6 in	5 in	10¾ in	8½ in	11 lb
	152 mm	127 mm	273 mm	215 mm	4·989 kg

With fixed oil lamp. Card Style 0-360° and ¼ points.
Not illustrated   Finish Grey – with Polished Brass finish add 'BR' to Cat. No.

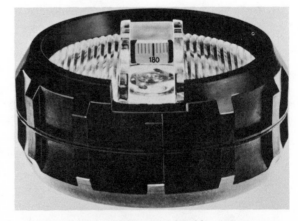

Above: Offshore Instruments' hand-bearing compsss. Includes an infinity prism to avoid parallax, 10x magnification, and beta illumination.

R/T

There is now a radiotelephone available for small craft that are without power or that have too little of it to support broadcasting electronics. No doubt the now-ubiquitous CB is considered adequate for most recreational communications on the water. But, with a radiotelephone, the same wattage can put you in touch with any place without having to battle your way through the "how-am-I-coming-throughers?" Marine Master-1 by General Aviation Electronics.

General Aviation Electronics, Inc.
4141 Kingman Drive
Indianapolis, Indiana 46226

Tell It to Me

There is something primeval about gauges. My boy had a boxful of them before he could talk, and it is no accident that the Six Million Dollar Man and the Bionic Woman wrest from us the devotions of our *Kinder*. (Seas are washing over the deck. The topmast has gone over the side. The boats are stove. The jumbo's blown. And even the coffee's boiling over. See here, the gauges say so. . . .)

Good gauges telling lots of stuff, from Telcor.

Telcor Instruments, Inc.
17785 Sky Park Circle
Irvine, California 92714

Right: The Master Mariner-1, from a General Aviation Electronics catalog.
Below: A sample of the hundreds of gauges and sensors featured in the Telcor catalog.

Marine Master-1

Here's a perfect radiotelephone for sailboats or other small craft that have only minimal or standby electrical battery power. The Marine Master-1 is completely self-contained, self-powered hand-held with 6 full channel capacity. 2.5 watts can be reduced to 1 watt as required by law. The MM-1 can be used with outside or mast-mount antenna, although low profile antenna is included.

125

SERIES 150 EXHAUST TEMPERATURE SYSTEMS

For single or twin gasoline or diesel engines. Operates on 12 or 32 vdc. System comes complete for installation with sensors, 20' thermocouple cables, electronic module and meter. Two meter versions are available. (A) Individual 3" Meter for single or twin engine installations, and (B) Combination 3" Meter with port and starboard meter movements in a single housing for twin engine installations. Repeater stations can be added to all systems. In twin engine installations, Combination 3" Repeaters can be added to a system with Individual 3" Meters and vise versa.

Individual 3" and Combination 3" Meters

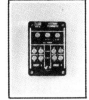

Electronic Module

Adjustable Depth Sensor

SERIES 150 EXHAUST TEMPERATURE

Single Engine with Individual 3" Meter

Model 151	Pyrometer	400-1200°F	$165.00
Model 152	Pyrometer	700-1500°F	165.00
Model 153	Pyrometer	0-1500°F	165.00

Twin Engine – Two Systems with (1) Combination 3" Meter

Model 151C	Pyrometer	400-1200/400-1200°F	285.00
Model 152C	Pyrometer	700-1500/700-1500°F	285.00
Model 153C	Pyrometer	0-1500/0-1500°F	285.00

The Ghost in the Machine

. . . looked at two of the better-known self-steering gears, and then the latest electronic one. The primary conclusion is that the price ratio of *mechanical* versus *electronic* cybernetics is 1:10.

QME (Quantock Marine Enterprises)
Import Marine Sales (U.S. agents)
P.O. Box 1060
Garden Grove, California 92640

Morriss Marine
Saltmarsh Lane
Hayling Island, Hants
England

Windtrack is a steering system that electronically integrates directional commands with respect to both wind bearing and selected compass courses. The system diagrammed is in the $4,000 range.

Safe Flight Instrument Corp.
P.O. Box 550
White Plains, N.Y. 10602

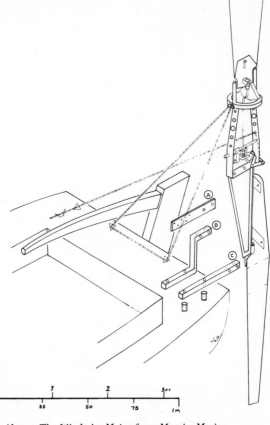

The Q.M.E. Wind Vane is efficient on all points of sailing — it tends however to be more workmanlike before the wind, this is why so many Ocean passages which are mostly down wind use our system. In fact we have had people take off more expensive vanes to put ours on to cross trade winds.

The design of the gear makes it virtually indestructible, and its life span is indefinite as working nylon parts are replaced for a matter of shillings with using the world wide available Holt Allen range.

Wind spills from vane when pushed over at a certain angle, so no strain is on gear at this point. The gear has in fact been used in mid Atlantic gales and still been in control of the boat.

Above: The Windtrim Major from Morriss Marine.
Left: A few words from QME on their mechanical wind-vane kit.
Below: Wind-Track diagram from a Safe Flight instruments catalog.

126

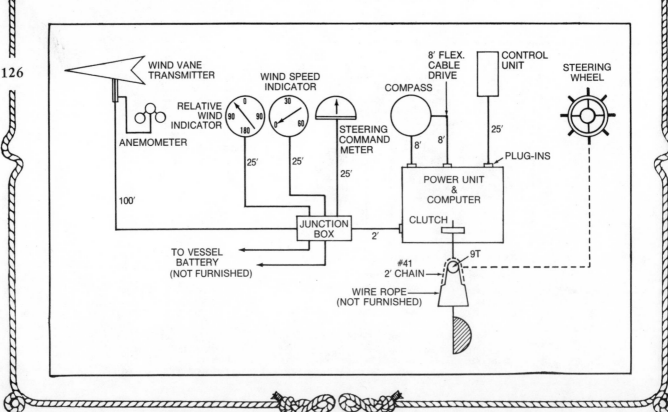

Dear Editors:

For the next *Mariner's Catalog,* please insert "air-push" air-powered windshield wipers from Sprague Devices, Inc., 500 Huron St., Michigan City, Indiana 46360. All-bronze for first class (or all-plastic for economy), no electrics, power enough to swing a street broom, pressure washers available with nozzles that mount on the arms with the blade, pantograph arms available for maximum coverage. Super quality, don't require a hole in the glass, and quite economical compared to a Kent clearview screen.

Space Age Electronics, Spalding Hall, Victoria Rd., London, England, makes very economical depth-sounders. 160 fathom, L.E.D. flasher in nonmetallic case for less than $100.00. Controls O-ringed watertight, very good, very realiable. One-year exposure on open bridge in tropics and never a problem, salt, rain, and all. Visible in sunlight, too.

W.M. Bertolet II
St. Thomas, Virgin Islands

Instant Wind Forecasting, by Alan Watts
Dodd, Mead, New York
119 pages, illus., 1975, $7.95

This is a companion volume to *Instant Weather Forecasting* by the same author, which we reviewed in the first *Mariner's Catalog.* The emphasis here is on predicting wind conditions from the tactical rather than the strategical point of view. In other words, the author is talking about short-term wind. Watts trains you to look at your surroundings—sea, clouds, shore, trees, obstructions, etc.—and use them as data to predict changes in the wind. For the sailor, being able to predict the weather accurately is important; to predict the wind is essential.

Below: Quote from Instant Wind Forecasting.

Warm—perhaps Thundery Days

Main recognition points: Beçause temperate latitude sea temperature cannot be excessive, a hot or warm airstream must have an origin in the sub-tropics. Thus expect layers of cloud together with sunshine, poor visibility or sea fog. Thunderstorms formed over a land mass can move over the sea, but few storms originate over the water. Expect skies like (71) or (103).

Typical morning situation 0800–1000 LST	Ways of recognizing change	Wind changes to expect
Warm and humid. Poor visibility and often fog on coasts if not at sea. Wind from a warm quarter (usually a southern quadrant) which is typically moderate or less. Deck heads and deck hands may sweat	Signs of change are wrought in higher clouds. Clouds of the high or medium levels, (103) or (71) are examples, must move from hot land mass and obey the rule that they come from left hand of the surface wind direction, e.g. East coast of US: medium level clouds from W over warm southerly. English Channel: medium level clouds from S over warm easterly. Such orientations breed thunder. Be suspicious of backing and increasing wind in sultry conditions (Right hand of surface wind in Southern Hemisphere)	If it remains sunny, or if there are sunny periods over the land, allow for a sluggish sea breeze (Inshore and Coastwise but perhaps not the latter) that may not start until afternoon. If thundery-type cloud thickens then surface wind will usually increase and perhaps back a little. When thunder heard, storms within ten miles. When sky like photo 17, then allow immediately for gusts to 30–40 knots (possibly more) torrential rain and hail etc. Storms ashore draw in air from seaward+ sea breeze? = moderate or more, on-shore wind. Most intense storms move up against a wind they are sucking into themselves. So wind that sluggishly shifts towards coming bad storm means intense thunder squalls later *from* the direction of storm

127

Polaris, contrary to general belief, is not located at the exact Pole of the Heavens, which is the extension of the earth's axis on the celestial sphere. As a matter of fact, the Pole Star is 1¼° from the true Pole. Polaris is a 2nd magnitude star of the solar type. It is 407 light years distant and about 2500 times as bright as the sun. It is approaching our system at the rate of about 11 miles a second. It revolves around the Pole once in 24 hours in a circle 2½° in diameter. Within this circle more than 200 stars have been photographed.

The North Star is about as many degrees above the horizon as the observer is north of the Equator. If you were at the North Pole, Polaris would shine directly overhead. If you stood on the Equator, Polaris would be on the horizon.

Polaris is a triple system of suns. It is a spectroscopic binary with a period of 30 years, and in addition has a 9th magnitude companion. Polaris itself is a Cepheid variable with a range of a little more than 1/10 of a magnitude, and a well determined period of 3.97 days.

Compare the light of the different stars in Ursa Minor as a means of estimating stellar magnitude.

The stars γ and β Ursæ Minoris are called the "Guardians of the Pole."

Owing to the Precession of the Equinoxes, the position of the true Pole is continually but slowly changing, following a circle around the Pole of the Ecliptic, which lies in the constellation Draco.

It takes the North Pole about 26,000 years to complete its great circle. About the year 7500 A.D. the star α Cephei will be the North Star. In 13,500 A.D. Vega will be the Polaris of the sky, and about the year 21,000 A.D. α Draconis will again be the North Star as it was about 4500 B.C.

The Oxford Companion to Ships and the Sea
Edited by Peter Kemp
Oxford University Press, New York, London
972 pages, illus., 1976, $35

There's an Oxford Companion to almost everything else—literature, history, art, film, music, theatre, etc.—so it's a wonder that they took so long to publish one on ships and the sea. That they finally did is good for them and better for us.

What is a "companion"? Well, it's not a dictionary and not an encyclopedia. It lies in the territory somewhere between. It's arranged alphabetically, with headings consisting of words, terms, names, places, and things. You might call it a reader's guide. In some cases the descriptions are short—perhaps only a sentence—in others they are long, some running long enough to be properly termed short essays. Because of the nature of the beast, it's easy to find fault with a companion (it's as easy to find praise, for that matter): limitations of space mean that the editor must be less than thorough, so items he finds necessary will find inclusion whereas those the reader finds necessary might not. We would never leave out biographical notes on McFee, Stevenson (both the author and the lighthouse engineer), Underhill, and Riesenberg, for instance; Kemp did. On the other hand, he included people we would never think of including, which testifies to his scholarship.

Field Book of the Skies
by William T. Olcott
G.P. Putnam's Sons, N.Y.
482 pages, illus., index, rev. ed. 1954, $5.75

Sailors and navigators spend enough time looking at the stars; they might as well know something about them. This is a small handbook that comes very well recommended and makes the stars something else besides dots of light to aim your sextant at. The text describes the stars, gives methods and charts for identification, provides historical data on their discovery, and, for the romantics, tells about the mythology associated with them. Take a copy along on your next cruise; you'll gain a new perspective.

Scientific Maps and Atlases—Catalog
The UNESCO Press
Unipub
Box 433, Murray Hill Station
New York, N.Y. 10016

The United Nations, through UNESCO, has a series of maps that might be of interest to mariners. Their catalog of maps and atlases lists and describes, among others, climatic and oceanographic maps. If you're seriously interested, send for your free catalog.

Boxed quote left above from Field Book of the Skies.
Boxed quote and illustration below from the Oxford Companion . . .

GNOMONIC CHART, a chart of great utility in *great circle sailing based on the gnomonic projection. This is a perspective projection in which part of a spherical surface is projected from the centre of the sphere on to a plane surface tangential to the sphere's surface. The principal property of this projection is that great circle arcs are projected as straight lines.

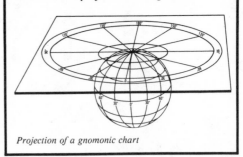

Projection of a gnomonic chart

But enough pedantry. Errors and omissions notwithstanding, *The Oxford Companion to Ships and the Sea* is an excellent reference book, one that has more than earned its place on the shelf next to De Kerchove's *International Maritime Dictionary* (see review in MC-1, p. 133). But at $35 a copy, it's not for everyone—if your interest in things marine is casual, pass it up; but if you are constantly going back and forth to reference books, as we are, then it could well nigh become indispensable.

Notes
from the Companionway

Good Stoves

Dickinson marine stoves have been a standby in the North Pacific fishing fleets since 1932. Only recently has the firm sought to distribute its excellent stoves to ships and boats in other waters. There will be good galleys in those ships and boats.

**Dickinson Marine Products
3737 Napier St.
Burnaby 2, B.C.
Canada**

Quote below and photo of the Bering stove from the Dickinson catalog.

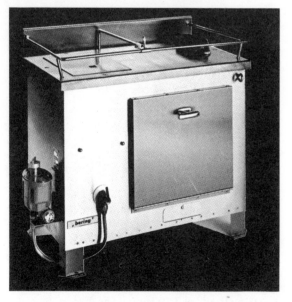

Oil fired for trouble free performance.* All Dickinson stoves are designed to operate well on diesel, stove oil or kerosene. This gives the boat owner important advantages: These fuels are readily available at almost any marina; it offers additional safety at sea. Heating oils in their natural state will not explode. The control valve is equipped with an overflow to prevent excess oil entering the burner. **(Note: Installed as recommended in Dickinson Installation Manual).*

Para-fin Distributors

The excellent Taylor's Para-fin stoves (reviewed in the *Mariner's Catalog, Volume 2*, p. 81) now have several American distributors:

Faire Harbour Boats
Scituate, Mass.

Johnson & Joseph
Oakland, Cal.

Windward Mark
Seattle, Wash.

Jay Stuart Haft
Milwaukee, Wisc.

Thomas Hardware
Grosse Point Farms, Mich.

Right: Taylor's Para-fin Cooker 030, available in brass or stainless steel.

The Sure-Fire, Two-Match Method

Many folks have great difficulty lighting kerosene or alcohol boat stoves of the variety that require "priming," or heating the burner with a fire of liquid fuel in order to get the thing going on a vaporized fuel. I, myself, have been a longtime member-in-good-standing of this group, but all that changed last summer. It was then that I invented, developed, practiced, and perfected my sure-fire, two-match method of outwitting even the most obstinate of boat stoves.

It works like this:

1. If the stove is of the pressure variety, pump up the pressure. On gravity-feed stoves, this step may, of course, be omitted.

2. Light match #1.

3. Open and shut the fuel valve to let liquid fuel into the priming pan, at the same time setting it afire with match #1 so that you can see exactly how much liquid fuel is going into the pan.

4. Shake out match #1.

5. Wait for all the liquid fuel to burn up and the fire to go out.

6. Light match #2.

7. Turn on the fuel valve and light the burner with match #2.

8. Shake out match #2.

You have now accomplished in a sure, certain, and controlled way with two matches what used to take you from one to 12 matches to accomplish in a totally out-of-control operation punctuated by sputtering from both you and the stove and, oftentimes, bright flames playing against the overhead.

The secret to the two-match method is, of course, that instead of being too, too clever and trying to show off by turning on the burner to light it by catching that last bit of priming flame (if you miss by two microseconds, you get either a sputter or a flare-up, depending on whether you were late or early), you calmly devote match #2 to increasing the possible time-span for lighting the burner from two microseconds to perhaps 15 full seconds.

Best of all, this method converts almost any old boat stove from an unpredictable adversary into a faithful friend.

—**Roger Taylor**

No More Strike and Pray

Dear Editors:

I recommend waterproof matches called "Greenlites," manufactured in Australia by Brymay. They are available in Bermuda in supermarkets and also down in the Caribbean islands.

Ginny Jones
Mystic, Conn.

(Does anyone know the address of the distributor, or that of the manufacturer Down-Under?—Eds.)

INTERVIEWING THE COOK

Common Stoves, Uncommon Values

Optimus-Princess stoves are among the most common brands one will find in most any fleet. Tens of thousands of boats have them, and we've no complaints. Their model 31 Interchangeable Gimbaled Dual Range at $382, for example, makes good, clean boat sense for those who live aboard at marinas. We believe their most useful item to be the model 455R One-Burner Sea Swing kerosene stove, which is a real godsend for the queasy cook in a seaway or the singlehander with a boat that won't balance on the course she has to make good. It's good for lots of coffee and soup that would not have otherwise been had.

Optimus-Princess, Inc.
P.O. Box 3448
12423 E. Florence Ave.
Santa Fe Springs, Calif. 90670

MODEL 45 SR ONE BURNER SEA SWING KEROSENE STOVE

All brass one burner kerosene stove mounted in the traditional stainless steel sea swing gimbal. The sea swing stove is preheated with Optimus lighting paste or methylated spirit. The rugged sea swing is equally handy as the 5 RM with salty old world charm besides.

SPECIFICATIONS
Tank capacity: 1¾ pints
Suitable filling: ¾ of tank capacity
Burning time: Approx. 4 hrs.
Height:
Shipping weight: Stove 3 lbs., Sea Swing 6 lbs.

Above: From the Optimus-Princess catalog.
Below left: From the Brookstone catalog.

Warmth Plus Beauty

A perfectly beautiful ship's heating stove, burning wood, coal, or peat, and made by Lange in Denmark, is distributed in this country by:

Southampton Stove Company
75 Herrick Road
Southampton, N.Y. 11968

Lunch in Advance

Of course, if one is expecting a slop, or one normally cruises in a naturally cranky boat, one can prepare lunch with breakfast in harbor and store it in something like these 1-quart stainless vacuum bottles from Brookstone. I can see a special rack for them within reach of the helm.

Brookstone
Peterborough, N.H. 03458

Above: The Lange ship's stove, 21" high, 13½" deep, 13½" wide, heating capacity 20-25,000 BTUs/hr.

Above: The Westerbeke boat heater.
Boxed quote below and heater at right from Remotronics brochure.

> NOW, at last, it is possible to buy an efficient and highly effective heater for boats. The Remotron is already well-known for its low-cost operation, high efficiency, low-noise level and its ability to give long, trouble-free service. The secret of Remotron's success is the fact that it operates on Propane, a clean-burning fuel with high thermal efficiency.
>
> The Remotron chimney is mounted on the gunwale or the freeboard in a boat. Both the exhaust fumes and the air for combustion are respectively vented and taken in from the open air outside of the cabin. (The combustion is not affected by weather and sea.) In marine applications, when the chimney is retracted, the heater stops automatically and in this position the chimney is flush with the surface of the deck and does not cause any obstruction to work on board.

Cutting the drum with homemade tool and ax.

Warmth Less Beauty

Westerbeke has entered the heating-unit market with this 6,150-BTU electrically fired kerosene-burning boat heater at $598. Write:

J.H. Westerbeke Corp.
Avon Industrial Park
Avon, Mass. 02322

Heat from a Bottle

The growing number who prefer bottled gas on their boats will be interested to hear of Remotronix, a bottled-gas-fired 5,350-BTU central heating system especially for marine applications. Cost of the system is around $620.

Remotronics
P.O. Box 456
Bellevue, Wash. 98009

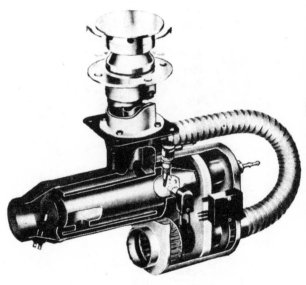

How to Build an Oil Barrel Stove, **by Ole Wik**
Alaska Northwest Pub. Co.
Anchorage, Alaska
24 pages, paperbound, illus., 1976, $1.95

Your shop needs a stove? You can't afford one? You want to build one from an oil barrel but don't have room for the entire 55-gallon drum? Ole Wik has developed a method of making a stove measuring 21″ x 17½″ x 10½″, cut from a single barrel using simple tools such as tin snips, cold chisel, hammer, file, drill, pliers, etc. No torch-cutting. No welding.

Left: From How to Build an Oil Barrel Stove.

Catalytic Heaters

The early days of catalytic heaters were not very confidence-inspiring—more than one ice-fishing house or camper became a tomb for the occupant. Lots of engineering has been applied to the problems involved since then, and several units are now on the market that have passed very rigorous testing for their ability to withstand abuse and poor control variation without emitting noxious fumes or leaking fuel. On principle, they are not our cup of tea, but then you know how weird we're prone to be sometimes.

Domestic brands are well known and not hard to find—most camping, outdoor, and sporting goods stores offer a choice of them. Two overseas brands that will not be well known but have good track records (the Atlantic singlehanded race, for example) are those of Atlantic Supply, made in Denmark, and Kontite-Therm'x, made in France. The Atlantic Supply line ranges from the "Minicat" model at 2,000 BTU to the "Maxigas" unit at 7,400 BTU.

**Atlantic Supply
Quintrel Downs
Newquay, Cornwall
England**

**Kontite-Therm'x
Kay & Co., Ltd.
Acresfield House
15 Exchange Street
Bolton, Lancs BL1 1RS
England**

Above: The Minicat catalytic heater from an Atlantic Supply brochure.
Below: An Aladdin lamp installed in gimbals by Faire Harbour Boats (see Faire Harbour's listing on the next page).

Kerosene Lamps at Their Best

That we have not mentioned Aladdin lamps 'til now is just carelessness. Aladdins, of course, represent the highest development of kerosene illumination. Their round wicks burn not to produce light, as in a flat-wick oil lamp, but rather to produce hot gases, which are then burned on a mantle above, much like those hideously intense gas lanterns, only with a much softer and more humane light, about like a 60-watt bulb when properly adjusted, enough for hours of reading or writing without strain. Too, the significant amount of heat they give will keep most northern evenings at bay without resort to other heat sources. Their adjustment is critical, and Aladdins are not to be left alone, ever, but they are the finest kind of present company. They are distributed nationally, and their home office for wholesale inquiries is:

**Aladdin Industries, Inc.
Heating and Lighting Div.
P.O. Box 7235
703 Murfreesboro Rd.
Nashville, Tenn. 37210**

133

GIMBAL STYLE ALADDIN LAMP

21" Tall

Model B-2315

These solid brass, double gimballed lamps are manufactured exclusively by Faire Harbour Boats using the Model 23, solid brass, Aladdin burner. The oil fount is solid brass and is authentic Aladdin size and style. The double Gimbal is heavy, solid brass and permits full swing on both axis. 21" tall, center of lamp 7½" from wall.

Heat and Light Dealer

Faire Harbour Boats was mentioned above in connection with Taylor's cooking stoves. They also carry the entire Remotronix and Aladdin lines of heaters and lights. Skippers fitting out in the Northeast will want to check them out.

**Faire Harbour Boats
44 Captain Pierce Road
Scituate, Mass. 02066**

Soapstone

After we promoted soapstone for home manufacturing of ship's stoves and fireplaces, a friend reminded us that laboratory countertops are often made of very high grade stuff. Alberene is one of the best lab-grade stones and the lovely flecked grey-blue-green color would have one consider countering the whole galley with it, too, if you could stand the weight. The quarry company is in Virginia, and their slabs are sold custom-cut by distributors: the one we contacted is in Massachusetts.

**Alberene Stone Corp.
Box 98
Schuyler, Virginia 22969**

**Everett Collins Corp.
197 Gardner St.
West Roxbury, Mass. 02132**

Left and quote below: From Alberene catalog.

This sink drainboard in the Atomic Energy Commission Laboratory at New Brunswick, New Jersey, shows the effects of 22 years of punishing service. But it took only two hours of hand rubbing with an abrasive stone to restore the surface to its original smoothness.

Only Alberene working surfaces can be refinished like this. The man-made materials cannot be restored in this manner when the surface finish has been worn away. Alberene is permanent.

134

If It's Organic, Smoke It

The "Little Chief Smoker" is not a youthful charismatic pothead down the block. It is an excellent device that works well and is the most practical solution we know for those who cannot have or share an old-fashioned walk-in, from:

**L.L. Bean, Inc.
Freeport, Maine 04033**

Left and above: From the L.L. Bean catalog.

You Knead It

Dear Editors:

Regarding the hard-tack crisis referred to in MC-4:
From *Chamber's Encyclopaedia*, 1881, recipe for common sea biscuit: 'Sea biscuit, or common ship's bread, is made from wheaten flour (retaining some of the bran), water, and common salt. The materials are kneaded together, either by manual labor—that is, by the hands and feet of the workmen—or by introducing the materials into a long trough or box, with a central shaft to which a series of knives are attached, and made to revolve rapidly by machinery. The mass of dough so obtained is then kneaded and thinned out into a sheet the proper thickness of the bread, by being passed and repassed between heavy rollers. This sheet is placed below a roller with knife-edge shapes, is readily cut into hexagonal or round shapes; the cuts are not complete but are indentations, and the slab remains in one piece. These slabs are placed in an oven for about 12 minutes and are then placed in a warm room for 2 or 3 days to dry thoroughly. The more modern ovens are fitted for continuous baking, the bread being drawn through in sheets on endless chains. These ovens have a capacity of 2,000 pounds of bread a day."

My own comments: no real proportions are given, and, as my old Ma used to say, being an expert baker, you can't be exact; flour varies, you have to go by feel. This seems a simple thing to do, experimenting in small batches—it seems the dough is mixed rather stiff.

Chamber's Encyclopaedia goes on to say that Cabin Biscuit had a little shortening, sometimes a little milk, and a very little yeast, which of course made a lighter and more easily spoiled biscuit. I wonder if this is really any different from the unleavened bread of the Bible?

If anyone wants to use his feet, go to it!

Pete Culler
Hyannis, Mass.

Dear Editors:

As soon as I came to your request for hardtack recipes (MC-4, p.101), I asked my wife if she knew anything on the subject. She dove into a cookbook and came up with the recipe for ships' biscuits below. After she cooked a batch, I had to fight off the kids to get any before they were gone. They are somewhat heavier than pilot bread, but similar in taste.

Ships' Biscuits
(makes about 2 dozen 1-to 2-inch biscuits)
2 cups all-purpose flour
½ teaspoon salt
1 teaspoon shortening
½ cup water

Preheat oven to 325°. Sift together flour and salt into medium-size bowl. With fingertips, work shortening into flour. Stir in water until dough is stiff. Beat dough to ½-inch thickness, preferably with a mallet. Fold dough into 6 layers. Beat down again, and refold about a half-dozen times until the dough becomes elastic. Roll once again to ½-inch thickness and cut out biscuits with floured biscuit cutter. Bake about 30 minutes. Cool. Store in tightly covered container.

Stephen Bird
Seattle, Washington

Hampton Crystal's decanter.

Decanters

Decanters for the receipt and medical application of the ship's spirits are fairly common in nautical gift shops. Most of them are made in Spain or Portugal, and their distribution is sewed up by the importers. But here is a beauty in lead crystal made in England. The price was £7.75 a year ago and probably somewhat more than that now; £10 perhaps would do it.

Hampton Crystal Co.
73 Station Rd.
Hampton
Middlesex, TW12 2BJ
England

135

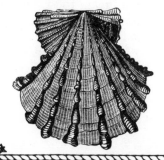

On several occasions we've noticed that various eastern Mediterranean and Adriatic products, especially things like olives and peppers, are shipped here in fine, stout, plastic barrels with heavy screw-top lids. There are several sizes of them; we've seen five, from five liters to what must be about thirty gallons or more. And then a friend showed us his larder in which 'most everything was stowed in them. Now we notice some of the local fishermen using them for bait. The word is to check with your local deli and find out the address of their Greek or Yugoslavian condiments distributor.

FLAKE MULLIGAN

Adding zest and tang to the flavor of the sea, this modern version of dogfish soup has warmed northern Irish fishermen for centuries.

```
DOGFISH     1 pound
POTATOES    3 cups sliced
ONION     2 cups sliced
WATER     6 cups
RICE    ½ cup
GREEN PEPPER    1 cup diced
BACON    ½ cup diced
SALT and PEPPER    to taste
PARSLEY    to garnish
CROUTONS
```

Cut dogfish into 2-inch pieces. Place fish, potatoes, and onion in a large kettle. Add water and bring to a boil. Add rice, green pepper, and bacon. Simmer, covered, for 30 minutes. Add salt and pepper. Garnish with parsley and float croutons on top. Serves 6.

136

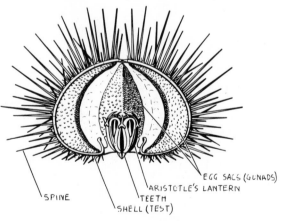

SPINE
ARISTOTLE'S LANTERN
TEETH
SHELL (TEST)
EGG SACS (GONADS)

Anatomy of a sea urchin.

The Dogfish Cookbook, by Russ Mohney
Pacific Search Books
715 Harrison St.
Seattle, Washington
108 pages, illus., index, 1976, paperbound, $1.95

Anyone who has gone fishing, either commercial or pleasure, knows how easy it is to catch dogfish. You catch them whether you want to or not. Most of us throw them back, but Russ Mohney thinks that's foolish. So he has written a book that describes how to catch, clean, cook, and preserve dogfish.

And why not? Euell Gibbons has been telling us long enough that we're missing out on something good by passing up periwinkles, limpets, sea urchins, and even dog whelks. Red-dog steaks, anyone?

Now that the ice is broken, so to speak, it would be criminal to confine your experimentation with exotic seafood to the lowly dogfish. You might like to spend some time with:

The Edible Sea, by Paul and Mavis Hill
A.S. Barnes, New York
276 pages, illus., index, 1975, $15

This book is in the same vein as Euell Gibbon's *Stalking the Blue-Eyed Scallop* (David McKay Co., N.Y., $2.95; reviewed in MC-1, page 180), though it differs in many respects: the variety of edibles is greater, the illustrations are more numerous, and the number of recipes is larger. *The Edible Sea* describes your quarry and tells you how to catch it, preserve it, prepare it, cook it, and eat it. The range of seafood goes from the common type, such as you might find in the local fish market, to the bizarre, such as barnacles, moray eels, ratfish, skates, limpets, and sponges. And for the romantically inclined, there are a few words about the aphrodisiacal qualities of some seafood.

Boxed recipe, left above, from the Dogfish Cookbook.
Illustration at left and quote below from the Edible Sea.

Sea urchin roe is an exotic, delicious, and nutritious repast. It can be eaten right from the shell either straight from the ocean or boiled first; it can be fried lightly, quickly baked in a scallop shell, mixed for dips and butters, or used in a variety of other dishes such as the Japanese nori maki sushi (kelp rice roll). Nori maki sushi sometimes features sea urchin roe alone but often includes raw fish and scallops also.

To open a sea urchin, simply crack it open at the bottom or cut it in half with a heavy knife.

RIGGING AND ROPE

Gangs

In this section, Pete Culler talks about making up gangs of rigging. When you consider the work that goes into such undertakings, it is not surprising that they were generally made up by gangs. And still are, for we found one, called:

The Rigging Gang
P.O. Box 1308
Wilmington, Delaware 19801

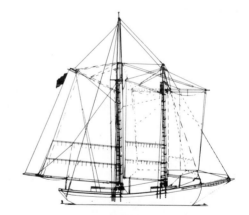

*Right, bottom: Two of the Riggins Gang's projects—*Chief Aptakisic *(above),* Western Union *(below).*

Basic Facts:
Proprietor: Nicholas S. Benton, Master Rigger
Number in Staff: 3 winter, 6 summer
Loft Location: Falk Fields Farm, Locust Grove, Maryland
Loft Phone: (301) 648-5643
Mailing Address: P.O. Box 1308, Wilmington, Delaware 19801
Products/services: Design of new rigs, rig details, fabrication of custom wire and rope rigging, fabrication of custom ironwork and blocks, outfitting of sailing craft, historical research, and technical consulting. In short, complete rigging services for traditional sailing ships and small craft. Rigging supplies: pine tar, marline, hempline.
Previous major projects: Pilot, 122-feet-on-deck Boston pilot schooner built in 1924 at Story's yard in Essex. Completely rerigged. Sail plan by Bill Baker. *Charlotte Ann,* 1888 oyster schooner built by Rice Brothers Shipyard, Bridgeton, NJ; and restored by John Woodside. 62 feet-on-deck. Complete rerigging including sail plan by N. Benton. *Western Union,* 1938 cable tender built from lines of 1886 Chesapeake-built cable schooner. 94 feet-on-deck and 126 feet-overall rig length. Rerigged 1976 to basic sail plan by C. Wittholtz with all details designed by N. Benton. *Chief Aptakisic,* 53 feet-on-deck training schooner. Complete rerigging to sail plan by N. Benton. *St. Margaret II.* Complete rerigging of 75 feet-on-deck schooner to sail plan by N. Benton.
Prospects: Currently we are preparing to rig a replica of the schooner *Columbia* now in the planning stages on Maynard Bray's drawing board. We are also preparing to rig the bark *Elissa* for the Galveston Historical Foundation under the direction of Michael Creamer. Numerous small projects come and go.

137

Rope Instead of Wire?

The development of stainless running rigging after WW II was part and parcel of the lascivious orgy thrown around marine craft then and since. No one can question the performance of this stuff overhead; strength-to-weight and (internal) stability indexes, windage characteristics, and weather resistance all give it superiority over anything else. But some will find the initial cost prohibitive, or object to the look or behavior of the (state of the art) gear that must attend wire overhead, or dislike handling wire, or object to the fishhooks that develop in strained or elderly wire, or resent the sounds it is wont to make in the night.

For these folks Marlow Ropes of Great Britain has developed pre-stretched rope designed to function satisfactorily where wire would otherwise be used. In this country, there are three distributors:

Imtra Corp.
151 Mystic Ave.
Medford, Mass. 02155

Inland Marine
79 East Jackson
Wilkes Barre, Penn. 18701

Seagull Marine Sales
1851 McGaw Ave.
Irvine, Calif. 92705

These three distributors can also supply Marlow-manufactured whipping twines made of rotproof Terylene.

COMPARATIVE STRETCH PROPERTIES OF MARLOW ROPES

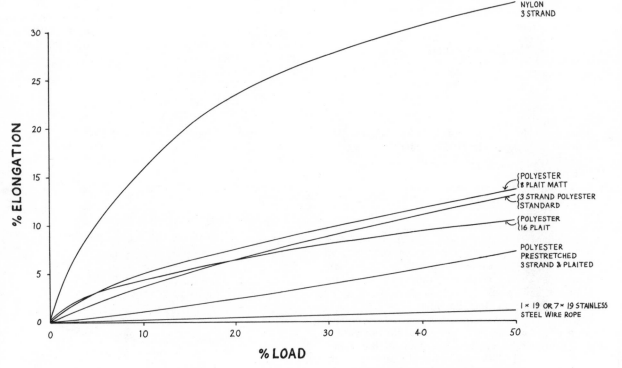

Graph above from a Marlow catalog.
Poly-foam line below from Nichols Net.

138

Sink or Swim Ropes

We can thank the gillnet fishermen for two fascinating developments in the ropeworks: foam-filled ropes, with high buoyancy that will hold stuff up along the line; and lead-filled line, which will sink and hold the same stuff down. Their use for gill and trammel nets is self-evident, but no doubt they've other yet-undiscovered marine uses, and we list them here to invite curiosity and invention. Various commercial fishing gear houses offer these ropes. We found ours at Nichols, which we've listed in earlier volumes for their nets and twines. A neat company to have on tap; all kinds of good stuff.

Nichols Net & Twine Co.
RR3, Bend Rd.
East St. Louis, Ill. 62201

(POLY-FOAM) FLOAT LINE

POLY-FOAM →

300 FT. $27.50
600 FT. $49.90
LESS THAN 100 Feet Add 15%

– FOR GREATER FLOTATION –

This is positively the finest float line we have ever sold or used. A core of Poly foam is encased in Braided Polyethylene. This eliminates all floats when used on Gill Nets or Trammel Nets. When used with a Leadcore Leadline it is practically impossible to tangle a net as the floats or leads are not available to Fall through the Mesh.

There's Rope and Then There's Rope

As we have often said or implied in other volumes of this *Catalog* the rope business is generally known and its distribution is thorough, not requiring our off-the-beaten-track treatment. But one rope company has come to our attention that is truly remarkable. This is Belfast Ropes.

Not only do they make the now-rare hemp, including four-strand (bells and sirens here), manila, and sisal stuff, but also they make very interesting and unique configurations of synthetic material, such as their Polyhemp Twine and Octoplat mooring rope.

The home office is in Northern Ireland, and all but one of their distributors are in the British Isles. The one North American distributor listed is in Ontario.

Belfast Ropework Ltd.
P.O. Box 80
Belfast BT4 1AN
Northern Ireland

Amjay Rope & Twines
361 Elgin Street
Brantford, Ontario
Canada

Sisal Rope

A traditional rope, still popular for general purpose use. Spun from high grade fibre. Available in a comprehensive size range.

Standard Make-Up: 220 metre coils.

Specific Gravity 1.50.

Manila Rope

Available in grades I and II. Laid in 3 or 4 strand construction. Used in the Marine and Fishing industries and as Lifting Tackle.

Standard Make-Up: 220 metre coils.

Specific Gravity 1.50.

(See Specification No. 8).

Best Hemp Boltrope

Manufactured from high quality Soft Hemp. The main application is as Gymnasium Climbing Ropes. Good grip, soft handling and non slip are the inherent qualities in this rope. The most popular sizes are 10, 16, 28 and 36mm dia. in 4 strand. Size range available in 3 or 4 strand.

Standard Make-Up: 220 metre coils.

Material above from the Belfast Ropework Ltd. catalog

SCRAPING DOWN.

Drawn by Arthur Briscoe.

Tarred Rigging
and Stropped Blocks

by Pete Culler

Mention of tarred rigging today brings forth mental pictures of *Old Ironsides*, clipper ships, and *Two Years Before the Mast*, which book, by the way, gives a good account of tarring down—how it was done, not so much why, as that part of it was accepted in those days.

To consider tarred rigging now might be taken to be reactionary in the extreme, yet with the high cost of boating gear, more and more do-it-yourself build-

ing and rigging, it makes good sense—it always did, but like so many things, good sense often goes to leeward. I have noticed many times, in most any harbor, that otherwise-well-kept craft have had standing rigging in deplorable condition, for no other reason than that the owners of them have no knowledge of rigging upkeep, or that properly maintained rigging can last as long as the vessel.

For classic craft, a return to tarred rigging makes sense, especially since pine tar is still available—we're lucky; some commission or do-good outfit has yet to declare it unfit for Man's endeavors!

Stainless steel wire and Dacron line are fine, just the thing for a racer. Though wonderful, they don't last forever. Both take well to tar, yet plain galvanized steel rigging, properly put up to begin with and kept tarred, will last every bit as long. Plain black iron will, too, if you coat and tend it properly, as pine tar is one of the most waterproof of coatings. Tar, by the way, was part of the makeup of the first Atlantic cable.

Rigging already made up and in use on a boat will benefit by being tarred, even if it has been totally exposed without protection. But for first class results, a new gang of rigging is made up with pine tar so that—and note this—with proper retarring, its life, as far as these things go, will be as long as anyone wants it around. Tarring is not for those who still think that new-notion boats don't require maintenance. Whether built by wood butchers, tin knockers, chemists, or masons, any craft to remain seaworthy must have maintenance, and taking care of the rigging is only a small part of it. Those preaching the no-maintenance boat cannot really have gone to sea; real seakeeping is most wearing on any craft.

I will not go into how to make up a gang of rigging for, say, a classic schooner; it's all available in many ancient works on rigging. There are still some riggers who know how to do it, and, with the printed matter available, it's no great feat for the self-taught person with desire to master it. Rather, I will describe the use of pine tar in making up a gang of rigging. It matters not if it's for a small sloop or a large schooner; the principle is the same.

My own system, though it may vary slightly from other practicing riggers in detail, is, or was, the standard of the past. Assuming you have quite a number of splices and servings to do, first you must get some marline of quality and suitable size, which is

(Continued on next page)

140

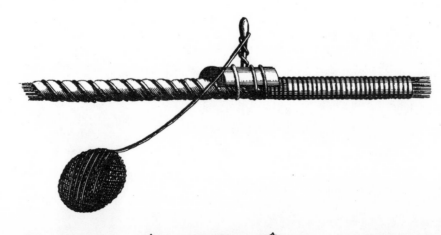

them up, is caused by a lack of lubrication and tar, plus a scant knowhow with tackles and seizings. Those who may want to make their own sails may well have to make their own tarred boltrope, now that real tarred hemp is about unavailable; they might also have to tar synthetic small stuff in place of hard-to-come-by real marline. Just how you do this is quite simple, messy, and wonderful smelling. Most people like the smell of pine tar, though some females profess to hate it.

Here are some pointers on the use and thinning of tar for various gear. In mild or warm weather, for making up a gang of rigging, pine tar can often be used as is, though some batches are thicker than others. Cold weather requires thinning in any case. I find several thinners work, but turpentine is best of all, for it's really a by-product of making tar (or maybe tar is the by-product of making turpentine). For making boltrope or lanyards out of new stuff, I make my tar "thin as water"; that is, so it sounds watery running off a stirring stick. Too thin is better than too thick. Often I mix it about like the old-time licorice water kids had as a treat in the distant past. I then simply pass the line through the bucket or can of watery tar and hang it in bights from a spike over the bucket till it has drained, then put it out in the air to dry. If anyone thinks he can dry this stuff in a closed building in the winter, forget it. Put the line out in the air; an open shed is good, though in good summer weather, just outdoors is fine, and it will set well before dew or rain falls. Thus treated it can be used for lanyards. The line is cut to lengths, the stopper knots are made, the line is well greased and stretched, then it is rove off and set up. Being new, the line may have to be set up a couple of times; then when things seem set, it's tarred all over. The soaking in the thin stuff first insures full penetration.

not an easy thing to do at the moment. Marline is quite expensive now, so you want it to last once it is put on. You will need parcelling—light stuff like drill or strong sheeting. Stout muslin also will do, or, if the rigging is large, light canvas can be used. I've seen friction tape used for parcelling more than once; my advice is, don't. Some riggers cut and roll their parcelling in bandage form, about 2″ wide, tying the roll with a bit of twine, then putting many rolls to soak in a can of linseed oil. When they are to be used, some are taken out and stood on end in a tilted pie pan to drain, and the parcelling is put on soaking wet. This is good practice. In the past, for big wire, we used to strip up sacking, which manila line came in at one time. This sacking was said "to hold the tar" in the big meshes. Having stripped much old rigging put up this way, I have no doubts but what it made a very waterproof covering.

I like to tar the bare wire or splice before parcelling, whether the cloth is soaked in oil or not. Very big wire may need tarring, then worming and parcelling, tarring again, then serving with well-tallowed marline. This is a most delightfully messy operation, and it's soon apparent, even to the novice, that the great pressure of the serving, using a mallet or board, has forced the concoction to the very core of the wire, and that it is totally sealed, with even the air pushed out. No other method that I know of, put on by hand, in a barn, under a tree, or aboard a vessel, or wherever is handy, can so secure a splice from moisture and air. Once this treated rigging has set up somewhat (it's always a little flexible), surface maintenance, with tar, is required, and the rigging will outlast you. Can anyone ask more of a simple hand operation?

The bare-wire parts that usually are not served take to tar just fine; the point is, tar it all—servings, bare wire, ratlines, and seizings, if any. The whole works, not forgetting the turnbuckles, or deadeyes if you use them. Turnbuckles and any other threaded fittings, opened up and the threads tarred, will always be workable later on. This applies to both bronze and iron threads—a mooring shackle with threads treated with pine tar will open up easily years later. This same system is great for any kind of threads exposed to weather, salt, road goo, and all the other crud much machinery is exposed to. Just why the use of this stuff on threads is little known is hard to fathom. Sometimes I think Modern Technology outruns common sense, at least where the ordinary boatman is concerned.

Naturally, all sorts of other gear can and should be tarred, as it was in the past—rope strops if you use them, certainly deadeyes and lanyards, for part of the trouble a novice has keeping these tight, or setting

141

If the line is to be used as a boltrope, and it seems a bit stiff after the dipping and drying (remember that cold makes it so), I often soak it again, this time in kerosene with some tallow dissolved in it, then hung and dried again. This limbers it up for sewing on as sail roping. I've had quite some success with using Dacron, or a cheap form of synthetic pot warp for tarred roping, as none of this stuff has any stretch. I'm often asked why I tar Dacron, as weather does not affect it and it does not stretch and shrink like

(Continued on next page)

(Continued from preceding page)

natural fibers. Not quite so—sun and salt do affect it. Untreated Dacron behaves just the opposite of natural fibers, stretching some when wet, and taking up when dry. Treat it right and it will last as long as you care for it. Manila line can be tarred the same way, and, if it's good stuff to begin with (much of it now seems poor), it works as well as any.

Well-tarred line, though it will chafe, is less subject to chafing than untreated line. Chafe is one of the big pains of maintenance in real open-water sailing. Working up a gang of rigging with pine tar, linseed oil, and tallow is hard on the hands in some ways, yet you will not have the dry and cracking skin some people get when working outside in cold weather—the stuff is good medicine in many ways.

Once a new vessel is rigged and in use, she will require several tarrings the first year, until there is considerable buildup, then she only requires tar each fall at layup or an occasional touch when something gets chafed in use. If you think you can tar, even in hot weather, and then go sailing the next day, forget it. Properly planned, in the North at least, once a coating is built up, putting on tar at layup time poses no problem.

If by chance you hate maintenance work of any kind, and must have instant dry, instant results, and don't care for marlinspike seamanship, forget all this and run your gear till it rots, then replace it frequently. Let's hope it does not let you down in a tight spot.

When I first started in with boats, some working knowledge of marlinspike seamanship was not uncommon among most boatmen; some were highly skilled at it, beyond the everyday needs of their profession, as it is an interesting and satisfying skill to acquire. I was fortunate to have Biddlecomb's *Art of Rigging* as a textbook at an early age, but best of all was learning from the many real seamen then around. I think for the finer details, a person can't go wrong now using *The Ashley Book of Knots* (Doubleday, N.Y. $16.95). This volume tends to floor some people on first glance. It's really quite easy to use. The section on applied marlinspike seamanship is the most important.

142

Stropped Blocks

I mentioned such things as tarring block strops and smaller gear, all of which benefit by the tar. Who uses stropped blocks now? You can, especially if you make your own. There have been some recent articles in boating magazines on making blocks, most showing the now-customary internal metal strapping; this is

fine if you want to do it that way. I've made many blocks of all sizes, both for boats and tackles for lifting and hauling, and have never made an internal metal-stropped block for my own craft. I only do it on order for boats I am building for others. I've found the rope-stropped block much more satisfactory than metal-stropped and easier and cheaper to make. I'm always asked by those who never have used them if they are strong. I've never had a failure, other than getting one fouled in the undercarriage of a truck, and even it was quite repairable. If such blocks could control the rig in a three-deck warship, or do for heaving-down tackles in careening, I for one need no assurance of their ability.

The various stroppings possible to suit different uses (see *Ashley*), the ready adjustability, the tendency to take a fair lead, and that lack of "fittings" that so much boat gear is cluttered with now, plus the simple and economical building, have made these blocks my choice for many years over the usual standard block. More than once on various craft, when I could not get a standard block to set properly, I've robbed its sheave and pin, junked the shell and metal, then made a rope-stropped shell, tailored and fitted to the job, always with good results.

I find, too, that there is now a rather limited choice in types of store-bought blocks. By making your own you can have all sorts of fine specials that just suit a certain place. I've made non-toppling blocks for boat falls, blocks that can't be fouled, and all the other types, with strops to suit the many purposes. A properly made and stropped block, kept tarred, is a tough bit of chandlery.

I am often asked what wood I use for blocks, and bullseyes, lizards, parrels, and deadeyes for that matter. The answer is: wood that is cheap and available. Most people think in terms of lignum vitae, which is expensive and unnecessary, or teak, which now seems to be the rage for block shells. In over 50 years of exposure to boats, I never heard of using teak for block shells until recently. Most teak splits too easily to make good block shells. If this last remark casts doubt on the knowledge of some modern block-makers, that's fully what I intend.

We are considering here the economical, the available, and the durable, and their workability in backyard shops, or on the deck of a vessel. One of the most available and toughest woods in New England is the common American elm, the one the beetles raise hell with. It's not a handsome wood, but it's quite available off wood piles and fellings. Its resistance to splitting needs no elaboration—anyone who has split elm or attempted to, for stove wood will get the message. In the South, live oak takes its place. Ash, hickory, maple, and beech are often on a wood pile; all have been used for blocks in the past, as was locust, of course. There is hornbeam and an oc-

(Continued on next page)

casional old walnut railroad tie. In other words, there is more block-making wood just hanging around than a large fleet could ever use.

I've used other types of wood for blocks: white oak, apple, and some I don't know what, except they're hard and tough. And then there's greenheart. Federal dock building, or other very high-class piling work, often calls for greenheart fender piles. The trimmed-off tops of these can often be cadged from dock builders, much battered and split by driving, but you might find some usable stuff for blocks, though there will be much waste due to the splits. This stuff won't float, so if you get hold of a big chunk, be prepared for a heavy lift. A lump of greenheart is not just the thing you toss lightly into the trunk of a mini-car.

I'm sure there are other easily acquired block-making woods, but since there is so much of the above available, I've not looked very far. If ruggedness is the main thing, probably elm is the choice; if varnished looks are the main thing, I prefer ash or locust, both being quite strong enough.

Once a block shell is made, regardless of the type of wood, it is put to soak for two weeks (a month is better) in linseed oil. Once the oil has oxidized, weather will have no effect on the wood. After about six months and some use, wood blocks can be cleaned up, varnished, or painted. If it is done too soon, the oil will lift the finish. This is planning ahead, something that seems to have gone out of style.

A bit of sea lore here: In the days of hemp lanyards for the deadeyes, a properly planned craft had her new lanyard stuff put on the stretch when her keel was laid, a strain being on it in the rigging loft while the hull was being built. There was little or no stretch left in her line when she fitted out; and lanyards were not set up for the final time in cold weather if it could possibly be avoided. Often there was more setting up required after the vessel had sailed some, but this was more because of the settling of the rigging eyes aloft and the splices, than it was because of stretch in the lanyards. And yes, the additional setting up was possibly because of the slight raising of the sides of the vessel as she found herself.

I often make wooden sheaves for blocks, and this works quite well. Such sheaves were commonplace in days long past. If I were to make blocks for a cruising boat, or a day boat of some size, I think it would be well worth buying roller sheaves of the proper size for the various blocks, at least for halyards and sheets. Downhaul blocks, lift blocks, and many others that don't have long, heavy hauls, do just as well with a plain sheave of wood, or metal, if you have a lathe. Scrap shafting of about the right size makes fine metal sheaves; for wooden ones I like elm or locust. Bronze pins are worth it, especially if the rollers are bronze, and I like them for wood sheaves. If the rollers are steel, use steel pins. In all cases, keep them greased, pack 'em with it. One exception: if you use blocks for hauling up on a sand beach, run them dry. Grease picks up sand, making a grinding compound.

I make my blocks differently than some recent articles show, not that those ways are not good. Since I have unlimited firewood, for all practical purposes, to work from, as much as possible I get my blocks out of solid pieces of wood—even doubles and an occasional triple. Simply mill out to thickness, width, and often in longish lengths; mark off and bore most

of the mortice in the squared-up state, which is easy to hold. Though the job can be done freehand using a half-baked jig, a drill press is best, using the power paddle bits; I find these best for this sort of thing. When all is bored, I clean out the mortices with a chisel and a rasp, then whack up the blocks in the lengths and shapes that meet my fancy on a bandsaw and sanding disc.

Just what shape I fancy is often guided by the kind of block and its use. I also make it a point not to leave much wood on in places where it does no good; some of the old shapes of the past are quite attractive. In the unfinished square state, it's best to bore for the pins, too, for obvious reasons. Scores for the strap are about the last thing to be cut. Shells can be riveted across as in modern blocks, or you can use a threaded rod if you have a tap long enough to reach through the block—this method was employed by a well-known yacht block maker years ago. He is now out of business, of course. Often small blocks I make out of good, tough stock skip the use of cross fastenings and seem to give no trouble. On the other hand, on very big blocks, for heavy lifts, I've not only cross-riveted, but also have fore-and-aft riveted across the sides of the shell, above and below the pin, and, in some cases, for certain uses, double-stropped them besides.

I've made blocks that range from less than 2″ long to 10″ long, and one old soaker of a snatch block maybe 14″ or 15″ long for use as a lead block when pulling with a truck.

That this sort of thing is worthwhile now, in these days of everything off the shelf, is a matter of individual choice. I think it well worth it for many reasons. You can have blocks to suit your type of craft exactly, from both artistic and mechanical standpoints. You can do it economically. If you like to make things, there is a lot of satisfaction in that alone. You avoid a lot of metal fittings; all that is really needed are sheaves, sometimes, and an occasional shackle or hook.

I must have six or eight block-and-tackles around, some all home built, others partly so, often using rebuilt manufactured blocks that have been salvaged. These rigs vary from quite small to large and are most handy around the shop, house, and in the truck. Things one is apt to bull around the hard way can, with a bit of imagination, be moved simply and safely with a block and tackle.

What sometimes passes for a block now—stainless straps, plastic shells, and composition sheaves—are simply not in the class of the old timers I take great pleasure in making and using. Each to his own.

Deadeyes, hearts, lizards, bullseyes, and all sorts of special wooden fairleads can be made the same way, out of solid stuff, from the previously mentioned woods. Much of this stuff is most suited to turning on a wood lathe; some, however, may not be needed in a true round shape, so it's worked up more or less like in block making. For those who have or can borrow the use of a wood lathe, much of the round stuff can be made quite rapidly. I will not discourse on the use of the wood lathe; it's assumed that if you use one, you will know how, or soon learn how, to hold various work.

End

Dear Editors:

I am a retired sea captain in my middle 80's. I spent many years in sailing ships, large coasting schooners, and square riggers. I learned my knots and sennit braiding in those vessels. I have made many things, such as all types of rope mats, bell lanyards, and large frames for pictures and fancy ropework. I have sold some to yacht clubs and seafood restaurants. One is in the Mariners Museum in Halifax, N.S. I would like to sell them if anyone is interested, for a very reasonable price.

Captain T.R. Picard
North Bay, Ont., Canada

*Above, right: An example of Capt. Picard's work.
Below, and below, right; From* Modern Rope Seamanship.

Modern Rope Seamanship
by Colin Jarman and Bill Beavis
International Marine Publishing Company
Camden, Maine
110 pages, illus., 1976, $9.95

Knotting, splicing, and decorative ropework with the modern synthetic-fiber cordage.

Fig. 9.5 Cleating – using slipped half hitch

Fig. 8.8 Flaking down (2)

144

Dear Editors:

Being a sucker for a genuine bargain, I bought a chunk of 1/2-inch 3-strand nylon twist about 78 feet long for $5.00, and threw it in the car trunk. Got a call from a friend at the plant, whose car had gone sick on him, and he wondered if I could possibly tow him home. I just happened to have this nylon string with me, so I said I would pick him up, and we could go fetch his iron mule home. Now, 1/2-inch 3-strand nylon is good for about 7,000+ lbs. of tension, so I had no qualms about pulling his free-rolling 2,000-lb. import down the road. Both of us have been in and out of the sports car caper for longer than I care to admit, and we do know both ends of the towline, so I was not worried. I told him I was going to tow with nylon, and it would be the softest tow he had felt in a quarter of a century. We set it up at about 25 to 30 feet between cars and hitched up. I eased forward until the rope was off the ground. He gave the high sign, and I eased forward again, slowly. I was watching pretty close, and I am sure I moved at least three feet before his car moved an inch. The tow

went without fault, and when we got to his house, he told me that he did not feel the tow rope come taut, but all of a sudden he was moving smoothly. He thought nylon was the best thing for towing cars since the invention of gasoline. Cars, yes. Boats, no. Cars have no cleats inadequately screwed into a too-thin deck like some boats.

People still want to use a nylon line to tow a boat with. Could you put a cautionary note about this bad practice in your next issue?

R.F. Peterson
Stanford, Cal.

Mr. Peterson has a point. Nylon towing lines *are* dangerous, especially if the line is secured to an improperly fastened cleat or bitt. If such a fastening point were to give way, the nylon line would act just like an elastic, and anyone on the other end could easily wind up eating a cleatburger or chrome-plated bitt sandwich.—Eds.

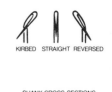

FISHING

Wherein we again ask why—as a cousin publication of the nation's largest fisherman's
journal—why is our coverage of the subject so
weird?

Atlantic Crossing Dept.

Howard Blackburn, if only you were alive today!
The Bass Buddy, from:

**K-Mac & Company
15404 Dooley Road
Addison, Texas 75001**

The basic Buddy is $59.95 plus shipping, but there
are many optional extras, including an outboard
trolling motor attachment. They also offer a lantern
holder for $16.95. Check state regulations; lantern
fishing is illegal in some.

145

Hook, Line & Sinker Dept.

To mention Mustad only in passing, as we did in
the last volume, was not fair. They are the world's
leader and standard for fishhooks of all types and
sizes. In the U.S. their home office is:

**O. Mustad & Son (USA) Inc.
P.O. Box 838
185 Clark Street
Auburn, N.Y. 13021**

*Above: Ah, yes. The Bass
Buddy.
Right: Hook terminology
from the Mustad catalog.*

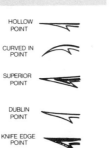

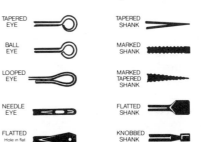

Supplies, Pure and Simple

All port cities with a fishing fleet have at least one commercial store selling wares of the trade. As often as not, these will be hole-in-the-wall places without bikinied-bombshell mannequins in the window—often there are no windows at all—and no advertising. When you write them you often get only a list of what they have. The game is not "Man versus Fish," it's "man makes a living," and that makes them very good places to buy, indeed. A few places to try in the northeast:

Parisi
27 Commercial Street
Gloucester, Mass. 01930

Island Fish Net Company
142 Railroad Ave.
Sayville, N.Y. 11782

Capt'n Supply Co.
Box 562, Ocean Drive
Cape May, N.J. 08204

```
No. 750 Tarred Gangin 2 lb. Spools
    550 Tarred Gangin 2 lb. Spools

Trawl Rigged with 6/0  8/0 Hooks
    325 Hooks per tub approx., 2,600 ft.
    Long - Ground Line of No. 16 Brownell
    Trawl Line Tarred (without tub)
```

Above, and right, above: From the Parisi catalog. They also have tubs.
Right, below: From the Lead Enterprises catalog.

Lead

We were curious to find a wholesale source of lead products, sinkers to keels, and discovered a big one— all manner of lead products for fishing and then some.

Lead Enterprises Manufacturing
3310 N.W. 29th St.
Miami, Florida

Small-Scale Gear

Western world fishing vessels tend to get smaller to remain profitable as inflation and oil prices bite, and Spencer Carter Ltd. is helping them with scaled-down gear. Their interest extends into gear, lead weights, hooks, ready-tied lines with plastic lures, line, swivels, gloves, trawl boards, blocks, drive shafts, flexible drive couplings, pulleys, and link belting. They also manufacture gantries, gallows, masts, deck fittings, davits, engine and hydraulic motor seatings, propeller shafts, sterntubes, rudders, and stocks. Seems like a progressive firm offering practical equipment.

Spencer - Carter Limited
Kernick Road
Penryn, Cornwall
England
TELEX 45489

—John Leather

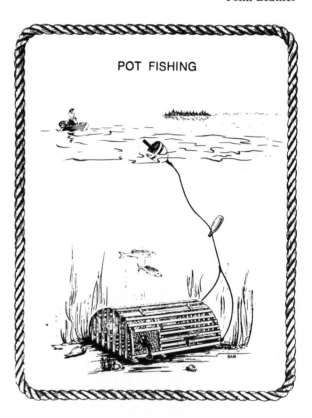

POT FISHING

THIS "CORNER" PYRAMID SINKER HOLDS . . .

and HOLDS . . .

and

H O L D S

IN THE SURF

Special Design

***Beautiful Swimmers,* by William W. Warner**
Atlantic-Little, Brown, Boston, Mass.
304 pages, illus., 1976, $10

It used to be that if you wanted an authentic, recent study of the doings of Chesapeake Bay watermen, you read Varley Lang's *Follow the Water* (see review, MC-4, P. 121). Lang's book is still valuable, but, since it was published in 1961, it just isn't recent enough. *Beautiful Swimmers* is, and it is one of the best books written on the Chesapeake Bay (it's also one of the best books written on anything during 1976—it won a Pulitzer Prize).

The title of the book refers to the Bay's blue crab, whose Latin name is *Callinectes sapidus* (tasty, beautiful swimmers). The focus of the book is the crab and the industry that surrounds it—one of the largest fisheries in the United States. Yet the real heroes of the story, if you can call them that, are the watermen whose lives revolve around the comings and goings of the crab. The narrative is, at once, the natural history of the blue crab, a study of the economy of the crab fishery, a portrayal of the waterman's life, and a description of the methods of catching, storing, transporting, and marketing crabs.

You would think that a book that did all that would be incredibly boring, but we assure you that it is not. The reason is simple: the author did his research, not out of books, but by visiting with watermen, working with watermen, eating and drinking with watermen, and, above all else, *listening* to watermen. The stories he has to tell as a result make fine reading.

Illustration and boxed quote below from Beautiful Swimmers.

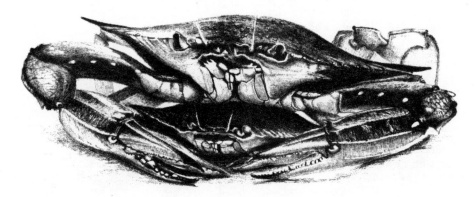

DOUBLERS AT REST

> Anyways they put one of them little sand fiddlers [the ghost crab] in the Derby. Now, you being a scientist-like from the Smithsonian Institute and a-studying of crabs, you know how fast they can go. Well, that little crab, he just shot over the line and kept going! Never did catch him, I don't believe. Then three or four years ago they flew in one of those big spider crabs from Hawaii — his name was 'Great Warrior' in Hawaiian, I heard it said — and you never saw a bigger nor more ugly looking thing. Well, now, that 'Great Warrior,' he took three steps and he was off the board. Then he goes for the judge and bites him on the shoe. It took two men to pull him off! I swear it! But, you see, he wasn't any kind of crab you could eat, so it come to us we could rule him out on that score. Seemed like a shame for a feller to fly that crab four thousand miles and then have him declared ineligible. But we had to do something; it wasn't no contest that way. That's how come we have the Governor's Cup now, for all of them foreign crabs. But they got to be edible, like you say. That's the only rule."

147

Coated Mesh

The inventive mind is always at home around the water and at those times when one has an idea requiring plastic-coated steel mesh (holding cages, traps, screening, pots, and so on), it's nice to know where to get it. Vinyl clad marine mesh in rolls—many mesh sizes, welded, woven, or hex, and the snips, crimpers, and clips to civilize it:

**Coatings Engineering Corp.
33 Union Ave.
Sudbury, Mass. 01776**

Fish Expo

Fishing gear freaks will appreciate knowing about Fish Expo, the biggest commercial fishing exposition in the United States. On display at the annual show are boats, gear, engines, and associated equipment, and during the course of the Expo there are seminars, talks, and movies. Fish Expo alternates between Seattle and Boston: Seattle in the fall of 1977 (Oct. 14-17), Boston in the fall of 1978, etc. For specifics:

**Fish Expo
21 Elm Street
Camden, Maine 04843**

Separation by Machine

A lot of Sea Grant and other funds are being expended these days on exploring ways to use better the fish we catch and also ways to eat species that we currently don't use at all. We are, as a culture, a fussy lot and usually demand that protein substances that are not red meat be *white*. This is why white cod meat, which tastes just so-so, gets a higher price at the landing than bluish-green pollock meat, which is delicious! Oddly enough, we'll eat any old trash if it's all ground up into a paste of any color. Read the label on your next can of "sandwich spread" or consider the contents of the next wiener you eat and see what we mean.

Anyway, the waste of many food industries, certainly fishing, has got to end soon, and machines such as those offered by Paoli are a small-scale means toward that end. Readers with a bit of capital, some time, and interest should write:

**Stephen Paoli Manufacturing Corp.
2531 Eleventh Street
Rockford, Illinois 61108**

...and a local fisherman—a very careful man—enough, in sailor's parlance, to eat the ship...

—Conor O'Brien
From Three Yachts (1928)

Now there's a nautical expression worth reviving!

—Eds.

Plastic-coated wire pots like the one above can be quickly assembled from Marine Mesh.

We're pleased to announce the availability of vinyl-clad Marine Mesh in the popular size for crabbing—24″ wide, 1½″ hex mesh, 18 gauge wire, in 150 foot rolls.

Now, crabbers can obtain a rugged vinyl-coated mesh from a source close by.

Crab pots made of Marine Mesh last many times longer than pots made of plain galvanized wire.

Marine Mesh is made of high strength galvanized wire, dip-coated with our own Cecoflex® vinyl and heat-cured (fused) at high temperatures right on the wire. Our coating is a thick vinyl plastic, not a paint.

Join the trend to vinyl-clad mesh. Wire rolls, accessories and assembly tools all are available, shipped FOB our plant. Write or call us for information and samples.

*Above: From a Coatings Engineering brochure.
Below: The Paoli 19-8 Separator System.*

Aquaculture

To keep up our growing list of aquaculture-related publications, we add *Farm Pond Harvest*, one of the older publications in the field, and most interesting reading for those with a spot of fresh going begging.

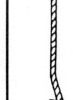

Farm Pond Harvest
c/o Professional Sportsman's Pub. Co.
Box AA
Momence, Illinois 60954

Most ponds, quarries and big lakes have one unfortunate thing in common—a large population of small sized bluegill. Until recently, this large population of small bluegill has been an undeveloped resource that no-one seemed to know what to do with.

Basically, the program amounts to distributing proper sized pellets for bluegill into the special floating tray-type feeder. Numerous experiments have proven the bluegill and some bass adapt to the free hand-out every bit as readily as the trout and catfish have. A large percentage of bass will also feed on floating pellets—the bluegill will "teach" them.

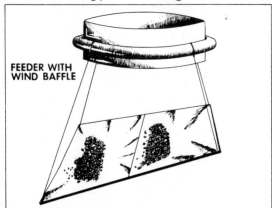

FEEDER WITH WIND BAFFLE

FARM POND HARVEST'S program is not designed to be the only source of food, but as a supplemental feeding that provides the needed amount of food that is not available naturally in most ponds, quarries, or lakes.

In only a few months of feeding bluegill, we were able to bring forth growth amounting to one-half again the original size of the bluegill. Proper protein must be present in the pellet to accomplish this.

Bluegill will stay in and around a particular area where food is readily available. This insures the feeding of the same bluegill day after day, so that maximum growth can be obtained.

This same desirable feature in the makeup of the bluegill, its "home-body" trend, means fishing near the feeder can be excellent. Many people are putting these feeders right off their docks on bigger lakes so they can have instant-fishing when they want it without going several miles by boat to find it.

FARM POND HARVEST'S program uses both a sinking and a floating type pellet. The floating ring at the top of the feeder holds the floating pellets at the feeding site. Without it, many pellets might drift away before they could be consumed. Sinking pellets must be held in a tray-type feeder at just the right position for feeding. Otherwise, they would sink to the bottom of the pond, wasted. The special feeder illustrated here does the job. The floating pellets and the sinking pellets stay right where they should—available for the bluegill to feed on whenever the desire for food hits them. Complete feeding instructions are included with the new floating-type feeder.

Above: From Farm Pond Harvest. *The feeder goes for $20; the feed for $14.*
Right: From Fishes of the World.

Fishes of the World: An Illustrated Dictionary
by Alwyne Wheeler
Macmillan, New York
366 pages, illus., glossary, 1975, $27.50

There are a number of fish dictionaries available today: some good, some bad, some expensive, some inexpensive. This is a good, expensive one that would fit well in a reference library, but, because of its physical size (9½″ x 12″), it would fare poorly as a field guide. It is thorough, well illustrated (color plates and line drawings), and organized so you can enter it with either the scientific or the common name of the fish—"Entries are arranged in alphabetical order, separate entires being made for families (cross-referenced to the genera included), and under the scientific name of the species of fish. Thus, the Atlantic salmon will appear under its scientific, Latinized name, *Salmo salar*, cross-referenced to the family Salmonidae, reference to which will lead to all the other members of the family included. Widely used vernacular names mostly in the English language are also given and cross-indexed."

M. productus PACIFIC HAKE 90 cm. (35 in.) This hake ranges from n. Alaska to Magdalena Bay in California, and offshore along the continental shelf. It is found in depths of 183–914 m. (100–500 fathoms). Like other hakes it is a schooling fish which migrates vertically each day feeding nearer the surface as night approaches. It also migrates offshore in the winter.

149

It feeds mainly on fishes, but eats squids and crustaceans; the young fish eat small crustaceans mainly. In turn it is eaten by many marine animals especially small whales, porpoises, seals, and sea lions, swordfish, sharks, and halibut. Its flesh is rated as insipid and soft if kept, although very fresh it is good. Much of the hake caught was used for pet food and the manufacture of fish meal, but of recent years fisheries for it have been expanded by Russian ships.

Fly Tackle: A Guide to the Tools of the Trade
by Harmon Henkin
Lippincott, Philadelphia
240 pages, illus., index, biblio., list of sources, 1976, $9.95

Sneakers resting after a day of wading

The *Mariner's Catalog* hasn't paid much attention to fly fishing in the past; what we have covered so far has been the antithesis of fly fishing and its own peculiar cult. Yet there are a few good things to say about the sport, so when we see something good, we'll mention it.

This book is the most sensible of its kind on the subject of fly-fishing tackle. The author is an aficionado, that's for sure, but he has the most essential type of commonsense when it comes to discussing the equipment you will need: "There may not be a direct causal relationship between the dissatisfaction we feel in our lives and the amount of impulse buying we engage in, but there is at least some connection. We all seem to believe subconsciously that buying things will make us happier." Or, "This mellowing process took place when I came to realize that fly-fishing, cleared of the muddle that envelops it, has a simple, primary aim—to catch fish."

The book is filled with the legend and lore of fine and not-so-fine fly tackle, and a liberal amount of practical advice on outfitting yourself for your own hedonistic fling at a stream.

The Complete Fisherman's Catalog
by Harmon Henkin
Lippincott, Philadelphia
463 pages, illus., index, paperbound, 1977, $7.95

"A source book of information about tackle and accessories for fly fishing, spinning, bait casting, surf casting, ice fishing, offshore fishing, and more." If there is a better catalog on the subject, we'd like to see it. This is a superlative effort, worthy of being referred to in the same breath as *The Whole Earth Catalog, The Explorers Ltd. Sourcebook*, and, of course, *The Mariner's Catalog*. However, the person who had the impertinence to put the word "complete" in the title should be given a short course in the stupidity and counter-productivity of inflated claims.

Top: From Fly Tackle.
Left and below: From the Complete Fisherman's Catalog.

Old reels work just as well

By Harmon Henkin

Recently a friend who is just beginning to fish watched as I rummaged around in the morass of assorted things in my garage.

An ancient Bache-Brown spinning reel turned up. The tarnished 25-year-old fellow was the first spinning reel I had ever owned. I put it aside one day when the handle fell off. The friend looked it over carefully, amazed at its age and manual half-bail.

He needed an all-around reel. Could he have it?

My first instinct was to defer on sentimental grounds. But then, looking around at the mounds of sentimentality, that didn't seem like a firm reason. So I explained the utterly simple mechanism. Just lift the slim bail handle, cast and replace the handle to retrieve. Nothing easier.

"But modern reels are so much better," I argued.

"Why?"

"They have ball bearings. They're smaller. They have automatic bails. All the latest gadgetry."

"Does that really make a difference?"

"The new ones have Teflon drags and stuff."

"This drag seems smooth."

"It was a great drag. Never slipped."

"Are the new ones really any better?"

"Ah. Umm. Well, you see . . . just take the reel. It's as good as you'll ever need. Send it back to White Plains and get the handle redone."

He seemed happy as he left with it. I pondered my reaction.

Are the new ones really better than the classics? Probably not better than the average angler would ever need. We don't buy Ferraris because they handle better than Chevies. We buy them for other, more metaphysical reasons. The same goes for fishing tackle.

You might as well get the best reel for the money, one that has all the latest deluxe features.

But that doesn't mean they're better. That's a different quality entirely.

*Microbial Seascapes: A Pictorial Essay on
Marine Microorganisms and Their
Environments*
by John McNeill Sieburth, PhD.
University Park Press, Baltimore, Md.
**216 pages, paperbound, nearly 200 photos,
1975, $9.50**

There's seeing, and then there's *seeing*; there's understanding, and then there's *understanding*. If we're not making ourselves clear, the concept will become more concrete if you walk down to the seashore, get down on your hands and knees or dive into the water, and look at the sea life. You will see it and quite possibly understand it. Next you could take a few samples back with you to the laboratory and study them under a scanning electron microscope. You will then *see* them and, one would hope, *understand* them.

John Sieburth, a professor at URI, did just that and took photographs of the results. Here, in an astounding book, are collected a series of micrographs that will stand you on your ear. For instance, first you might see the eggs of a dog whelk magnified 10 times; then you might see succeeding photos of a single egg magnified 53, 653 and 5,230 times. And it's a guided tour—with captions and diagrams, Sieburth tells you exactly what you are looking at.

Excellent picture books are many times alluded to as visual feasts. This one is.

Below: From Microbial Seascapes.

Plate 2-6. Plankton net-tow concentrated on filter
Site: Narragansett Bay, RI
Magnification: 1,800X

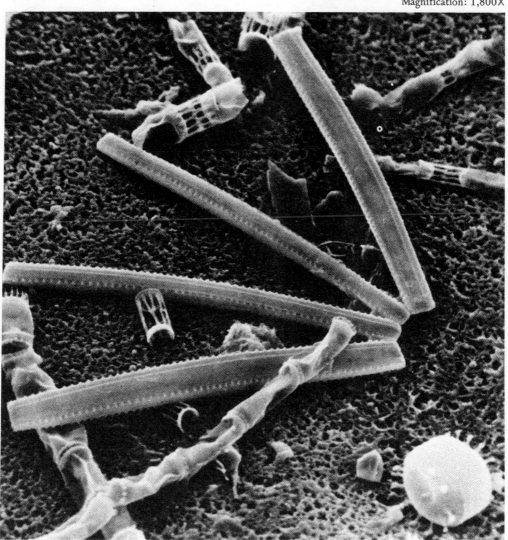

*Collecting phytoplankton by net eliminates much of the debris and phytoflagellates but captures the
larger diatoms, which are free of attached bacteria—*

151

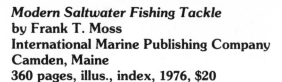

Modern Saltwater Fishing Tackle
by Frank T. Moss
International Marine Publishing Company
Camden, Maine
360 pages, illus., index, 1976, $20

Detailed examination of all saltwater gear and tackle, including why it works as well as how it works.

Below: From Modern Saltwater Fishing Tackle.

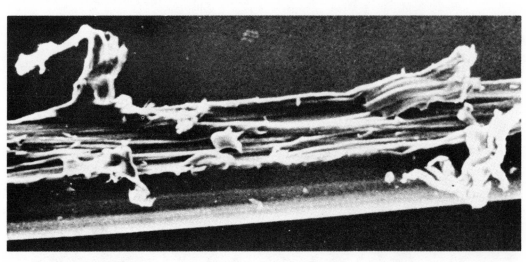

This is what happens to monofilament when it is pulled over a sharp edge, like a grooved rod guide. Electron-microscope photo was made by the Du Pont Company during line tests.

Garcia Outdoor Library

For sportfishermen, the Garcia Corporation publishes a range of how-to books on specialized subjects. The books are written by well-known outdoorsmen, and, at $1.50 each, are attractively priced. Get them from:

The Garcia Corporation
329 Alfred Avenue
Teaneck, N.J. 07666

Making A Living Alongshore, by Phil Schwind
International Marine Publishing Company
Camden, Maine
160 pages, illus., 1976, $7.95

How to make a living gathering shellfish, and engaging in small-time commercial fishing; emphasizes practical rather than pie-in-the-sky advice.

Fiddler crab at right and quote below from
Making a Living . . .

With the emphasis on Norwegian sardines, Icelandic haddock, Canadian salt codfish, South African lobster tails, Japanese crabs, and so on and so on, what has happened to the American "alongshore fisherman," the little fellow who provided his neighborhood with fish and shellfish that were fresh, *fresh*, FRESH, right out of the water with their tails still wagging, or with their shells clamped shut? The fish and shellfish are still there, but the fine art of making a living along the shore has gone the way of blacksmithing and candle making. Mass production may have done away with the handcrafts, but the fish and shellfish are still there, waiting to be caught. They may exist in smaller numbers because of competition, but they are more valuable because of higher prices, and they are more vulnerable because of better equipment.

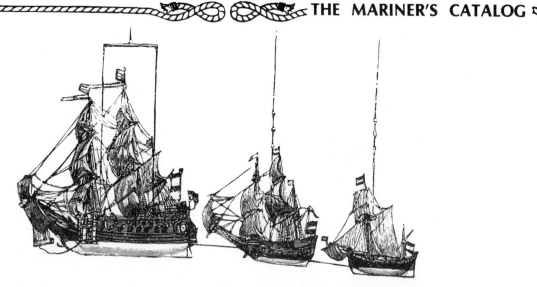

MODELS AND MODELING

The most impressive modeller's source to come to our attention during the past year is Helmut Breisinger of West Germany. They have their own series of models, primarily of German ships and small craft, but most notable are their plans and photo collections from all over the world, including the Plans de Marine Ancienne of Le Musée de la Marine of France, the working drawings of Harold A. Underhill (some of them by other draftsmen), the Ausgesuchte Geschenk-Bucher series on German naval vessels from 1848 to 1945, and page after page of Breisinger's own plans of many vessels from many places and periods. Their 144-page catalog is jammed with vessel and craft types one hasn't seen available before, and usually there is a selection of plans within each type to boot. For example, there are over a half-dozen royal barges from which to choose.

Helmut Breisinger
Schiffsmodellbau
Uhlandstrasse 7, Postfach 26
7441 Grossbettlingen
West Germany
Catalog is $5 (U.S.) postpaid.

The ordering department at Breisinger had this to say: "Payment of the catalog can be effected by enclosing a check or the cash (dollars) when placing the order. Moreover, bank or post transfers are possible (Account No. 132033 with the Kreissparkasse Nürtingen). In case deliveries are to be made by airmail, the extra charge will have to be paid by the customer and will have to be included."

Admiralitätsanker : Metall
J 100/25   25 x 25 mm
J 100/35   35 x 35 mm
J 100/50   50 x 50 mm

Above and below: From the Helmut Breisinger catalog.

153

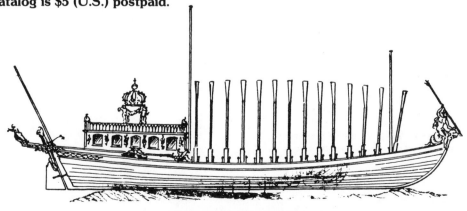

Admirers of English hull forms will wish to know about Hands which, appropriately enough, hand-makes model boats:

Hands Products
11 Dryburgh Mansions
Erpingham Road
Putney, London S.W. 15 1BE
England

Above: Thames spritsail sailing barge Nautilus *by Hands Products.*
Above, left: From a Hands Products brochure.

At present, there are 5 models in the Hands range:
A Bristol Channel pilot cutter, a simplification of the pilot *Marguerite T,* £26
A Falmouth working oyster boat of small scale, taken from the vessel *George Glacen,* £30
A Hastings lugger of small scale, taken from plans and remaining information of the vessel *Industry R.X. 94,* £34
A spritsail sailing barge, taken from plans and current model of the barge *Nautilus,* £50
A spiritsail barge taken from the original vessel *May.* £68.50
Hands expects to increase the number of models offered soon. New offerings will be a Brixham trawler, a Morecamb Bay prawner, an East Coast smack, a Liverpool pilot, and a Norfolk wherry.

Metrication for Modellers
Model & Allied Publications
13-35 Bridge St.
Hemel Hempstead, Herts
England

A 40-page pamphlet on just that, metric equivalents for model work, where it makes only slightly more sense than it does for full-size boatwork, that is to say, a one on a scale of ten.
Working in a 3/4″ scale, 1/16″ is an inch on the full-sized craft. Pretty neat. Let's do this metrically now. Remember, we don't want to change the size of our model. O.K., here goes (pulling out a slide-rule calculator): an inch equals 2.54 centimeters. On a 1.905 centimeter scale model (equivalent to 3/4″), 2.54 centimeters on the real thing equals .015875 centimeters on the model. Gee, that's really slick.

More Paper

154

Perhaps there are secret vices that are less expensive than paper models, but how inexpensive can a thing become before being classified as a virtue? That little pensioner down the street with a satiated smile on his face all the time probably has an attic full of paper models. Here is another source with a *Providence*, a *Morgan*, and a *Viking Ship* at $2.50 each.

Seacraft Models, Inc.
160 Gibbs Ave.
Newport, R.I. 02840

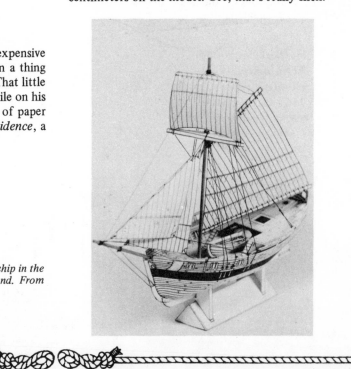

Right: Paper model of the Providence, *the first ship in the U.S. Navy and John Paul Jones's first command. From Seacraft Models.*

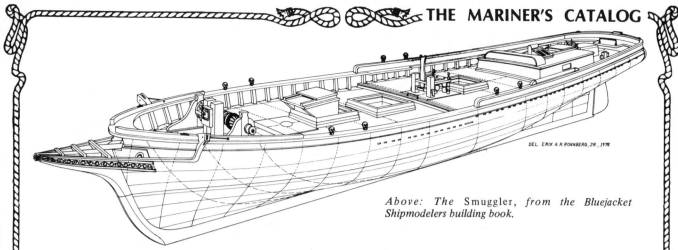

DEL. ERIK A.R.RONNBERG, JR., 1976

Above: The Smuggler, *from the Bluejacket Shipmodelers building book.*

A Notable Kit

On page 125 of the *Mariner's Catalog, Volume 4,* George Putz has a note about kits, and what he had to say is usually true. After looking at the drawings and instruction book from Bluejacket's kit of *Smuggler,* an 1877 Gloucester schooner, I'd say he'll have to take back the bit about more research needed for kit models. No additional research is needed for the *Smuggler.* The book is a fine job of background material, explanations of fittings, and detail sketches, and it's a construction manual to boot. The drawings are well done and show almost everything needed. To me, this is what a model kit should be. The scale is standard museum, 1/4" = 1 ft., which makes the parts large enough so there is no excuse for leaving out detail. Erik Ronnberg, Jr., the author of the book, is to be congratulated on his drawings and instructions.

From the photographs of the model, I'd say the fittings were well done except for the wheel. That looks a little heavy, but thank goodness a kit manufacturer is turning out Britannia metal castings. Again, museum specs.

The kit price sounds high ($74.55), but I don't think it is if one considers the work that went into it. If someone objects, he can always buy the plans and instructions ($12) and go from there. There's more satisfaction that way, but not everyone who wants to build a model has the tools, casting equipment, and other gear needed for doing the whole job.

Bluejacket is to be congratulated on this one. (Bluejacket has more than 30 other model kits besides the *Smuggler.*—Eds.)

Bluejacket Ship Crafters
145 Water Street
South Norwalk, Conn. 06854
Catalog is $1

—Jay Hanna

Lower left: Diagram for making a comparator, which is used for checking scale, from the Techniques of Ship Modelling.

The Techniques of Ship Modelling
by Gerald A. Wingrove
Model & Allied Publications
13-35 Bridge St.
Hemel Hempstead, Hertfordshire
England
£4

If you already have several books on modelling, you probably don't need this one. It's a matter of your own working style. One book, just to get the idea, will suffice for many, who will take off from there and do just fine. Others try to collect every wrinkle they can, and a half-dozen new tricks will justify the purchase of a new title.

This one is full of tooling and technical advice by one of England's foremost model builders. It is "targeted" at the medium-advanced craftsman, and the work as a whole reminds one of the several modelling titles that *Popular Science, Popular Mechanics,* and various Fawcett publications produced in the 1940s and 1950s.

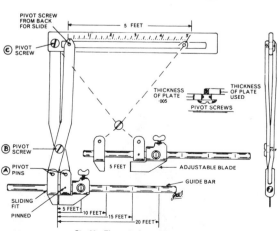

Fig. 29   The parts for making a comparator

155

Seventeenth Century Rigging
by R.C. Anderson
Model & Allied Publications
13-35 Bridge St.
Hemel Hempstead, Herts.
England
£1.50

156

Much recommended for ships of the period. All the exquisite books that constitute the "must haves" (Lever's, etc.) are wonderful, of course, but their richness and completeness almost work against them from a practical standpoint. In a way, their illustrations have too much, and one can go cross-eyed trying to figure out how a particular bend or fitting is actually supposed to "go." This book takes each problem and isolates it, using thin-line, somewhat-expanded drawings to show leads and articulations. Not pretty. Very useful.

New Magazine

Model Ships and Boats is a new journal on the shelf. Beginning as a slim thing early in 1976, recent issues have shown health. Response from its readership is enthusiastic, and its technical departments are useful from the beginning through medium-advanced levels.

Model Ships and Boats
415 Lexington Ave.
New York, N.Y. 10017
$9.15 per year

FIG. 280

Above: Art by Buck Smith.
Left: From Seventeenth Century Rigging.

Painting and Lining Scale Models
by Ian D. Huntley
Model & Allied Publications
13-35 Bridge St.
Hemel Hempstead, Herts.
England
£1.75

This 94-page soft-cover book on model finishwork is really good. Not only does it deal with the techniques of *applying* finishes, but also it goes into remarkable depth on the *nature* of various finishes. Where else can you find a straightforward source describing, in one chapter, acrylics, alkyds, amino resins, asphaltic bitumens, cellulose, vinyls, and styrenes, as well as discussions of the whole commercial inventory of pigmentation, solvents, thinners, driers, and plasticizers? There is a section on "weathering" and "griming" techniques, a field in which our aircraft and railroad modelling friends are way ahead of us. Though there is little mention of watercraft per se, it is a good book.

Radio Control for Model Yachts
by C.R. Jeffries
£1.25
and
Radio Control Model Boats
by Philip Connolly and Vic Smeed
£1.50
Model & Allied Publications
13-35 Bridge St.
Hemel Hempstead, Herts.
England

RC is very popular in England, and these two books provide a picture of the English developments of the craft and sport in sail and power, respectively. Generally, English electronics are on a par or a bit less than those here. Some of their engines, however, are most interesting mills on which to ponder.

The National Watercraft Collection
2nd Edition
by Howard I. Chapelle
International Marine Publishing Company
Camden, Maine
416 pages, illus., biblio., index, 1976, $20

Revised edition of the detailed catalog of the Smithsonian Institution's ship and boat models: merchant sail, merchant steam, and fishing craft.

A magneto-equipped Gannet 15 c.c., 4-stroke petrol motor showing the sparking plug, pushrods, tappets and valve springs—all unique to this type of motor

Above: From Radio Control for Model Boats.
Below: From the National Watercraft Collection.

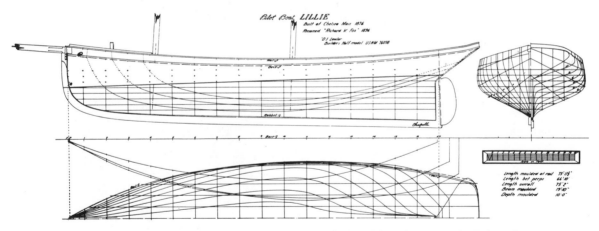

LINES OF THE BOSTON PILOT SCHOONER *Lillie*, built at Chelsea, Massachusetts, 1876. Taken off the builder's half-model USNM 76038.

157

The Baltimore Clipper, by Howard I. Chapelle
Edward W. Sweetman Co.
Box 1509
Largo, Florida 33540
192 pages, illus., index, $9

We've been under the impression that Chapelle's study of the origins and development of the Baltimore clipper has been long out of print. It turns out that there are two reprints available (the other is by the Augustus Kelley Co., Clifton, N.J., $27.50, but we haven't seen a copy). This edition is reduced in physical size from the original, but it's all there. Like other books by Chapelle, the text is fairly dry, but if you're looking for well-researched history with plenty of plans to back it up, you'll find it here.

Below: Kessel Neuchatel from the Kurt Holzapfel catalog.

Steaming Mad

A German-language catalog of model steam plants and boilers:

**Kurt Holzapfel
Dampfmachinen
CH-8401 Winterthur
Switzerland
price of catalog is 5 International Reply
Coupons**

158

Custom model boiler services; one here, another in England:

Dear Editors:

Generally we do not build boilers for full-sized boats; our preference is for models. We can make copper or steel boilers, in smaller sizes, to a known design; or we can design to suit the builder. Prices, since all the work is more or less "custom" built, will be given on request. Most of our work has been in the locomotive field. To give an idea of size, the largest boiler in diameter is 10".

**Robert W. Maynard
3825 Virginin Court
Cincinnati, Ohio 45211**

Dear Editors:

I am a one-man business and all my work is issued with a test certificate. All the marine boilers I make are to customers' drawings or sketches. I specialize in boilers only, therefore I keep up to date with all the latest equipment.

**R.R. Chambers
37 Wyke Oliver Road
Preston, Weymouth
Dorset, England**

Below: Marine-type engine designed and constructed by Maynard for use on a geared locomotive: bore 1¼", stroke 1½".

THE STUART TRIPLE

A Triple Expansion Engine with cylinders ¾-in. 1¼-in., and 1¾-in. × 1-in. stroke. Length 9-in., height 6⅛-in., width 4-in. The finished weight is 10-lb.

Left: From the Carolus catalog.

This is an accurate and very complete model of a Marine Engine. It is a robust working model; feed and air pumps work correctly. It is an ideal engine for a model liner. Above all, to an amateur who has skill in the use of his tools it is a delightful model to build.

Carolus is another name to add to your list of Stuart steam-model sources. They offer a book entitled *Building Steam Engines from Castings*, priced at $2.00.

Carolus Model Engineering Works
3082 South 200 East
Bountiful, Utah 84010

A fine, stout, and fast model steam unit is available from:

Seaward Models
P.O. Box P 76
South Dartmouth. Mass. 02748
(Be sure to include an addressed, stamped envelope when writing for information.)

An interesting engine model is the ST-1 steam turbine kit at $27.95 and a boiler for her at $19.95, by:

Hobson Tiny Engines
P.O. Box 283
Visalia, Cal. 93277

Anyone who likes models will enjoy building this little steam turbine. It has only one moving part and takes only a few pleasant hours to build. The fun, though, comes in operating it after you have it assembled. The high speed at which it turns at full throttle, accompanied by its business-like whine, exhausting steam from the stack and the immediate response when thrown into reverse will bring a grin to almost anybody's face. Using an electronic counter, no load, we have clocked it at speeds over 10,000 R.P.M. The turbine operates on 30#-40# steam pressure and is all metal. It has been carefully engineered. All lathe work, machining, and reaming has been done. So has the frustrating work requiring jigs and dies. The kit is complete and contains *everything* you need to connect to your boiler, except a little solder. A soldering torch, drill, and ordinary shop tools are all you will need. Overall height including stack is 5″. The rotor is 3/8″ by 2-11/16″ diameter. The diameter of the housing with trim ring in place is slightly over 3″.

—Hobson Tiny Engines

159

Left: The Hobson ST-1 engine with front cover off.
Below: Seaward's model engine.

Dear Editors:

In your discussion of models on pages 126-127 of the first *Mariner's Catalog,* you seem to favor wood models over plastic models. I warrant that if I built a plastic model of the USS *Kearsarge,* and you built a wood model, mine would be a better model. You could not afford to make the planking look authentic, and if the waterlines, buttock lines, and half-breadths were compared, the plastic model would be much more accurate. Sure, the scientific hull will be approximately the correct shape, but the Revell hull will be as accurate as good designers can make it, working from the best data they can get their hands on—and Revell's toolmakers are darn good!

I have two models. One is a wood model of the *A.J. Fuller,* a full-rigged ship launched in Bath, Maine, in 1889, I believe. This model appears to have been built by a member of the crew. The rigging is very well done and is all there. The hull is a typical piece of carved wood that shows the grain through the paint. The paint, by the way, is gold or brass below the waterline.

My other model is a Revell *Cutty Sark.* Each piece of copper sheathing is detailed. Pretty neat. The rigging plans of the *Cutty Sark* are in several stages, and if you want to do a proper job, Revell provides a sheet showing which belaying pin takes which line—by name, or sheet, or halyard, or lift. When I sat down with this Revell sheet and the *A.J. Fuller,* I was surprised to find the two agreed—line for line and belaying pin for belaying pin. As I thought about this, it became pretty apparent that this kind of standardization was essential, considering the origins and languages of crew members. (See also *Standard Seamanship for the Merchant Service,* Felix Reisenberg, 2nd Edition, Van Nostrand Company, Inc., pp 179-220.)

If you want to model a specific ship and are interested in copying the prototype, stick to the plastics; if you want to make a "model boat," I guess wood is all right.

R.F. Peterson
Stanford, California

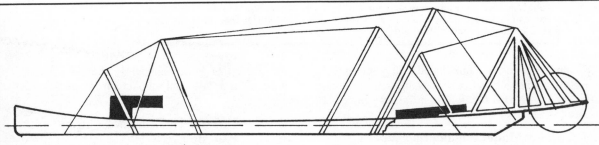

Add braces for paddlewheel Complete hog chain system.

FIG. 36

This is fine as long as the wheel remains at rest. When it runs, however, a lot of other stresses come into being. Water is lifted and thrust back or forward. Vibrations are set up. To resist these forces wood braces are added as shown in Figure 36.

160

Steamboat Book

People who have no living experience with steamboats often have buried in their psyches the inability to believe the physics of these platforms. There are those who don't think man has been to the moon, either. One has to admit that those special-effects fellows are truly clever.

A delightful and sympathetic book on how they *did* do it is:

The Western Rivers Steamboat Cyclopaedium, or American Riverboat Structure and Detail, Salted with Lore With a Nod to the Modelmaker
by Alan L. Bates
Hustle Press, Leonia, N.J.

Above: From the Western Rivers Steamboat Cyclopaedium.

Planbooks

The Louis Davidson Waterline Shipmodeler's Planbook Series has just added *U.S. Battleships* ($3.75). Other titles in the series are *U.S. Cruisers* ($3.50), *U.S. Destroyers* ($3.00), and *Bronze Age Ships* ($3.00). Each book presents photos and drawings to help give life to miniature vessels and fleets. Useful, but the printing should be better. Some of the photos are too muddy for detail work.

Louis Davidson
3531 Milford
Pensacola, Florida 32506

Modelling Tools

Dobson has developed two tools of possible use: a mitre box for small work, and a solution to the enraging aspects of seizing and serving model gauges of rigging wires and threads—a real arthritis fighter.

Dobson
1416 So. Courtland
Park Ridge, Illinois 60068

MITER-RITE is ....
Precision in Miniature

a DOBSON product

THIS "MITER-RITE" IS A PRECISION HAND-CRAFTED MITER SAW IN MINIATURE THAT HOLDS THE SAW BLADE PRECISELY PERPENDICULAR TO THE BASE AT ANY ANGLE WITH A RANGE OF 65° ON EACH SIDE OF 90°. A POSITIVE LOCKING POSITION IS ALSO FEATURED AT 90° AND 45°.

THE OVERALL SIZE OF THE "MITER-RITE" IS 7¾" WIDE x 5¼" DEEP x 4" HIGH, AND IT COMES COMPLETE WITH A SAW BLADE THAT IS CAPABLE OF CUTTING BRASS TUBING AS EASILY AS WOOD. (SAW BLADE IS A STANDARD ITEM IN ALL HOBBY SHOPS.)

THE CUTTING CAPACITY OF WOOD IS: ½" x 1¼" AT 90°, ½"x7/8" AT 45° AND ¼" THICK x 3" WIDE AT ANY ANGLE. A REPLACEABLE CUTTING BOARD IS PROVIDED SO THAT THE MAIN BASE NEED NOT BE CUT.

THE SPECIALLY DESIGNED BLADE HOLDER HAS A SECTION 4¼" LONG THAT GRIPS AND GUIDES THE BLADE BUT NEVER COMES IN CONTACT WITH THE SAW TEETH, THUS ASSURING NO WEAR WHATEVER. IN ADDITION, 2 NYLON SCREWS SERVE AS ADJUSTABLE PRESSURE PADS.

THE "MITER-RITE" ALSO FEATURES A "MEMORY" STOP GAGE, BOTH LEFT AND RIGHT. THIS MEMORY GAGE CAN BE SET THEN MOVED ASIDE FOR A LONGER CUT AND LATER SET BACK TO EXACTLY THE SAME POSITION.

MAKE CHECK OR MONEY ORDER PAYABLE TO:

DOBSON **$29.95*** 1416 SO. COURTLAND PARK RIDGE, IL 60068 * PLUS POSTAGE

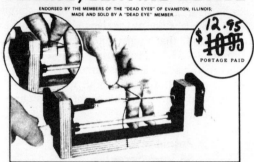

for Model Shipbuilders
the "STRING-ALONG"
A SEIZING/SERVING DEVICE

ENDORSED BY THE MEMBERS OF THE "DEAD EYES" OF EVANSTON, ILLINOIS; MADE AND SOLD BY A "DEAD EYE" MEMBER.

$12.95 ~~$10.95~~ POSTAGE PAID

A QUALITY FABRICATED DEVICE TO SERVE AND SEIZE LINES FOR MODEL SHIP BUILDERS. TURNING THE HANDLE TURNS THE CORD (INSTEAD OF JUST TWISTING) AND PERMITS YOU TO SEIZE A LINE IN A FRACTION OF WHAT IT TOOK TO DO BY PASSING THE LINE HAND OVER HAND. USE THE ALLIGATOR CLIP TO HOLD A BLOCK, OR MAKE A LOOP, IT SNAPS OFF TO ALLOW YOU TO PASS THE LINE THROUGH BOTH ENDS AND SEIZE ANY LENGTH OF LINE.

CONSTRUCTED WITH 4 GEARS, ALUMINUM TUBING, 6 NYLON BEARINGS.
THE WOOD FRAME IS MADE WITH AN 11 PLY BIRCHWOOD THAT'S PHENOLIC LAMINATED.
* AS AN INTRODUCTION, 12 "OK" CLIPS ARE ENCLOSED. YOU WILL FIND THEM EXTREMELY HELPFUL IN RIGGING.

MAKE CHECKS · MONEY ORDERS PAYABLE TO **DOBSON** 1416 So. COURTLAND PARK RIDGE, ILL. 60068

Above and above, right: From a Hobson catalog. Note the price change on the "String-Along".
Below: The inner workings of a Badger airbrush. From a Badger Airbrush Company catalog.

You can find Badger Airbrushes at the better hobby shops and art supply houses, or write:

Badger Airbrush Co.
9201 Gage Ave.
Franklin Park, Illinois 60131

161

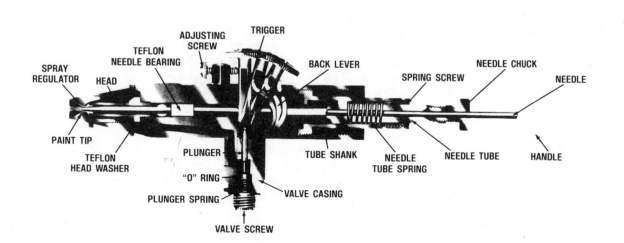

Above: From a Zakoske brochure.
Below: Boxed quote from a Shipyard Half Models brochure.
A sample of their work is at the bottom of the opposite page.

Pre-built Models

As modelling has caught on, so has *having* models. Relatively speaking, there never were very many of them, and as the fad has spread, so have the model sharks. There are now several outfits peddling models to whomever will fall for their litany of "hundreds of hours of research goes into each . . . ," "master craftsmen plying their ancient . . . ," "museum quality throughout . . . ," and so on and on. It's all blather, of course, but we are afraid that lots of redecorated offices, institutions, restaurants, and fireplace mantels are to be cursed by these perversions. The fact is that if you are to have a truly excellent model, you must be rich, lucky, or do it yourself.

We've found only one organization that seems to be producing *acceptable* display ship models on a mass-production basis for less than an arm and a leg: Zakoske, Ltd., in Hong Kong. They offer completed display models, some fully planked, others built on a fiberglass hull, that range from $250 for a model of the *Spray* to $3,250 for a fully built *Victory*. They also accept museum and custom orders. Most of their line is at the $1,000 mark, about what it would cost to have a professional in this country do a fair job on a commercial kit.

Zakoske Ltd.
86 Lam Street
Third floor
Kowloon, Hong Kong

Half Models

In the same vein, Shipyard Half Models of Marblehead offers an extraordinary deal on half-models. They offer custom work to your specs, but their "series" offerings quoted here are most impressive, and they have on file virtually any one-design that you name, many famous racers, cruisers, and voyagers, including the best-known Universal Rule and International Rule boats, all the *America*'s Cup craft, fishing schooners, pilot schooners, and dozens of the most beloved traditional American small craft types.

Shipyard Half Models
Box 304
Marblehead, Mass. 01945

The "series" designation refers to alternative methods of construction. The Standard Series offers reasonably priced half models constructed from a solid epoxy/wood composite using master patterns. Hulls are finished in white with a black waterline and include the design name and particulars engraved on the brass nameplate. The Official Series are similarly constructed but are custom finished in the owner's colors and also include the vessel's and owner's names engraved on the nameplate. The Designers Series offers built-up half section models traditionally called hawk's nest models. These are constructed with varnished basswood centerline, sheer, and waterline plane, and half sections. The Collectors Series are traditional block models custom finished in the owner's colors and with a varnished basswood sheer (deck) plane. The Heirloom Series are varnished mahogany lift models with the addition of basswood inlays to designate the sections, waterlines, and buttocks.

THE PHYSICAL EXERCISE WITH WHICH MODEL YACHTING PROVIDES ITS DEVOTEES
IS WORTHY OF THE CONSIDERATION OF THE ENERGETICALLY-MINDED.

Competition Sails
for Model Sailing Yachts

All classes, and both have big winners in their record books.

West Coast

Black Sails
4761 Niagara Ave.
San Diego, California 92107

East Coast

Carr Sails
76 Gresham Street
Springfield, Virginia 22151

Above: The Carr Sails Factory Team Boat M66 in the thick of it at a regatta.
Below: A selection of Shipyard half models (see opposite page).

163

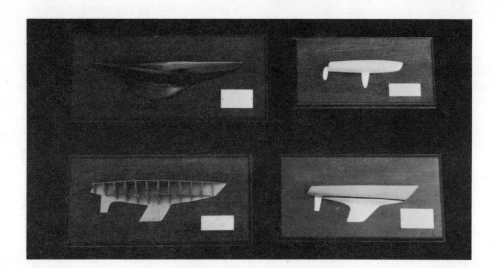

Above: Ron Packman's waterline model of the Orchidea.

An English Modelmaker

Models by Ron Packman have an honored place in the exacting craft of ship representation. Working at his studio by Hampshire's historic Hamble River, Packman produces fine scale models of ships of all types, besides magnificent carvings of animals and birds. Packman could not be better qualified for his craft; trained as a yachtbuilder, he became manager of a yachtyard and eventually a surveyor. His craftsmanship in wood is matched by his wide knowledge of other materials, many used in his models.

The 30-inch-waterline model of the refrigerated cargo liner *Orchidea*, at a scale of 1/230, is typical of his work, which is well researched, thoroughly accurate, and available to order.

> **Ron Packman**
> **Southerly, Orchard Road**
> **Locksheath, Southampton**
> **Hampshire**
> **England**

—John Leather

Yachtsman's Choice: The Best of Rudder
edited by Gurney Williams III
David McKay Co., N.Y.
212 pages, 1977, $10.95

There are some first-rate articles in this anthology—especially some by John Hanna, Thomas Fleming Day, and L. Francis Herreshoff—but it takes some kind of gall to call this book the "best" of *Rudder* magazine. *Rudder* is this nation's oldest and onetime best yachting magazine, and the wealth of material to be found in its pages is truly astounding. We realize that, if you took twenty editors and put each in a room with all of *Rudder*'s back issues and told them to compile an anthology of the best, you would get twenty completely different books. But we do believe that the most successful editor would create a book that demonstrated the essence of the publication. What that essence is, in our opinion, can be demonstrated only by recreating pages from the magazine, complete with illustrations, ads from the era, boat plans, etc. Williams did not do this—there is not an illustration in his book, even though some of the articles he reprints were splendidly illustrated—and the result is a sterile collection of material that could easily have been taken from the pages of *Yachting*, or *Motor Boating*, or *Boating*. Too bad.

Another anthology of boating articles is:

The Sea Chest: A Yachtsman's Reader
edited by Critchell Rimington
W.W. Norton, N.Y.
355 pages, 1947 (reissued 1975), $10

We assume the material came from the pages of *Yachting*, but nowhere in the book does the editor say this, so maybe not. The book suffers from the same weakness as Williams', but at least there is no claim that this is the "best" of anything. And we do believe that the stories, poems, and essays are as a whole more worthwhile and satisfying than those in *Yachtsman's Choice*.

Shoreside Notes

... I have MY OWN RAILROAD ...
—Lord Buckley

A reader sent us this note:

Dear Editors:

I am writing to see if you would have information on where we could obtain replacement wheels and wheel carriers for a marine railroad. We have a steel railroad track bed on which a wood carriage runs via a winch. The carriage is supported on steel wheels with double flanges. The wheel, in turn, is held by a bracket cast and drilled to carry an axle for the wheel.

David Bruce Falconer
Rowayton, Conn.

SINGLE FLANGED CAR WHEELS		DOUBLE FLANGED CAR WHEELS		FLAT FACE TRUCK WHEELS	
Diameter	Tread	Diameter	Tread	Diameter	Tread
5″	1⅜″ to 2¼″	6″	1⅞″	4″	1¼″ to 2″
6″	1¼″ to 4½″	7¼″	1¼″	5″	1¼″ to 2″
8″	1¾″ to 4½″	8″	2¼″	6″	1¼″ to 4″
9″	2⅛″ to 2½″	10¾″	1⅜″	7″	1½″ to 2″
10″	1¾″ to 2¾″	10¾″	2⅛″	8″	1½″ to 3″
11″	1⅞″ to 2⅜″	12¼″	2¾″	9″	2⅞″ to 3″
12″	2″ to 3″	12⅜″	2¾″	10″	2″ to 3″
14″	2″ to 3⅞″			12″	2″ to 4″
16″	2″ to 5½″			14″	2″ to 4″
18″	2¾″ to 4½″			16″	2″ to 3½″
20″	3″ to 4″			18″	2½″ to 3½″
				20″	2½″ to 3½″

We make many other sizes — send us your specifications

It was rather a tough one to track down—the *Thomas Registry* finally bailed us out. We found two practical sources.

U.S. Steel makes wheels in the upper size limits for practical marine railway use, 12 inches in diameter and larger. The home office can direct you to a local warehouse supplier.

**U.S. Steel
600 Grant Street
Pittsburgh, Penn. 15230**

A more likely and easy source is Chase, which makes flanged wheels down to five inches and up to 20 inches in diameter and carries all the attendant axles, bearings, etc.

**The Chase Foundry and Manufacturing Co.
2300 Parson's Ave.
Columbus, Ohio 43207**

Left and below: From a Chase Foundry catalog.

High-strength gray iron wheels are available in a wide range of sizes and styles, including single and double flanged and flat face. Wheels can be equipped with Chase flexible bearings or Timken, ball, bronze or other bearings of your choice. Hub diameter and lengths can be made to your requirements. Wheels can be supplied rough or machined, as desired. Axles and attached brackets are available for all styles of wheels.

INDUSTRIAL CAR AND TRUCK WHEELS

Ramps

Our friend Steve Hammond is often heard to chuckle when driving past dock ramps, and he has caused us to notice how often expensive labor and materials are wasted on improper engineering design and that some new ramps sag and sway under their own weight alone. He also mentioned that the swing staging used by industrial builders and painters comes all ready to go and at comparable cost to the hand-made wood structures, rails included. Which led us to Louisville Ladder.

If readers have good ramp designs, send them along . . .

—Eds.

LOUISVILLE LADDER DIVISION

of Emerson Electric Co.

Home Office
1163 ALGONQUIN PARKWAY,
LOUISVILLE, KY. 40208
TELEPHONE 502/636-2811

Eastern Regional Warehouse
279 CANAL RD.,
FAIRLESS HILLS (PHILA.), PA 19030
TELEPHONE 215/736-1151

Southeastern Regional Warehouse
4569 WINTERS CHAPEL ROAD,
ATLANTA, GA 30360
TELEPHONE 404/447-9424

Midwestern Regional Warehouse
1129 ERIE STREET,
NORTH KANSAS CITY, MO 64116
TELEPHONE 816/421-2450

Data below from a Louisville Ladder brochure.

SCAFFOLD PLANKS & SWING STAGE PLATFORMS

2000 Series 500 Lb. Rated Load 2 Man Unit

SIZE	DEPTH	12" WIDE CODE	WT.	PRICE	20" WIDE CODE	WT.	PRICE	24" WIDE CODE	WT.	PRICE	28" WIDE CODE	WT.	PRICE	GUARDRAIL 1 SIDE	WT.	GUARDRAIL MIDRAIL TOEBOARD 1 SIDE	WT.
10	3½"	D1210	30	$ 95.00	D2010	37	$127.50	D2410	42	$143.50	D2810	47	$160.50	$ 75.00	15	$122.50	28
12		D1212	36	105.00	D2012	44	138.00	D2412	53	167.00	D2812	53	191.50	106.00	21	163.00	36
14		D1214	47	150.00	D2014	58	189.50	D2414	62	212.00	D2814	70	231.00	110.00	22	176.50	40
16	4½"	D1216	53	167.00	D2016	66	214.00	D2416	72	238.50	D2816	79	258.00	114.00	23	190.00	43
18		D1218	59	183.00	D2018	74	238.50	D2418	80	265.50	D2818	88	285.50	118.50	24	204.00	47
20		D1220	77	245.00	D2020	93	304.00	D2420	99	341.50	D2820	110	341.50	119.00	23	214.00	48
22	5¼"	D1222	84	267.50	D2022	101	328.50	D2422	108	374.50	D2822	120	403.50	123.00	24	227.50	51
24		D1224	91	290.00	D2024	109	363.00	D2424	117	407.50	D2824	130	436.50	127.00	25	241.00	55
26		D1226	114	356.50	D2026	134	445.00	D2426	143	506.00	D2826	156	549.00	131.50	26	255.00	63
28	6"	D1228	123	383.00	D2028	145	479.50	D2428	155	542.50	D2828	170	588.50	155.00	30	288.00	65
30		D1230	132	410.00	D2030	155	513.50	D2430	166	579.00	D2830	180	628.00	159.00	31	301.50	68
32		D1232	141	436.50	D2032	165	550.00	D2432	177	616.50	D2832	192	667.50	163.00	32	315.00	71
34		Not Available In 12" Width Over 32'			D2034	217	681.50	D2434	228	751.00	D2834	245	808.00	167.50	33	329.00	75
36	6½"				D2036	229	723.50	D2436	241	796.00	D2836	260	855.00	191.00	37	362.00	81
38‡					D2038	243	767.50	D2438	255	843.00	D2838	274	904.00	195.00	38	375.50	87
40‡					D2040	255	813.50	D2440	268	892.00	D2840	288	955.00	199.50	39	389.50	89

NOTE: Shaded Area Indicates U.L. Listing.   NOTE: Actual Length 3" Over Specified Length.

500#
Rated Load
ALL UNITS DESIGNED FOR CENTER WORKING LOAD WITH A SAFETY FACTOR OF 4.

Floats

After successfully negotiating the ramp, we come to the float. Tedford and Martin manufacture spruce and Styrofoam floats 3' x 16'. There are several such firms around the country, and we would like to hear about those that have given satisfaction.

Tedford & Martin, Inc.
Brown Square
Ipswich, Mass. 01938

Right and below: From a Tedford and Martin brochure.

These rugged, lightweight, floats have been designed to give many years of service, either on the salt water or on our many lakes. Floatation is provided by Styrofoam billets and located to give maximum stability.

The Styrofoam is protected from abrasion by skirtboards at the waterline and skids on the bottom. The skids make it possible to haul out in off season and pile to conserve space.

The relative lightweight and low maintenance make this float especially desirable. A few standard sizes may be combined to meet the demands of most all marinas. Floats may be coupled together to give finger floats, access floats, or main traffic floats.

166

Chainsaw Drill

Those who do build and maintain their own shore-side structures know the terrors of that long, threatening extension cord leading to the half-inch power drill with which you drill for bolts and drifts. We've listed rather expensive gas-powered timber drills in the past, but here is a device for converting your chainsaw into a drill, E-Z-Tach, from:

Nelson Maine
Hillsboro, N.H. 03244
$40.00

Installing Time Less Than 5 Minutes

Remove Bar & Chain With Wrench Furnished By The Saw Manufacturer.
The Allen Wrench That's Furnished With The Attachment Is All That Is Needed.

Speedy Drilling

Holes From ¼ inch To 1½ inch Can Be Drilled With Ease. Flat Speed Bits Are Used and They Are Ground To Cut Counter Clockwise. A 1½ inch Hole Can Be Drilled In Hard Wood At About 1 inch per Second.

Boxed quote above and photo below from Nelson Maine.

167

Rail Saver

So-called Mooring Whips have been used in Florida waters for years. They seem superfluous at first glance, but if you have had your rails chewed to a pulp by a float or a half-submerged neighbor a time or two, the feeling fades. There is also a Dinghy Whip configuration.

**Mooring Whip Sales
1554 North Federal Highway
Pompano Beach, Florida 33062**

Above and below: From a Mooring Whip Sales brochure.

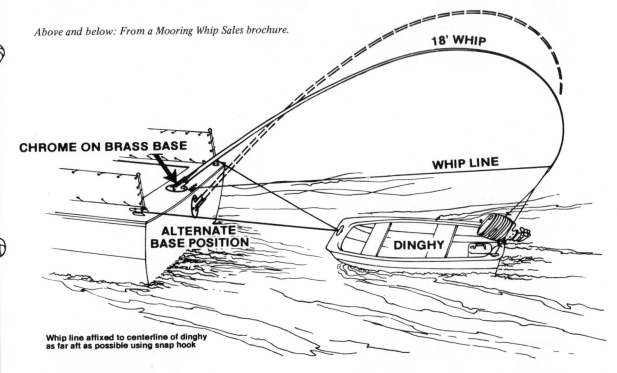

CHROME ON BRASS BASE

18' WHIP

WHIP LINE

ALTERNATE
BASE POSITION

DINGHY

Whip line affixed to centerline of dinghy
as far aft as possible using snap hook

168

Marina Costs/Revenues—1974
**National Association of Engine and Boat Manufacturers
Box 5555, Grand Central Station
New York, N.Y. 10017
6 pages, 1974, paper, $2**

Thinking of starting up or buying an existing boatyard or marina? Not sure of the economics? This might help you out. It's "a survey revealing revenue sources, indirect costs and their profitability, profit ratios, slip rental and storage rates (by region), launching fees, and labor rates for 75 marinas and boatyards in all parts of the U.S." Just keep in mind that inflation since 1974 must be taken into account when interpreting these statistics.

They (the Ceylonese) dynamite coral from reefs and burn it to make lime. But the broken reef lets in the sea to erode the shore. The government had begun a program to cement the reefs, but the paradox is that cement is made with lime, and, as no cement can be imported, the reefs that are dynamited for lime to mend the others must themselves be replaced. They call it the cement industry; it is an industry that is entirely self-consuming: nothing is achieved.
—Paul Theroux in *The Great Railway Bazaar*

MARINE MAMMALS

In the last volume of the *Catalog* we concentrated primarily on whales. Here we turn our attention to other sea mammals.

Manatees and Dugongs

Sea elephants and sea cows are perhaps *the* least understood of the sea's mammals. We contacted Dr. Daniel Hartman, a leading expert on these species (he spends months at a time in the water with them), and he responded to say that very little information is generally available, what there is being in obscure articles in hard-to-find journals. So, until a "popular" literature develops, we can only remind ourselves that they are there, sensitive and slow animals, many of them graced with deep scars left by the outboard wheels directed over them on purpose by the moronic and despicably bored.

Porpoises

Porpoises really get it in the tuna fishery. Though some improvements have been made in net design, many still drown in the industry's efforts to capture the symbiotic species. *The Porpoise News* monitors developments in the porpoise/tuna controversy and related matters. They also distribute the disturbing comicbook *Net Profit*, a production of *Save the Dolphins*.

The Porpoise News
Chipmunk Falls
Weare, New Hampshire 03281

Save the Dolphins
1945 20th Ave.
San Francisco, Cal. 94116

Left: A sea cow in an awkward position.

169

Lilly on Dolphins, by John C. Lilly, M.D.
Anchor Press/Doubleday, New York
1975, 500 pages, bibliography, index, $3.50

John Lilly's studies of dolphins are familiar classics in the field and so it must have seemed strange that they weren't among the books reviewed in *Volume 4* of the *Mariner's Catalog*. We realize that it would take more than a fleeting paragraph to describe his work and so gave precedence to *Mind in the Water*, which arrived as an instant classic and a comprehensive survey of many scholars, poets, scientists, and friends of whales and porpoises, including John Lilly.

Lilly on Delphins is the publication of several pieces written between 1961 and 1968 including "The Mind of the Dolphin" and "Man and Dolphin," which describe the studies made at his Communication Research Institute in St. Thomas. These and other essays in the book discuss both the physio-

(Continued on next page)

(Continued from preceding page)

logical facts and the imaginative leaps that make communication with dolphins seem possible. Above all, Lilly asks us to try to assume that another mammal could be as intelligent as man, that dolphins could be approached as equals, and that the varied sounds that dolphins produce could contain patterns of language. He acknowledges the possibilities for deciphering their language with the help of recording instruments to translate their sounds into an audible range or a visual image; unfortunately, he isn't fully committed to the effort, and he leaves it to those trained in linguistics for another time and place. Instead, knowing that captured dolphins tend to lower the frequency of their sounds to an audible range for humans and to imitate the human speech they hear, Lilly concentrates on teaching dolphins to speak English. His premise is that only with shared language can intelligence be tested, that language means speech, and that only a brain as large as man's is capable of speech.

Lilly's experiments seem full of contradictions. He claims to test for a higher level of understanding than the mimicking of a parrot or the responses of an obedient dog, yet he designs experiments that seem to confine the dolphins to these activities. Thus they often demonstrate their intelligence in ways for which they are not being tested and, when impatient and frustrated with the speech classes, they invite their trainers to attempt a little imitation of dolphin sounds instead. Though Lilly advocates that we go halfway in understanding dolphins, he won't act on these cues.

He seems unduly concerned with treading some middle ground between anthropomorphizing and objectifying his subject. Rather than approaching the dolphin's world as an anthropologist, as one might justifiably meet an equal, he tries to boil the whole exchange down to the physical properties of our respective voices and definitions of noise, signals, information, and sonic bursts. It is a frustration to the reader to see that Lilly is perhaps more interested in "interspecies communication" as a tool for other applications than in dolphins and all that they could teach us. In his attempt to seem scientific and credible, I suspect that he avoids telling us all his best insights about dolphins, the ones he wasn't testing or that couldn't be recorded on his sonic equipment.

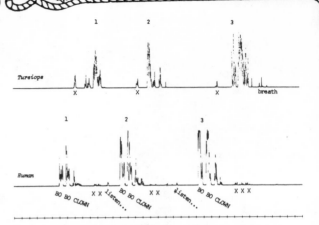

PLATE 28. *Another Sample of the Analyses of the Margaret-Peter Exchanges During Peter's Learning Period.* The upper trace shows the amplitude of the sound emitted by Peter and the lower trace of the sound emitted by Margaret. First Margaret says the words "bo bo clown" and Peter replies with three bursts of sound. The part of his curve showing an "X" is where some of Margaret's voice shows in Peter's channel; "X's" on her trace show where Peter's voice shows in her channel. This example illustrates that Peter will work many times to perfect the same words. He does not copy Margaret when she says "listen." He copies only when she say, the words "bo bo clown." Each of his copies is quite different as can be seen by the top trace. He varies them as she varies the use of the same words. This figure illustrates some of the complexities of evaluating the vocal performance of a dolphin with his great degree of flexibility, plasticity, and quick learning (from manuscript cited).

Above: From Lilly on Dolphins.

Science may be partly a matter of having proof of your hunches, but it would have been worth hearing Dr. Lilly's hunches before he left dolphin research and moved on to other fields. Even as unproven hypotheses, they would have been more valuable than all his rambling and repetitive definitions, premises, and rejected biases. In contrast, his contribution to *Mind in the Waters* is a beautiful and clear expression of the surprising, early experiences with dolphins that raised his expectations of what they might be capable of learning from or teaching to humans.

— **Charlotte Putz**

Grey Seal, Common Seal by R. M. Lockley
October House, New York, N.Y. 10010
175 pages, illus., index, 1966, $7.50

Lockley compares these two species, giving attention predominantly to grey seals and basing most of his information on his own observations along the shores of the British Isles. From craggy cliffs and bouldered beaches he stands watch for hours at a time, recording the activities of the seals in careful detail. As a field naturalist, Lockley has the magical combination of the adventurousness to explore inaccessible places, the patience and scientific discipline to spend hours observing, and enthusiastic and compassionate concern for his subject. The chapter about the breeding season reads like a play director's blocking script; the one on intelligence is full of anecdotes about seal pets; his discussion about the varying tendency of seals to herd together in dense populations demonstrates his capacity never to overgeneralize but to interpret, surmise, and make comparisons with human behavior. The chapter on seals and men begins with familiar themes of hunting vs. conservation but swiftly turns to myths and legends about clans of men descended from seals and about various misfortunes resulting from harming a seal. Thus the book is full of rare surprises as well as scientific facts.

—Charlotte Putz

COMMON SEAL.

HARP SEAL.

The World of the Walrus by Richard Perry
Taplinger Publishing Co., New York, N.Y.
162 pages, photos, bibliography, index, 1968, $5.95

Perry's *World of the Walrus* represents an energetic sort of research in which any observation on record has a place, no matter how offhanded or ancient. Log entries of explorers and experiences of natives and travelers throughout the Arctic all contribute to the information about walrus behavior, yet references to sources are woven into the text unobstrusively so that the book remains a study of walruses, not a history of man's interaction with them. Everything known is there: how walruses care for the calves, feed and move with their tusks, attack or ignore people, migrate along their respective Arctic routes and more, as well as man's hunting techniques, use of the animals, and conservation problems. Never knowing what will come next, you are lured to read on.

—Charlotte Putz

Learning, it is said, begins when we realize how little we know.

—Maurice Griffiths

171

Dolphins, Whales and Porpoises
by D. J. Coffey
Macmillan Publishing Co., New York, N.Y.
223 pages, illus., index, 1977, $17.95

Above: A whale breaks the surface (photo by Bob Simpson).

Dolphins, Whales and Porpoises is subtitled as, and tries to be, an encyclopedia of sea mammals but covers too much too briefly. Coffey's training makes him cautious, opting for empty generalizations rather than details and real occurrences. The three sections, cetacea, pinnipledia, and sirenia, start with an A-to-Z discussion covering headings such as aging, behavior, captivity, distribution, evolution, mythology, and some aspects of physiology. What follows is possibly the most complete dictionary of species available, alphabetical by Latin names. If you don't know the Latin names for blue or grey or humpback whale, you won't find them in the index and you might miss the single entry for each of these great species. The many species of dolphins, porpoises, and seals, however, are indexed in English and give the impression that there's a contest among explorers to spot one of these creatures in a new place and name it after themselves. I thought only sparrows, warblers, and birdwatchers could create such confusion. Unfortunately, the many photographs are not organized to illustrate this dictionary. The conditions necessary for keeping sea mammals in captivity are discussed more thoroughly than in other books I've seen. With his veterinary background, it is understandable that this would be Coffey's best documented contribution. He feels that capturing these animals for commercial entertainment is "distasteful and degrading" and dangerous to their well-being; but if research, education, and studies that assist conservation efforts are involved, it is justified.

—Charlotte Putz

Brother Whale by Roy Nickerson
Chronicle Books, San Francisco, Cal.
155 pages, illus., bibliography, index, 1977, $4.95

Brother Whale is intentionally an introduction, not in the sense of a summary of basic information, but like a greeting to a guest: welcome; follow me here; I'd like you to meet my brother. Nickerson writes about the experiences of whalewatching in the Pacific which have sparked his own curiosity and compassion for whales and assumes, correctly I believe, that these accounts will fire up his readers to plunge into the subject, too. As a beginning he provides information about whaling history and restrictions, identification of whale species, evolution, diet, songs, and intelligence, just to name a few areas. In a few paragraphs about migration and distribution, he conjures up clearer images than many other sources of the various species oscillating over the globe from season to season in their respective territories. His coverage of conservation organizations and activities is excellent and understandably current, since Nickerson is in the business of gathering news. Likewise, he is good at tracking down information and debunking faulty rumors and myths. Like other writers, Nickerson warns that the future of whales and men may be long or brief and ultimately linked together, depending on our management of ocean resources.

—Charlotte Putz

A Natural History of Marine Mammals
by Victor B. Scheffer
Illustrations by Peter Parnell
Charles Scribner's Sons, New York
157 pages, appendixes, bibliography, index,
1976, $7.95

Scheffer's *Natural History of Marine Mammals* is as comprehensive as an encyclopedia. It rounds up information absorbed from untold numbers of sources and touches the peaks of *Mind in the Waters* and his own *Year of the Whale*, both reviewed in *Volume 4* of the *Mariner's Catalog*. He writes for readers with no background in the subject and aims to create a new interest and to teach. Terms such as metabolic rate or lactic acid tolerance, speaking of adaptations to deep water, or echo location and sonograms, in connection with senses, are thoughtfully explained. Reminiscent of his imagery in *Year of the Whale* are his descriptions of sounds of various marine mammals as "a ballpark racket" or "a booming pile-driving sound" or "the slow creak of a rusty hinge," and more. Many unfamiliar facts, plus the chapter about new directions in research and how studies are made, and the appendix about where to see certain species, and the eight-page annotated bibliography, make the book unique. For illustrating the mammals as they are discussed, Scheffer has selected the artwork of Peter Parnall; it is the opportunity to enjoy almost four dozen examples of Parnall's very special style of drawing that makes this book a treasure.

—Charlotte Putz

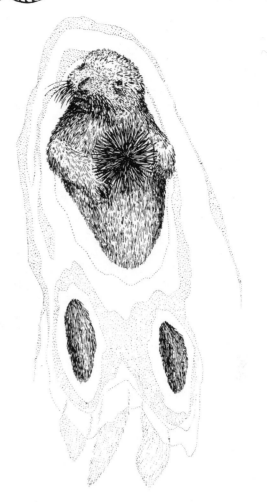

Above: Sea otter feeding on a sea urchin. From A Natural History of Marine Mammals.

AN INTRODUCTION TO BOOKS ON WHALING

by
Kenneth R. Martin

Whales and whaling have always held wide topical appeal. Consequently, much of the publication in these fields has been lightweight and pop-oriented, long on romance and short on information. But in the last few years, several forces have combined to change this: a virtual explosion of hard data on whales, which have made these mysterious creatures all the more fascinating; a growth in public alarm over the disastrous consequences of whaling; and finally, a more scholarly approach to the history of whaling. In the flood of recent printing and reprinting have come a few gems that offer any interested novice a solid background.

Whaling titles may be divided into three categories: general surveys, regional studies of whaling ports or whaling grounds, and primary accounts (mostly journal or memoirs of Yankee whalemen). Titles in all three categories bear down heavily on America's whaling industry, once predominant but now vanished. Even general surveys are somewhat un-

balanced in this regard. The relentless, worldwide, mass-produced whale slaughter of the 1960s and 1970s, led by Japan, the U.S.S.R., and Norway, has yet to be properly documented in an American trade book.

Publications on whaling have another built-in liability: it is almost impossible for an author to discuss any aspect of whaling without lengthy digressions on taxonomy and cetology. In view of the colossal fascination of cetaceans, this is quite understandable. But readers will note an inordinate amount of slippage as they proceed from volume to volume. Nonetheless, the experience of reading one's way through whaling history is fascinating—how could such a subject be dull?

Readers unacquainted with whaling should begin with two general surveys, both in print although somewhat outdated. F.C. Ommanney's *Lost Leviathan* (New York: Dodd Mead & Co., 1971) explains the nature of cetaceans and offers a comprehensive history of whaling. Leonard H. Matthews, et al., *The Whale* (New York: Simon and Schuster, 1968; New York: Crescent Books, 1974) is a coffee-table book replete with color illustrations and smart design. The quality of its narrative and illustrations is uneven, but the volume is handsome and will stand

173

(Continued on next page)

(Continued from preceding page)

up to repeated browsings. Since *The Whale* is selling on discount tables in many bookstores, its reduced price makes it a bargain. Another bargain reprint still seen on discount book tables is Albert Cook Church's classic, *Whale Ships and Whaling* (1938; rpt. New York: Bonanza Books, n.d.). This is a volume of remarkable period whaling photographs. While the reproduction quality of this cheap edition is not high, new readers should not miss Church.

The best single source on America's whaling industry is Elmo Paul Hohman's *The American Whaleman: A Study of Life and Labor in the Whaling Industry* (1928; rpt. Clifton, New Jersey: Augustus M. Kelley, Publishers, 1972; or Evanston, Illinois: Richard S. Barnes Bookseller, original edition newly bound). Hohman has yet to be surpassed for care and comprehensiveness in unravelling the complex economic affairs of Yankee entrepreneurs and exposing the basically exploitive nature of Yankee whaling. Readers who see nineteenth-century whaling as Melvillesque adventure will find Hohman eye-opening indeed. The book also contains many classic, true whaling anecdotes.

America's most important whaling ports were first Nantucket and later New Bedford. Edouard A. Stackpole's *The Sea Hunters: The New England Whalemen During Two Centuries, 1635-1835* (1953; rpt. Westport, Connecticut: Greenwood Press, Inc., 1973) recounts in detail the rise of Nantucket whaling and emphasizes that the particular knack it took to excel in so specialized a fishery was directly related to the particularity of Nantucketers themselves. By mid-nineteenth century, however, New Bedford had superseded Nantucket. Everett S. Allen very stylishly covers New Bedford in *Children of the Light: The Rise and Fall of New Bedford Whaling and the Death of the Arctic Fleet* (Boston and Toronto: Little, Brown and Company, 1973), in which he dramatizes both the resourcefulness and tunnel vision of Yankee whaling.

Whaling buffs, familiar with the generalities of the fishery's history, never tire of reading primary accounts. There are many in print to choose from. The most ripsnorting of these is Nelson Cole Haley's *Whale Hunt: The Narrative of a Voyage by Nelson Cole Haley, Harpooner in the Ship Charles W. Morgan, 1849-1853* (New York: Ives Washburn, Inc., 1967), and it is highly recommended as nonfiction adventure. Haley's account is in the manner of a memoir, as is William M. Davis' *Nimrod of the Sea: or The American Whaleman* (1874; rpt. North Quincy, Massachusetts: The Christopher Publishing House, 1972). Davis' book is packed with good-humored lore and lively whaling encounters. An opposite mood is struck in *"There She Blows": A Narrative of a Whaling Voyage in the Indian and South Atlantic Ocean*, written and published by sadder-but-wiser whaleman Ben Ezra Stiles Ely in 1849, and now attractively republished for the Marine Historical Association, Inc., with annotations by Curtis Dahl (Middletown, Connecticut: Wesleyan University

(Continued on next page)

174

Press, 1971). Ely's tale is worth reading because, as a well-bred youngster, he was scandalized and outraged by the routine brutality of life aboard a Yankee whaler. An unusual viewpoint is that of a whaling captain's wife: Mary Chipman Lawrence, *The Captain's Best Mate: The Journal of Mary Chipman Lawrence on the Whaler Addison, 1856-1860*, edited by Stanton Garner (Providence: Brown University Press, 1966), which consists of diary entries and makes up in immediacy what it may lack in after-the-fact stylishness. Some of the most memorable primary descriptions of old-time whaling have been excerpted and anthologized in a single volume: Edgar L. McCormick and Edward G. McGehee, *Life on a Whaler: Selected Source Materials for College Research Papers* (Boston: D.C. Heath and Company, 1960). This book has just gone out of print, but readers would be well advised to scrounge whatever copies remain. *Life on a Whaler* is a bargain and offers a high concentration of original narratives. Readers wishing to be updated may find Robert B. Robertson's *Of Whales and Men* (1954; rpt. New York: Touchstone-Clarion/Simon and Schuster, 1969) useful. It is a first-person, novelistic, admiring account of modern Antarctic whalemen.

There are a few books in print that transcend the above categories, volumes so important that readers in the field must be familiar with them. One is Charles M. Scammon's monumental study, *The Marine Mammals of the Northwestern Coast of North America, together with an Account of the American Whale Fishery* (1874), which has been reprinted in a luxury edition (Riverside, California: Manessier Publishing Co., 1969), and in paperback (New York: Dover Publications, Inc., 1968). Scammon, a Yankee whaling skipper, made careful observations and drawings of cetaceans during his celebrated career.

His book remains one of the most important on the subject, and his description of whaling's technical aspects is authoritative. Of similar importance is Alexander Starbuck's *History of the American Whale Fishery from its Earliest Inception to the Year 1876* (1878, rpt. New York: Argosy-Antiquarian Ltd., 1964). Starbuck arranged a remarkably thorough table of American whaling voyages by year, port, and ship names, with inclusive voyage dates and cargo tallies. Starbuck is the bible for anyone doing serious research on American whaling. There are several publications on scrimshaw, the folk art of the whaling industry; but the most thorough by far is E. Norman Flayderman's *Scrimshaw and Scrimshanders, Whales and Whalemen* (New Milford, Connecticut: N. Flayderman & Co., Inc., 1972). This volume's profusion of photographs depict an astonishing variety of tools, curios, whimseys, and art objects made by whalemen.

The devastation of world whale stocks has not been matched historically by prudent conservation. With many species threatened or endangered, and with the rush of biological research that documents the awesome complexity of whales, it is time for a new public sensibility. Everyone interested in whaling should digest Joan McIntyre, ed., *Mind in the Waters: A Book to Celebrate the Consciousness of Whales and Dolphins* (New York: Charles Scribner's Sons; and San Francisco: Sierra Club Books, 1974), a sensitive, disturbing anthology, that dramatizes the uniqueness of whales, reminds us that our relationship with them continues to be a predatory one, and rightly suggests the need for change. It is important that the last few centuries of whaling be viewed from this perspective. *Mind in the Waters*, then, is a necessary complement to the volumes recommended here.

175

"CUTTING IN."

Museum Publications Update

Frederick P. Schmitt, the curator at the Whaling Museum in Cold Spring Harbor, New York, reminds us that we failed to note the publications of that museum in our roundups in the 3rd and 4th *Mariner's Catalogs*. They have an impressive list for such a small museum, including: *Scrimshaw, Folk Art of the Whalers*, by Walter Earle ($1.75); *Out of the Wilderness*, by Walter Earle, history of Cold Spring Harbor to the Civil War ($1.95); *Mark Well the Whale*, by F.P. Schmitt ($6.95); *The Whale's Tale*, by F.P. Schmitt ($6); and a number of prints and maps.

Send for a free list of publications to:

**The Whaling Museum
Cold Spring Harbor, N.Y. 11724**

Picking Sides

We're living in an interesting time. Right now, before our eyes, there's a battle going on in the maritime museum industry. That in itself isn't interesting—there's always a battle or two raging inside museums—but the nature of this one is. Basically, it comes down to money (as if you needed to be told), and the antagonists disagree on how it should be spent. Should the museums spend big money on preserving a few big ships or on building a lot of small boats? People on both sides of that question are breathing fire, enough so that listening to any of them, or reading their essays in defense of their positions, can leave one in a state of confusion, especially since there are sub-battles going on around the main event—replication or restoration? (definition of terms is important for museum folk), static exhibition or working craft?, preservation of artifacts or preservation of skills?

Since the money to be spent will eventually come out of your pocket through government grants, subsidies, and tax deductions, you might want to study up on the problem. A series of articles, both pro and con, appeared in the *National Fisherman* during 1976; see the February, May, June, and July issues.

DIVING AND UNDERWATER

We have some editorial weak spots, and diving is one of them. Though we have many friends and acquaintances who dive, we don't; always wanted to, meant to, but haven't, and no reader has yet set down to synopsize his passions on the subject. We shall, then, limit our entries in this field to a rather gross level: organizations and information sources.

Men Beneath the Sea
by Hans Hass
St. Martins Press, N.Y.
$12.95

Of the many underwater and diving titles to be published (and that we've seen) in the past few years, this one is the most ambient. The author, one of diving's pioneers, rambles easily through the history of diving, then through the usual human interest aspects of diving (dangers, treasures, etc.), and, finally, through some intelligent discussions, debunkeries, and prophesies concerning a host of underwater subjects—from dolphins and the law to the effects that a life of diving has on the consciousness of those who do it.

Quote below from Men Beneath the Sea.

As far as I personally am concerned, my many years of diving have undoubtedly wrought a kind of change of consciousness. Under water you have a strange freedom which is never possible on land. As soon as you penetrate the surface of water you pass into another life, into another way of thinking. Down there you gain a detachment from the human world such as is scarcely to be found elsewhere. In my case years of underwater research awakened an interest in land creatures, simply because from the perspective of the underwater world I saw them differently—as exiles from the sea. My underwater interest spilled over into the world of air and thus retraced the path of evolution. I then gave up diving completely for more than a decade and occupied myself solely with land creatures, especially the most astonishing one—man; I sold my ship and took an abrupt interest in what for a biologist are remote areas—industrial economics, political science, law, art, and the rest. This happened because I still remained under water in principle. Our watery abode, the starting point for this whole development, remained constantly before my eyes and virtually forced upon me a different and unaccustomed way of looking at things.

An Impressive Magazine

Like the rest of the sporting press, diving publications are packed with hype, boobs, and buns selling do-dads and gizmos, beaches and drinks. They emphasize a world where people don't become older, speared fish cost $500 apiece, and rubber fetishism is legitimized. I suppose that this isn't too bad when the issue is fishing tackle or, within limits, boats or even skis. But then you come to mountain climbing or diving, where everything is fine as long as everything is right—no mistakes—and everyone in an adult frame of mind knows most assuredly that boobs and buns are often mistaken. So to hell with the diving press.

The one magazine in this field that genuinely impresses us is *Undercurrent*, a newsletter that comes out monthly; it sells no advertising and solicits no goodies from the industry. They review and test gear, places, programs, and developments contingent to all aspects of sport diving. For example, in the Nov.-Dec. 1976 issue they published the results of a highly detailed questionnaire on the performance of every brand-name wetsuit made in the United States. One thousand readers responded, and we cannot imagine a more incisive product evaluation for the would-be purchaser of a wetsuit than the compilation of all those comments. Likewise, when reviewing places, such as a well-known diving resort in the Caribbean, they even tell you to stay away if that is their conclusion drawn from their research. Having read three issues, we're determined to subscribe, even as nondivers.

Undercurrent
P.O. Box 1658
Sausalito, Cal. 94965
$15/yr.

Below: From Undercurrent *magazine.*

WET SUIT EVALUATION BY OWNERS

Respondents rated their reaction to their own suit on a scale of Excellent, Good, Fair and Poor. "Excellent" responses were multiplied by four, "Good" by three, "Fair" by two and "Poor" by one, and then divided by the number of responses, giving a "mean." Bayley, White Stag, Imperial and Harvey are primarily custom-made suits, a factor which contributes to their higher overall rating. However, comparisons of custom-made only and off-the-rack suits only suggest that the ranking would remain nearly identical, although the range between suits might be reduced.

I. WARMTH
Imperial	3.47
Bayley	3.44
White Stag	3.34
Harvey	3.33
Parkway	3.32
U.S. Divers	3.04

II. DURABILITY
Bayley	3.45
Imperial	3.26
Harvey	3.21
White Stag	3.18
Parkway	3.17
U.S. Divers	2.96

III. COMFORT
Bayley	3.40
White Stag	3.40
Imperial	3.38
Harvey	3.24
Parkway	3.12
U.S. Divers	2.83

IV. FIT
Bayley	3.52
Imperial	3.40
White Stag	3.19
Harvey	3.15
Parkway	3.06
U.S. Divers	2.79

V. WORKMANSHIP
Bayley	3.42
Imperial	3.33
Harvey	3.28
Parkway	3.26
White Stag	3.18
U.S. Divers	3.08

VI. WOULD RECOMMEND
White Stag	90%
Harvey	88%
Parkway	88%
Bayley	86%
Imperial	86%
U.S. Divers	78%

Certification

All appearances would indicate that sport diving is taking pretty good care of itself, especially with respect to its monitoring of training programs. There are five major certification organizations in the country.

By the end of 1976, the National Association of Underwater Instructors had certified some 5,000 instructors, who in turn had certified about 550,000 divers. The NAUI is a spearhead on instructional quality and a legislative watchdog with a very large package of information services, including discount books (an impressive list of titles) and a monthly newsletter.

NAUI
P.O. Box 630
Colton, Cal. 92324

Another similar organization is the Professional Association of Diving Instructors. Eleven years old and with some 6,000 members, PADI offers 12 levels of certification and nine specialty certifications. Generally, its stress seems to be on firming up the top of the diving population rather than spreading out the base of it.

PADI
P.O. Box 177
Costa Mesa, Cal. 92627

What PADI does for instructors, the National Association of Skin Diving Schools does for institutions with diving programs. The purpose of its ten-week, $1,600 college course is to provide the industry with full-time "diving instructor-equipment counselors."

NASDS
1214 Rosecrans St.
San Diego, Cal. 92106

The three organizations above, plus the YMCA diver's instruction program (National YMCA Scuba Program, 127 Peachtree St. N.E., Atlanta, Georgia 30303), are combined in a super-organization called the National Scuba Training Council, which coordinates the work of each group and, no doubt to leaven rivalries, deals with the complaints of enrollees and watches the politics.

NSTC
P.O. Box 7996
Long Beach, Cal. 90807

STANDARDS FOR THE TRAINING OF BASIC SCUBA DIVERS

1. Every student shall have a minimum of three (3) open water training dives prior to certification. Of these dives one (1) is to be a skin dive and two (2) are to be scuba dives. No more than two (2) dives per day may be counted toward this requirement.
2. During the open water training dives there is to be at least one (1) instructor in the water for every ten (10) students in the water.
3. All students are required to have an approved diving log book with information on the importance and procedures for use of the log book.

STANDARDS FOR UNDERWATER INSTRUCTORS

1. In order to function as an underwater instructor or as an assistant instructor or provisional instructor during the teaching of sport diving, the instructor is to have met the requirements for certification and renewal by a member association of NSTC and be a current active member in good standing of that association.
2. In order to teach sport scuba diving the instructor is to obtain insurance coverage under an instructor's professional liability policy that protects the instructor and the member association.
3. Instructors are to support only retail store/-schools that require certification cards for air fills and rentals.

Above: From an NSTC brochure.
Below: From an NAUI brochure.

Diving instruction is often offered through diving equipment stores, almost always in fact. Often these programs (offered by the store personnel) are part of the Scuba Schools International Certification Program for advanced open water diving, instructor's programs, or underwater photography.

SSI
1634 S. College Ave.
Ft. Collins, Colorado 80521

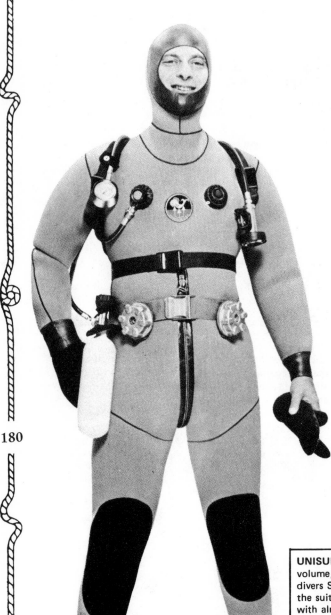

Speleology

Advanced divers with a special interest in caves will want to know about the services and publications of the National Association of Cave Diving.

NACD
2900 N.W. 29th Ave.
Gainesville, Florida 32601

Mail-order Equipment

There are hundreds of small diving shops around the country and dozens of big ones. Two that deal in volume mail-order business are New England Divers, *the* giant in the industry, and Aqua-Craft, which has to be described as large.

New England Divers
(Mail Order Div.)
Tozer Road
Beverly, Mass. 01915
free catalog

Aqua-Craft
3280 Kurtz Street
San Diego, Cal. 92110
***Wishbook* is $1**

Sub-Aqua Illustrated Dictionary
by Leo Zanelli and George Skuse
Oxford University Press
London and New York
114 pages, illus., 1976, $7.95

This is a dictionary/glossary of terms for scuba divers. We're not knowledgeable enough to say whether it is good or not (though a little cross-checking of other sources indicates that the former is the case), but the striking feature of the book is the diving bibliography included as a bonus. If you want to chase down diving literature, this is a place to begin.

UNISUIT SYSTEM. Unisuit combines all the best features of constant volume, dry, wet, and hard hat suits. The unisuit is an integral part of the divers Scuba System. Air from the Scuba is fed, at the diver's command, to the suit for warmth, comfort and buoyancy trim. The Unisuit can be used with almost any popular regulator and with Hookah, band masks and lightweight hats. With the Poseidon Cyklon 300 regulator—and interchangeable full face mask—any pro can have an economical all-purpose rig. Surface air hook-up. Bail-out-bottle for safety. Full face protection. Even an independent suit inflation system for very deep gas dives. Visit your local New England Divers store for full details or write for a descriptive brochure.

Above: The Unisuit, from the New England Divers catalog.

Aqua-Bell

The Aqua-Bell is a very interesting little diving helmet to be used in waters *35 feet and shallower*. The basic unit is fed air with a hand pump from above by someone who loves you, and there are also electric and gas air pump options. The mother company is Aqua-Bell, but there are franchise outfits too, like Captain Nemo's.

Aqua-Bell Corp.
P.O. Box 221
Windsor, Wisc. 53598

Captain Nemo, Inc.
951 Country Club Blvd.
Cape Coral, Florida 33904

Basics of Underwater Photography
by Doug Wallin
American Photographic Book Publishing Co.
Garden City, N.Y.
$5.95

This book is just that—it's about *basics*, the whole shtick on getting light recorded on emulsions through optics. 128 pages, and not one is wasted on the romance or fun of it—just how to get good photographs and why the hows work the way they do.

Left: The Aqua-Bell.

A Shepherd of the Abalone Herd

by Alan Graham

I had just sighted a ling cod the size of a submarine when the earthy bellow of a foghorn nudged me into existence. It is 7 a.m. and looking up at the tallest redwood tree . . . not a leaf is rippling . . . no wind. Six miles down the road lies the Great Mother . . . the Pacific . . . hopefully flat. I kiss my lady, hello-hello . . . goodbyegoodbye. Down the ladder from our loft to our child, Raven's, room. Another ladder, up this time, to our dome, which serves as our living room, kitchen. Make breakfast—coffee—up the quarter-mile trail to Fred and Bobbie's bus. Fred, who plays the foghorn, is building a beautiful cat-boat—delayed somewhat by his addiction to diving. After warming up the only Chevy pickup, we threw in our gear, and down the ridge we go toward the Pacific. As luck would have it, the sea was flat before us, and the coffee was royal in us. Twelve miles to our diving spot . . . a sliver of paradise . . . slightly chilly . . . surrounded by a pasture . . . a beautiful part of the not-too-known world. We stop at the cliff's edge, off with our clothes, on with our wetsuits. Life warms up considerably as we pass the flask. Down the cliff with our gear, tubes, gun, etc.

We sit on a log and put on the hood, gloves, booties; put on the speartip, hold the fins, mask, snorkel . . . walk to a rock at water's edge. The sun makes the Pacific flitter and throb . . . it looks good. Everything on—all together—off the rocks, into the sea. A panorama of another world shows itself . . . kelp dancing gently . . . sea urchins resembling psychedelic grapefruits . . . then I'm yelping from the rush of freezing water. The water next to my skin and suit gets warmer; peeing in my wetsuit makes it warmer yet. Swim . . . jump down, spin around, look around. Praise the Lord: Thank you, Father, for this day and this garden.

A ling cod shows himself on the bottom . . . he's a beauty. Pulling back the rubbers of my gun . . . praying without ceasing . . . down I go. He/she appears asleep, dreaming only the dreams ling cods dream. About two feet away from his head I squeeze the trigger . . . got him. Then it's up to the tube . . . put the stringer through his cheek . . . take the spear out of him . . . reload . . . down again. The ever-elusive abalone shows himself; disguised as a rock, he does not escape the watchful gaze of Captain Fathom. On the surface again, look for Fred. I see he's hunting along with the other cormorants close by. I have my ab iron on another stringer, and it's now in my hand. Down I go under the abalone . . . off it goes . . . run with it, up to the top . . . glad for a gulp of air. Measure the ab—it's oversize . . . good . . . into the net, into the tube . . . off we go.

Sitting on a rock down 20 feet, I see a large sea trout . . . a school and university of black snapper, hear a few chords of a Charlie Parker tune. Everything is so bright, so quiet, with a beat of life going back before eternity. Diving in the sea is visiting in another world . . . flying in a universe . . . a garden . . . a shepherd of the abalone herd.

Several hours pass and my toes start to get numb. It's time to head my vessel back to the beach. So I turn me homeward and thread my way through the rocks back to the beach. Fred lands a few minutes before me and has the flask in readiness as I hobble back to the log. After gutting our fish, we climb the mountain, to the truck, to the flask . . . out we go, to the road, spreading seafood, reaping gourmet lunches, whiskey, eggs, cheese, weed, vegetables, et al.

Back to our Community, wash our gear—wonderful dinner—catch distributed, surplus frozen; water the garden, sauna tonight, swap lies. Smoke the good smoke, go back home with my favorite girl and make love, and praise the Living God for a wonderful day.

—**Captain Fathom**

181

INDEX

185

189